To Go Into the Words

POETS ON POETRY

Derek Pollard, Series Editor
Donald Hall, Founding Editor

TITLES IN THE SERIES
Norman Finkelstein, *To Go Into the Words*
Major Jackson, *A Beat Beyond*, edited by Amor Kohli
Jane Miller, *From the Valley of Bronze Camels*
Tony Hoagland, *The Underground Poetry Metro Transportation System for Souls*
Philip Metres, *The Sound of Listening*
Julie Carr, *Someone Shot My Book*
Claudia Keelan, *Ecstatic Émigré*
Rigoberto Gonzalez, *Pivotal Voices, Era of Transition*
Garrett Hongo, *The Mirror Diary*
Marianne Boruch, *The Little Death of Self*
Yusef Komunyakaa, *Condition Red*
Khaled Mattawa, *How Long Have You Been With Us?*
Aaron Shurin, *The Skin of Meaning*
Kazim Ali, *Resident Alien*
Bruce Bond, *Immanent Distance*
Joyelle McSweeney, *The Necropastoral*
David Baker, *Show Me Your Environment*
Marilyn Hacker, *Unauthorized Voices*

ALSO AVAILABLE, BOOKS BY
Elizabeth Alexander, Meena Alexander, A. R. Ammons, John Ashbery, Robert Bly, Philip Booth, Marianne Boruch, Hayden Carruth, Amy Clampitt, Alfred Corn, Douglas Crase, Robert Creeley, Donald Davie, Thomas M. Disch, Ed Dorn, Martín Espada, Annie Finch, Tess Gallagher, Sandra M. Gilbert, Dana Gioia, Linda Gregerson, Allen Grossman, Thom Gunn, Rachel Hadas, John Haines, Donald Hall, Joy Harjo, Robert Hayden, Edward Hirsch, Daniel Hoffman, Jonathan Holden, John Hollander, Paul Hoover, Andrew Hudgins, T. R. Hummer, Laura (Riding) Jackson, Josephine Jacobsen, Mark Jarman, Lawrence Joseph, Galway Kinnell, Kenneth Koch, John Koethe, Yusef Komunyakaa, Marilyn Krysl, Maxine Kumin, Martin Lammon (editor), Philip Larkin, David Lehman, Philip Levine, Larry Levis, John Logan, William Logan, David Mason, William Matthews, William Meredith, Jane Miller, David Mura, Carol Muske, Alice Notley, Geoffrey O'Brien, Gregory Orr, Alicia Suskin Ostriker, Ron Padgett, Marge Piercy, Grace Schulman, Anne Sexton, Karl Shapiro, Reginald Shepherd, Charles Simic, William Stafford, Anne Stevenson, Cole Swenson, May Swenson, James Tate, Richard Tillinghast, C. K. Williams, Alan Williamson, David Wojahn, Charles Wright, James Wright, John Yau, and Stephen Yenser

For a complete list of titles, please see www.press.umich.edu

To Go Into the Words

NORMAN FINKELSTEIN

University of Michigan Press
Ann Arbor

Copyright © 2023 by Norman Finkelstein
All rights reserved

For questions or permissions, please contact um.press.perms@umich.edu

Published in the United States of America by the
University of Michigan Press
Manufactured in the United States of America
Printed on acid-free paper
First published October 2023

A CIP catalog record for this book is available from the British Library.

Library of Congress Cataloging-in-Publication data has been applied for.

ISBN 978-0-472-03941-8 (paper : alk. paper)
ISBN 978-0-472-22130-1 (e-book)

Because, to him who ponders well,
My rhymes more than their rhyming tell . . .

    —W. B. YEATS, "TO IRELAND IN THE COMING TIMES"

Contents

Acknowledgments   ix

Introduction   1

William Bronk   6

Helen Adam   29

Ronald Johnson   48

Michael Palmer   70

Nathaniel Mackey   108

Paul Bray   137

Lawrence Joseph   153

Total Midrash   173

Secular Jewish Culture and Its Radical Poetic Discontents   182

The Master of Turning   202

Acknowledgments

Acknowledgment is made to the following publications, where material from chapters in this book originally appeared, sometimes in earlier forms:

William Bronk: "William Bronk: The World as Desire" originally appeared in *Contemporary Literature* 23.4 (Fall 1982). "The Singular Achievement of William Bronk" originally appeared in *Sagetrieb* 7.3 (Winter 1988).

Helen Adam: "Helen Adam and Romantic Desire" originally appeared in *Credences* 3.3 (Fall 1985). The review of *The Helen Adam Reader* originally appeared in *Rain Taxi Review of Books* 13.2 (Summer 2008).

Ronald Johnson: The review of *The Shrubberies* is previously unpublished. "The New ARK" originally appeared in *Notre Dame Review* 37 (Winter/Spring 2014). "'He did not call himself an artist': Johnson's Outsider Aesthetic" originally appeared in the *Journal of Foreign Languages and Cultures* 3.1 (June 2019).

Michael Palmer: "The Case of Michael Palmer" originally appeared in *Contemporary Literature* 29.4 (Winter 1988). "From C to D: Michael Palmer from the Eighties to the Nineties (and Beyond)" was presented at the Poetry of the Eighties Conference at the University of Maine, June 2012. The review of *Little Elegies for Sister Satan* appeared on Restless Messengers: Poetry in Review (https://www.poetryinreview.com/?post=little_elegies), 5 June 2021.

Nathaniel Mackey: "Nathaniel Mackey: Poetry Terminable and Interminable" originally appeared in *Talisman* 43 (2015) (https://talismanarchive.weebly.com/finkelstein----mackey.html).

"Mythos, Quest Romance, and Mackey's 'Wandering We'" originally appeared in *Nathaniel Mackey: Destination Out*, ed. Jeanne Heuving, © 2021 by the University of Iowa Press. "Introduction to *Double Trio*: A Restless Messengers Symposium" appeared on Restless Messengers:

Poetry in Review (https://www.poetryinreview.com/?post=symposium_introduction), 24 April 2021.

Paul Bray: "The Marvelous Adventures of Paul Bray" originally appeared in *Annals of Scholarship* 19.1 (Winter 2009). "Glyphs from Beyond: Paul Bray's Gnostic Poetry" originally appeared in *Talisman* 42 (2014) (https://talismanarchive2a.weebly.com/finkelstein.html).

Lawrence Joseph: "Ground Zero Baudelaire: 'Into It' and the Poetics of Shock" originally appeared in *Jacket* 2, 9 February 2012 (https://jacket2.org/article/ground-zero-baudelaire). "Lawrence Joseph's Credo" originally appeared in *Jacket* 2, 30 March 2018 (https://jacket2.org/reviews/lawrence-josephs-credo).

"Total Midrash" originally appeared in *Religion & Literature*. Reprint permission granted by the University of Notre Dame, *Religion & Literature* 43.2 (Summer 2011).

"Secular Jewish Culture and Its Radical Poetic Discontents" originally appeared in *Radical Poetics and Secular Jewish Culture*, eds. Stephen Paul Miller and Daniel Morris, © 2010 by the University of Alabama Press.

"The Master of Turning" is previously unpublished.

I would also like to thank Derek Pollard, the editor of the Poets on Poetry Series, for his enthusiasm, encouragement, and support. This book would not have come into being without him.

Introduction

"'TO GO INTO THE WORDS TO EXPAND THEM' The Voices said ..." So begins "Beam 28, The Book of Orpheus," in Ronald Johnson's epic poem *ARK*. I have always identified with Johnson's vision in *ARK*, and I take the instructions that he receives from "The Voices" very seriously. Not only do they inspire my own poetry, but my criticism as well. For over forty years, through six books and well over 100 articles and reviews, I have tried to go into the words to expand them; that is, open up the work of a given poet, a given poem, so that other readers may reach a greater understanding and appreciate the work even more. "Not system but *commentary* is the legitimate form through which truth is approached," writes Gershom Scholem in his magisterial essay "Revelation and Tradition as Religious Categories in Judaism." Scholem, founder of the modern field of Kabbalah studies and himself a revisionist Gnostic commentator on Jewish textuality, recognized that secular literature was as open to such commentary as religious texts. I have tried to build on this understanding, writing about modern poetry in search of the gnosis which it may contain. And by "gnosis" I follow Elaine Pagels in *The Gnostic Gospels*, who tells us "we could translate it as 'insight,' for *gnosis* involves an intuitive process of knowing oneself." "Like artists," Pagels notes of the ancient Gnostics, "they express their own insight—their own *gnosis*—by creating new myths, poems, rituals ..." And such may well be the case for the poets about whom I have written.

According to Harold Bloom in *Agon*, "To ask how poems can be the Gnosis is to ask what is it that poems know, which in turn is to ask what is it that we can come to know when we read poems?" Bloom, who famously claimed to be a Jewish Gnostic, and who based his vast readings of "the Western Canon" on what he understood to be Gnostic and kabbalistic (as well as Freudian) principles, complicates our knowing through elaborate exegesis and dizzying acts of interpretation, engaging ancient and modern religious, philosophical, psychoanalytic, and literary texts. Yet he also argues for a pragmatic literary criticism, which is Gnostic insofar as it broadens our self-knowledge, deepens our inwardness, and aids us in locating our place in the cosmos. Like Hans Jonas before them, Bloom and Pagels both quote the Gnostic formula that:

What makes us free is the Gnosis

> of who we were
> of what we have become
> of where we were
> of wherein we have been thrown
> of what we are being freed
> of what birth really is
> of what rebirth really is

If this sounds like a rather tall order for the critic (to say nothing of the poet, whose visions presumably offer us the potential for such wisdom), our perspective changes somewhat when we as readers look in a sustained and careful way at individual poets and poems. This involves a steady awareness of form, structure, rhetoric and style (here we are heirs to both New Criticism and deconstruction), insight regarding the play of psychic forces in language (here psychoanalytic criticism often comes to our aid), and knowledge of the material historical circumstances which led to the production of the work (I'm still something of a Marxist, though not to the same extent as at the start of my critical career).

In *The Serpent's Gift: Gnostic Reflections on the Study of Religion*, Jeffrey Kripal makes the following audacious declaration: "I no longer want to study mystical literature. I now want to write it. But this, I suggest, can be done today only in and through our own (post)modern forms of consciousness and criticism." This passage resonates strongly with me, and I am reminded, as I write in the afterword to my book *On Mount Vision*, of a reader report on one of my articles (I believe it was about either Robert Duncan or Nathaniel Mackey) in which the reader declared that "there are times at which the author confuses reading poetry with spiritual exercise and presumes a reader who is too much a worshipper at the temple." In my response to that comment, I wrote that "my critical practice, if not a demystification of this poetry, is at least an *unveiling* of a partly hidden, partly repressed, partly neglected dimension of the work." So although I would not go so far as Kripal and claim my commentary as mystical literature, I would say that the work gathered in this book seeks to unveil, through commentary, the gnosis that is to be found in modern American poetry.

But why this body of poems in particular? The short answer is that as a poet, I have always felt a need to examine the work of my contemporaries and immediate predecessors in an effort to understand its importance to me. What in the work resonates for me? What can I learn from it? If the qualities I admire in the work inspire me, I want to explain those qualities to other readers, so that they too can appreciate them. But this is not only a matter of critical evaluation, as important as that may be. (And it is important—this is why I started my poetry review blog, Restless Messengers.) On a deeper level, as I reflect on the kind of commentary I write, I am led back to a passage from Walter Benjamin's essay on Kafka, which may seem at first glance to be rather remote from modern American poetry, but is actually quite relevant to the search for gnosis that I conduct among these texts:

> The gate to justice is learning. And yet Kafka does not dare attach to this learning the promises which tradition has attached to the study of Torah. His assistants are sextons who have lost their house of prayer, his students are pupils who have lost the Holy Writ. Now, there is nothing to support them on their "untrammeled, happy journey."

I first cited this passage many years ago, in the introduction to my book on modern Jewish literature, *The Ritual of New Creation*. Thinking about these assistants and students, however, it occurs to me now that the "untrammeled, happy journey" which results, as Benjamin ironically notes, from the experience of spiritual loss, is a journey, if not a quest, upon which many of the poets I write about have embarked. It certainly describes the path my own poetry has taken. In this respect, much of the poetry I discuss in this book has especially strong affinities to my own.

The spiritual loss which ironically serves as a creative impulse for these poets may be understood in relation to what Max Weber famously calls "the disenchantment of the world," which has led to a secular cultural milieu. What then constitutes spirituality in a world where "disenchantment" and secularism are supposedly a given? How does belief, broadly speaking, shape poetic practice for those poets who question, if not challenge, secularism, remaining at least partially in an "enchanted" psychic realm? These are questions I have posed in many ways throughout much of the criticism I have written, including most of what is gathered in this volume. Reflecting on this work, it occurs to me now that I have been practicing a mode of criticism which parallels Jeffrey Kripal's understanding of religious studies. As Kripal argues, "we can detect within certain moments of the (post)modern study of religion a certain explosive fusion of faith and reason—a kind of mental matter and antimatter, if you will—that produces a distinctly third realm of knowing that resembles but cannot be reduced to what has traditionally been called gnosis." If this applies to my critical practice, it is due to the fact that the poetry about which I offer commentary is the source, the ur-text, from which this "explosive fusion of faith and reason" comes. The modern gnosis of this poetry, as well as any commentary upon it, inevitably entails this "matter and antimatter." This is, to borrow the title from my own volume of selected poems, *the ratio of reason to magic*, which I seek to determine in the poetry I discuss here.

"*I was appointed the poet of heaven*": so begins the prefatory poem to Lawrence Joseph's first book, *Shouting at No One* (1983). Like a more severe version of the introduction to Blake's *Songs of Innocence*, Lawrence's poem recounts a Gnostic myth in which the poetic soul is judged by God to have failed in its task, and is sentenced to material embodiment, to "*be pulled from a womb / into a city.*" That city is mid-twentieth-century Detroit, depicted in gritty, realistic detail as a violent, polluted hellscape. Joseph, the poet-prophet of this fallen world, is indeed "shouting at no one," but still declares that "I don't want / the angel inside me, sword in hand, / to be silent. / Not yet." Joseph, raised in the Lebanese Maronite Church, is one of our most brilliant poetic voices, a poet whose vision of political history remains, even at its darkest, infused by a redemptive light. He is also a perfect example of Kripal's "explosive fusion of faith and reason," and the bitter wisdom he seeks to impart to his readers is a truly contemporary kind of gnosis. Poetry such as his speaks to me—so he is not quite "shouting at no one"—and when I am addressed in this way, I have always felt an obligation to respond. So it is with all the poets I address herein.

A few words about the chapters of this book. There are ten in all. The first seven focus on some of the poets who have meant the most to me, and are largely made up of critical essays and reviews I have published in various forms over the span of my career. Each chapter presents the pieces in chronological order. In a number of cases, these are poets to whom I have returned repeatedly over the course of my career, and indeed, some parts of these chapters go back to my earliest published criticism. For instance, the chapter on Michael Palmer consists of the original article I wrote on him, published in *Contemporary Literature* in 1988, followed by a piece that began as a conference paper, and concluding with a review of his most recent book, *Little Elegies for Sister Satan*. The chapters on William Bronk and Helen Adam reach back even further. I should also note that I wrote about some of these poets in my first book, *The Utopian Moment in Contemporary American Poetry* (1988, rev. ed. 1993), and in a later one, *On Mount Vision: Forms of the Sacred in Contemporary American Poetry* (2010).

The last three chapters are about being a Jewish poet, and how my relation to the traditions of Jewish thought and writing have shaped me as poet and critic. Here, I bring my critical instruments to bear upon myself. Three of the critical books I have published are about Jewish literature, and two of those are specifically about Jewish American poetry. These chapters, however, are more personal and reflective; they depart from a scholarly mode, though the scholar within me still finds a home within them. "Poetry is the scholar's art," Wallace Stevens tells us. He is an unsettling figure for a Jewish poet, for despite the rabbis who occasionally appear in his work (as I discuss in my book *Like a Dark Rabbi*), he had the standard antisemitic attitudes of his class and time. And yet, in "The Auroras of Autumn" he writes of the imagination as "that crown and mystical cabala," understanding full well that to be a Gnostic poet-quester is to be a poetic commentator as well. Such a vision of the imagination is at work throughout this book. I hope I have presented it in all its volatility and power.

William Bronk

I first met William Bronk (1918–1999) when I was in my twenties; with my teacher, the poet Henry Weinfield, I made what amounted to a pilgrimage to visit him at his spacious home in Hudson Falls, New York, where he lived all his life, and where he frequently welcomed literary visitors. Though I would see him infrequently, he became a mentor to me, and, as I say below, a model of poetic integrity. I regard him as one of the very most important poets of the second half of the twentieth century. I have written about him on a number of occasions; the two pieces here are my most comprehensive, and indicate why I see him as a major poet. Despite special issues of literary journals, books, and articles devoted to him, and two conferences held on his work, he is still not widely read.

I

William Bronk: The World as Desire

The recent publication of William Bronk's *Life Supports: New and Collected Poems* finally confirms what a small but ever-growing number of readers has known for some time: that Bronk is one of the most significant poets writing in English today. His formal and intellectual integrity unmatched in contemporary poetry, Bronk, at sixty-four, is at last beginning to gain the general recognition of a literary community whose praise has been lavished on poets of lesser stature; thus the centrality of his vision for our age now may be argued without raising the cries of astonished ignorance that would have been heard as a massive chorus even ten years ago. My intentions here are primarily celebratory, but the significance of Bronk's literary status is so compelling that I will reserve some few last words for this subject. I hope to convince, however, through example and explanation. Bronk's work has been occasionally reviewed, and has received some more exacting critical attention. This essay may therefore serve partly as an introduction, yet I hope also to suggest some crucial areas of the poetry that will bear much further critical exploration. The best way to accomplish both these goals is to examine the most important (and most enduring) of Bronk's poetic ideas. Through them we may gain insight into his literary history, his formal rhetoric, and his metaphysical vision.

The single great constant in the poetry of William Bronk is desire; specifically, desire for the world, which can never be known as a totality. Despite the self-limiting fact that consciousness is aware of its inability to experience this totality, it continually struggles to achieve its goal. Cut off from any ground of belief, secure only in its desire, consciousness therefore creates a world, which despite its insufficiency in metaphysical terms nevertheless allows for the rendering of form: the poem. Within the limits of their self-created worlds, Bronk's poems unfold as a phenomenology of desire, and this is why, when they are read as a single body of work, they echo each other so hauntingly that they seem like endless variations on the same theme. Bronk's poems actually move through wide registers of emotion, emerging from many essential human situations. But these are all abstracted into a kind of intellectual music, sensuous in its meditative complexity and at times overwhelming in the force of its rhetoric. Regardless of their "subjects," however, almost all the poems embody that philosophical moment adumbrated in the last stanza of "At Tikal," the final poem in Bronk's first published volume, *Light and Dark* (1955):

It is always hard like this, not having a world,
to imagine one, to go to the far edge
apart and imagine, to wall whether in
or out, to build a kind of cage for the sake
of feeling the bars around us, to give shape to a world.
And oh, it is always a world and not the world.

In adopting this paradigm, Bronk may certainly be considered an heir to the tradition of Romantic interiority, in which consciousness turns from the outside world and, out of lyrical fragments, creates its own world. As Bronk says in "Some Musicians Play Chamber Music for Us":

We commune with one another and the world.
Breath, bow and finger sing our true responses.

We elevate and offer up
the broken pieces chosen from our days.
So by such sacrament is the world made real,
a true presence caught, never reduced
to final elements, nor totaled up,
and yet composed, oh wholly and well composed.
In a broken, evasive world, reality
is what we mean to celebrate, to be
partakers of, within this music's sound:—
look, where the world comes, listen, hear.

Drawing on the ritual of the mass, Bronk presents music as a kind of secular sacrament which offers us "a true presence" in an otherwise "broken, evasive world." In his work, music becomes a frequent metaphor for this process, for in its seamless and sensuous character (and its origins in discrete tones), music appears as the perfect medium for the movements of desire. Music is complete within itself; it is its own world.

Much has been made of his links to Wallace Stevens, and there is no doubt that Bronk, in his earlier poetry especially, enters into that same rarefied realm of discourse as such Stevens poems as "Tea at the Palaz of Hoon" and "The Idea of Order at Key West." Indeed, Bronk is the more rarefied of the two poets, as should be evident from such a poem as "For an Early Italian Musician," from *The World, the Worldless* (1964):

Listening now to his music, how
one wishes to have been the musician, and so
to be beautiful forever as his music is,
and he in it, who is now
only his music, which is his world.

How one always wishes for an end
—to be complete.

And   there is also this:
that one wishes to last, that one needs to make
a world for survival, which cannot be done
simply, or soon, but by a slow

crystal on crystal accretion of a made
world, a world made to last.

One is nothing with no world.

In a poem such as this, we can see how, by limiting himself to a single pervasive fiction, Bronk makes a place for himself that is unique among modern poets. With no need to dwell upon the immediate particulars of the subject (usually considered to be the matter from which the poem is made), Bronk moves directly to the more relevant sensuous content: the ideas that the subject matter creates in the mind, which simultaneously "take form" as completed utterance. In this case, Bronk's careful use of enjambment and repetition reflects the "crystal on crystal accretion" which is the creative process for both the music and the poem. Yet because of Bronk's unswerving capacity for negation, which both as motive and rhetorical technique is based upon his unsatisfied desire, the poem seems to unwrite itself with its last line, recalling that its language has resulted merely from a fantasy, a wish "to have been the musician." This last line, of course, provides the strong sense of closure typical of Bronk's lyric style. Yet we also sense that the poem is bound to summon forth another utterance, another world ironically "made to last." Although the poem seems to posit the existence of such a world only in the past (since it is "for an early Italian musician"), it actually implies that in the future, such worlds will continue to come into being.

As his work evolves, Bronk realizes that the process of composing *a world* is of the utmost importance, because, for all his skepticism, it is this act of composition which binds him to *the world*—and in doing so, makes him a master of the sublime. One way in which the sublime may be understood is as an intense, elevated emotion that we feel when we are suddenly able to identify with the fullness or enormity of existence. We are rarely conscious of this enormity, but when such moments come upon us, they are both terrifying and transcendent. As Edmund Burke notes in his classic *A Philosophical Enquiry into the Origin of Our Ideas of the Sublime and Beautiful* (1757), "Another source of the sublime is *infinity*; if it does not rather belong to the last [that is, vastness]. Infinity has a tendency to fill the mind with that sort of delightful horror, which is the most genuine effect, and truest test of the sublime. There are scarce any things which can become the objects of our senses, that are really and in their own nature infinite. But the eye not being able to perceive the bounds of many things, they seem to be infinite, and they produce the same effects as if they were really so." Here then is Bronk's "Of the All with Which We Coexist," from *The Empty Hands* (1969):

Looking around me. I see as far to
one sky as another. The limitations of the eye:
we know the sky goes farther. Yet instruments
give us the same view and absolve the eye.

If I am not central to the world, then it fails
to make any difference whatever I feel.
The universe is large: to be eccentric is to be
nothing. It is not worth speaking of.

If I am anything at all, I am
the instrument of the world's passion, and not
the doer or the done to. It is to feel.
You, also, are such an instrument.

You speak of justice and injustice, and well you might.
You speak of grief, of ecstasy. This
is a cruel world and a gay one. We are. Feel
There is nothing to do, to be done, to be done to.

This magnificent poem, which may be justly compared to the transcendental lyrics of Shelley and Blake, articulates a vision of human desire with a purity and force unequaled in contemporary poetry. In declaring himself to be "the instrument of the world's passion" (the intensity of the diction overrides the omnipresent use of the conditional), Bronk becomes allied with the source of human creativity. Passion is central to the world; in claiming for himself and for all others that instrumentality, he centralizes his argument. Regardless of issue, regardless even of emotion, desire becomes the determinant of human value. I will return later to the fact that Bronk concludes "There is nothing to do" once this potential is discovered. Suffice it to say that this poem, in which the poet almost casually assumes a prophetic voice, creates the impression of an unmoved mover, whose lofty project is no longer premised on despair but on the exuberance of sheer feeling. In this way, Bronk abandons the deliberate marginality of his earlier stance, declaring in "The Way of the World," which immediately follows "Of the All with Which We Coexist," "I reject, at least, the implication, the two / idea, the conflict, the adversary, the will / of the world, my will. It isn't that." He is ready to bring his notion of the world to fulfillment, and he does so in "The Abnegation," from *That Tantalus* (1971):

I want to be that Tantalus, unfed
forever, that my want's agony declare
that such as we want has nothing to say to the world;
if the world wants, it nothing wants for us.
Let me be unsatisfied. Hearing me scream,
spare me compassion, look instead at man,
how he takes handouts, makeshifts, sops
for creature comfort. I refuse. I will not
be less than I am to be more human, or less
than human may be to seem to be more than I am.
I want as the world wants. I am the world.

The inevitability of such a statement makes it all the greater. If passion is the central force of the world and the poet is the instrument of passion, then he is, with implacable logic, the world itself. Like Tantalus, Bronk cannot be satisfied; "handouts" are not to be considered, for they cannot assuage genuine human want. Bronk is so uncompromising that he will identify himself only with the Absolute: if to be the world is to know unsatisfied desire, then he will accept nothing less. Therein lies his humanity. For although he seems to distinguish humanity from his act of identification ("I will not / be less than I am to be more human"), he actually declares that true humanity can do nothing more than accept the unending desire that makes it central to the world ("or less / than human may be to seem to be more than I am"). The totality of the world is the totality of human desire, and in this belief alone will Bronk sometimes posit his faith. The affirmation to which the poem attains roars forth in its last line; the vigor of its syntax and its shudderingly direct language are the formal correlatives to the world of hope and despair that the poet finally assumes.

But if the poet succeeds in assuming a position of centrality for his world, such a struggle in itself may have only limited worth. As I have indicated, Bronk's skepticism is so profound that it generates a power-fully self-negating rhetoric, which at its best embodies a sense of totality, despite the void to which it always refers. There are numerous occasions in the work when that skepticism is so passionate that the poem turns on itself, declaring our ultimate insignificance, the insignificance of the human world and all that we may do. At such moments we encoun-ter another of Bronk's seminal ideas, that "Something Matters But We Don't," from his volume of unrhymed sonnets, *To Praise the Music* (1972):

In man, I can see no substance solidly;
it is as if what we call man were no more
than an oddly angled look at something else.
Or is it my limitation, being man,
not to be able to see whatever is there?
And aren't these two alternatives the same?

Let me leave off speaking, unknowing as I am,
but not before I speak of the limits of speech,
or tell of man there is nothing to tell,
or tell of what we discern perhaps there could be
to tell that we know too little except it is there

and, if anything happens, it must be it happens there
and not to us, not by us: good or evil, it doesn't matter what we do.

It would appear that such a statement, reiterated in every one of Bronk's volumes, would contradict his world-creating project. But no: what we must realize about Bronk's work is that it is above all dialectical in nature. If at one point he affirms the centrality of human effort, at another point he must deny, with equal virtuosity and conviction, that human effort could even approach the center of reality. Such vacillation (and indeed, one thinks of Yeats) is a sign of poetic integrity, given that desire must encounter the entire range of experiential vicissitudes as it achieves form. Bronk's genius in part resides in the articulation of these changing moments; thus Bronk is able to write as thoroughly paradoxical a poem as "The Real World":

The real world is no world though without
our knowing it may well be. We can't
say anything about it: how it is
or why, what way it may, but it is there.

They studied the animals, how they react,
earth sciences, measured the interplay
of energies, money matters, how man
treats man, or has in time,—his history.

Nothing we say makes sense, finally.
All right; we believe certain things.
There are things we can say within that belief
unless they negate it. None of them deals with a real world.

There is a real world which does make sense.
It is beyond our knowing or speaking but it is there.

By acknowledging the human propensity for self-negation, Bronk calls into question the validity of all human endeavor. Nevertheless he also acknowledges the necessity of belief as founded upon such endeavor; this is all we have, though we may overturn our beliefs again and again. Bronk's "All right" here resonates with resigned futility, but he goes on to reiterate his own belief in the last stanza of the poem: "There is a real world which does make sense. / It is beyond our knowing or speaking but it is there." The "real world" to which he refers, unknowable despite all of history, seems to emerge from the tension between these otherwise irreconcilable positions; it is a utopian trope that comes into being to affirm a cosmic order that we can sometimes sense if never articulate. Immanence is withheld from us by our own limitations, but the "real world" keeps us from the void into which our perpetual negations would otherwise hurl us. The "real world" is also the "far country" of "Truth As a Far Country; As a Piteous Ogre," the country of which we are only a distant colony, the ogre whom when we encounter it we slay. This is our fate: in our hunger for reality we create those structures that set reality apart from us, that hypostatize it into an Absolute to which we can never attain.

If we are in the world only to be apart from the real world, so too we live only to be lived by life. The latter idea is emphasized in *Life Supports*, Bronk's collection of twenty-line poems, which appeared after a series of volumes in which the lengths of the poems dwindled from fourteen lines to three. The poet's most recent assaults against the silence that has always surrounded his utterances often turn on the dichotomy between individual existence and life in the abstract, "The Destroyer Life," whose motives and movements can be brutally at odds with individual exis-tence. Life may have meaning, but it is alien to that which we wish it to have. As is said in "The Wants of Life":

... Life is aside from us,

though we are lived: such doubtful presences,
so slight in ourselves, we lend a hand in our own
destruction, alive more then than other times,
glorying in the hustle and stir of things.
It's this to be alive! It uses us
without our knowing what it means to do.
Nothing tells us; nothing asks. We aren't
even servants there but furniture of the house,
food to be eaten, fuel, materials
of life. Or pictures watching from the walls.

So one is consumed by life, treated as an object or empty shell, to be discarded at the slightest whim. At worst, as in "Evaluation," "It wants a death and waits on the street for it / and follows it home and kills it in the corridor there." The final line of this poem offers a biting understate-ment that is all the more painful in its obviousness: "Life doesn't ask us its values."

These poems would seem to be among the darkest Bronk has written. Filled with disturbing images of violence, they would appear to be almost a celebration of negativity were it not for the very passion with which they are voiced. In the passion of their confrontation with death, they are reminiscent of Hegel's words from *The Phenomenology of Mind*:

> But the life of the mind is not one that shuns death, and keeps clear of destruction; it endures death and in death maintains its being. It only wins to its truth when it finds itself utterly torn asunder. It is this mighty power, not by being a positive which turns away from the negative, as when we say of anything it is nothing or it is false, and, being then done with it, pass off to something else: on the contrary, mind is this power only by looking the negative in the face, and dwelling with it. This dwelling beside it is the magic power that converts the negative into being.

It is this heroic quality, of course, that has always characterized the lyric sublime. One has only to think of Keats, "half in love with easeful death," to understand the unsettling sensuality and sudden, almost suicidal conclusion of "The Destroyer Life":

I know there are things: crystals, fossils, basalts,
certain metals, that seem as though they last
eternally and I know it is not so.
But we think of them so. I think also of logs
in the woods, tree-trunks, their bark whole
still and, inside, soft as suede, their strength,
their hard solidity wasted, years away.
I saw on the back porch a mold on a squash,
tiny magnificences yesterday
and, today, mold and squash together slime.

These poems that, once, I thought might be
support and comfort to me, come bad times,
are now an emptiness. I need to know
that all their strength is only as a strength
fills them, some strong life, and my
strong life is down as living things
show life so, do drive down.
And I hasten it: my impatiences

bristle why it takes so long, open the veins
of feeling, pulse let go, let go, let go.

For Bronk and Keats equally, death is the master who comes as a lover as well; and this is why Bronk, in emptying himself before the destroyer life, takes an unholy delight in declaring the vanity of human endeavor, especially his own poems. Such passion comes from desire's impatience with mere mortality: when the world, when life, cannot respond to the force of desire, death becomes its final residence.

Bronk offers a more felicitous alternative to his vision of the destroyer life in his poems about light. This is not to say that the essential ambiguity of the human position is ever resolved, but that the poet, in comprehending the otherness of life as man lives it, perceives its fullness as well as its emptiness, the light as well as the dark. For as sublime a poet as Bronk, the perception of life's plenitude is as radical, as devastating an experience as its antithesis, and must involve negation to bring forth a positive assertion. Hence in "The Annihilation of Matter,"

. . . it was always the light
that mattered, and only the light. Once, it had seemed
the objects mattered: the light was to see them by.
Examined, they yielded nothing, nothing real.
They were for seeing the light in various ways.
They gathered it, released it, held it in.
In them, the light revealed itself, took shape.
Objects are nothing. There is only the light, the light!

The idea of a vessel, a form, again appears: light enters and vitalizes matter, giving it significance, just as life enters the living. The rhetoric at such moments tends towards stark, unadorned assertions that impress by their direct, cumulative syntax, reaching to the final outcry. The rhythm generated by such sentence structure is a rhythm of passionate intellection, Pound's logopoeia in its purest and most abstract form. "Where It Ends" is perhaps the most lovely of these poems:

The gentleness of the slant October light
cancels whatever else we might have thought.

It is a hard world, empty and cruel;
but this light, oh Jesus Christ! This light!

The maple leaves, passive in front of the house,
are laved in it, abandoned, green gone.
That nothing else should matter but this light.
Gentleness, gentleness, the light.

The poet is so swept up by his luminous vision that he gives himself over to it entirely by the fourth line, breaking into the common expression of astonishment in what becomes, ironically, a religious poem in spite of itself. The second stanza rushes forward breathlessly, then dies down, ending in a sentence fragment that can only echo in an awed tone what the poet continues to feel. The structure of the poem enacts the emotional experience and creates its own totality, embodying all that it must express.

In coming to terms with Bronk's work, however, one must finally look beyond the dialectic of sufficiency and desire that gives form to the poems. With their strong sense of closure and totalizing structure, they seem to achieve a kind of rest that contradicts the ceaseless motions of desire which is their only subject. The poet Henry Weinfield, one of Bronk's ablest critics, observes of this contradiction that "it reveals a counterpoint and a hidden opposition between the discursive reasonings of the poet and what we can only call desire, since it is embedded not in argument but in form. What the pathos, the hidden music, of Bronk's poetry is, we can only establish by extrapolation, for his conceptual framework never goes beyond its agnostic negations. But in fact Bronk's irony is always self-consuming, for beneath it lies desire in search of a positive ground which, however, is never arrived at explicitly." This clarifies some of the most troubling aspects of Bronk's poetry. Because it can never arrive explicitly at that "positive ground"—which is to say it has never become aware of such a ground in history—the poetry, as in "Of the All with Which We Coexist," inevitably arrives at the point at which "There is nothing to be done." Desire, therefore, must perpetuate itself from poem to poem, a phenomenon that has both its positive and negative moments. In its negative moment, we have Bronk at his most resolutely antihistorical, as in "The Greeks, the Chinese, or Say the Mayans":

We can think of them as being here
in a long immediate present at no
distance, or somewhere else in another world,
some equivalent world, a world not reachable
from here, no direction there to here.
They moved in no direction. They didn't move.
Nothing builds; or if it builds, it falls.
It doesn't reach to here. . . .

With historical time perceived as "a long immediate present," only the force of desire at the instant it imposes itself can have any lasting significance for the individual ("It is to feel," as he writes in "The All with Which We Coexist"). Thus the importance Bronk places on erotic love, as in "That Something There Is Should Be":

Things have; we have no history:
we are men. You are a woman, but even so.
No, even so. It sounds like a kind of joke,
but that's what I mean: we are human. Human is not
to be something we know, but to be as the Jews say God
must be, without an image. What happens takes
no care for how we look, what part we take,
or whether we can. Something there is will be.
Caress me, be kind. We have no history.

This is the opposite of Bronk's antihistoricism, for "Something there is will be" although "We have no history." The individual can feel this way, and most often does, but humanity at large, given the nature of creativity, does not. In terms of poetry, historical awareness manifests itself in the notion of a poetic tradition, the forms that desire takes from poet to poet, from poem to poem. Bronk understands this deeply:

I used to think that Shakespeare didn't exist,
that all his works were part of Original
Creation if such could be said to be. There are those,
now, who say he was someone else: well,
he was someone, whether else or not, and we don't

know who he was but it doesn't matter at all.
We don't have to believe in him the way
we are asked sometimes to believe Drake's drums,
in that story, can be heard at crucial times. We know
that, wonder of wonders, Miranda is still alive.

These lines are from Bronk's "The Lives of the Poets," dedicated to Henry Weinfield, a poem that is a response to Weinfield's own "The Lives of the Poets," especially the following stanza:

Shakespeare (as in the well known parable
by Señor Borges) was invisible.
At Stratford-on-Avon he built himself a house,
And there he lived and died—anonymous.
He was not Hamlet, nor was meant to be
The heroic figure of a tragedy
Whose life becomes the symbol for an age—
Because he disappeared into his page.

The lives of the poets are my life—
I am the lives of the poets.

Bronk then is responding not only to the past poetic tradition, as embodied by Shakespeare, but to the future of the tradition too, as embodied in the younger poet's work. Both Bronk's and Weinfield's poems turn on the idea that desire is evoked and revived every time we write with historical awareness. As Eliot puts it in "Tradition and the Individual Talent," "the historical sense compels a man to write not merely with his own generation in his bones, but with a feeling that the whole of the literature of Europe from Homer and within it the whole of the literature of his own country has a simultaneous existence and composes a simultaneous order." The discrete identities of individual poets are less relevant than the fact that they contribute to the perpetuation of the creative continuum. Shakespeare may be invisible, unknown to us as a personality; but what matters is that Miranda is still alive, and that a new poet may always justifiably declare that "I am the lives of the poets." For all of Bronk's skepticism, his opus offers ample proof.

It should become clear now why the greatness of William Bronk's poetry is still not given its due. Even in the *New York Times* review of *Life Supports* (13 December 1981), Hayden Carruth called Bronk "reticent"; I hope that I have proved, incidentally, that this is simply not the case. Bronk, the man and the poet, is an uncompromising individual who perforce lives in a compromising time. This is most painfully true for poetry, that sad patchwork of schools and styles against which the original (the genuinely traditional) figure tends to disappear. For one who has survived, in George Oppen's words, "the shipwreck / Of the singular," discovery is a long process. Bronk, of course, understands this, and perhaps has even written about it. The name of the poem is "Unsatisfied Desire":

I have seen such beautiful things in the world which, apart
from desire, I should never have seen. I bless desire,
the fault of its satisfaction: the fault of the world.
I bless that fault: that, in its offering
denying us all, denies us nothing,
offers the world to us, not to have.

(1982)

II

The Singular Achievement of William Bronk

I can think of no better place to begin a discussion of William Bronk's distinctiveness among the poets of our time than with "The Substantive," in which Bronk plainly addresses his reader:

Reader, listen: I use the I and you
in order to tell you we are, neither, there,
speaker nor listener. No: listener yes;
we listen or miss it. However. There it is.

Never as actors, never children who show
someone how good they are: look! Look!
I can do it! Yes. Of course, you did.
You could. What way would it matter if you don't?

Or I and you: incredible: discrete
coordinates who conspire to meet on the grid
which was nowhere and is not,—nor are we.

In the beginning was the word and the word was adjective.
Attribute is everything we know.
Listen. Look. Not do. It is there.

In Bronk, one is never far from a point where the poet is stating his terms as clearly and directly as possible. In "The Substantive," Bronk's concern is with language as predicated upon that which is anterior to language; hence the ironic "In the beginning was the word and the word was adjective." But what is anterior to language, especially for a poet? Bronk's reader, his listening "you" who is no more a listener than the poet's "I," knows well enough, though in this particular poem it does not bear one of its usual names: the world, life, desire, reality; Bronk has many nouns and pronouns to employ, and for him, they are all inadequate. Although they may indicate or point to what lies beyond or before them (and Bronk has another poem on this subject called "The Gnomon of the Pro-Nouns"), they are incommensurate with the task of expressing "the substantive." Language is not substantive, and the poet's figures are woefully pathetic because he is compelled to do more than listen; he is compelled to produce utterances which appear to him as children showing off. The metaphor is paltry, and deliberately so: Bronk is always suspicious of metaphor because it is not merely language but reality as we perceive it that is metaphorical: "Attribute is everything we know." That the poem is worth writing is questionable ("I can do it! I did! Yes. Of course, you did."); that the poem meets its reader somewhere is "incredible." But because it does, Bronk must provide instructions—or a warning: "Listen. Look. Not do. It is there." The poem is not an action in the ordinary sense; indeed, for Bronk, all action is elsewhere, apart from us and unknowable. (Thus in "Of the All with Which We Co-Exist," "There is nothing to do, to be done, to be done to"; thus in "The Plainest Narrative," "What happens to us is not / what happens"). The writing of the poem is as much a matter of listening as the reader's reception of it, given its skepticism regarding its own nature as utterance. And as for the substantive? "It is there."

If I find that in my discussions of Bronk's poetry, especially in the light of modern poetry in general, I am quickly and inevitably led to close examinations of individual poems, it is because I am always confident that Bronk's poems can bear such scrutiny, in a way that most poems by most poets cannot. Not only does Bronk exploit rhetoric to its fullest, but his pervasive self-consciousness leads him to subordinate such rhetorical exploitation to an equally thorough engagement with the most important ideas of our time. As in "The Substantive," what Bronk understands is that such ideas often turn back upon themselves, demanding an interrogation of the conditions or ground upon which they are predicated. Bronk's poetry is often labeled "philosophical" or "abstract," and as little useful as such labels are, they are true. Unfortunately, they may also serve to keep Bronk from those readers, well-intentioned but misguided, who believe that a poetry of ideas is somehow peripheral to lived experience. In poetry, however, the relationship between ideas and lived experience is always mediated by language. It is the poet's task to discover those formal strategies which will lead the reader, paradoxically, to the most immediate perception of this relationship. Another paradox is found when one considers the expression of significant ideas in poetic language: such ideas call forth the most distinguished language, but they are only understood to be significant because of their distinguished expression.

This strange logic is of the utmost importance in understanding Bronk's poetic achievement. Confronting the conventional formal strategies (and concomitant aesthetic ideologies) of his time, Bronk chooses to situate his poems precisely in the space between abstract philosophical speculation and the immediacies of lived experience. Bronk's discourse largely consists of language variously challenging not only the assumed generic and epistemological limits of modem poetry, but the occasions of its utterances as well. Even the many Bronk poems which nominally focus upon the discrete, the particular ("My House New-Painted," "The Beautiful Wall, Machu Picchu," "The Tree in the Middle of the Field," etc.), soon pass into a realm of abstraction, which almost miraculously retains the sensuousness of the object-world through the poet's mastery of his linguistic instrument. Thus to a reader accustomed to most recent poetry, Bronk's work may not appear very much like "poetry" at all. But it is just those qualities of the verse which put some readers off—its tremendously compressed but flexible syntax, the radical austerity of its diction, its relentless suspicion of metaphor, its disdain of mere imagery, its seamless sense of measure, and the resolution of its closure—which make other readers sigh in relief and exclaim "At last!"

In any case, there is no mistaking the urgency and relevance of "The Opposition":

All right! So it doesn't make sense; we still
are disposed to talk about it in terms as best
we may, and that means rational. If not
to make sense, what are we talking for? And yet
we have to know that what we talk about
is more, is less—is other—than rational.

All the opposition there is in the world
is nothing much to this one: the way we try
to talk in sensible terms—what else?—of what
we know escapes (and we want it to) from sense.
Suppose, for example, we were born, as we say we are,
and died, in the end, after a reasonable life:

No would be all I could say to that, which I want
more than anything else that I could want.

Today there are those who resist the poet's "we," and perhaps rightly so. For much contemporary poetry has undermined the coherence of the lyric self or simply trivialized it; and once such integrity is challenged, then the imaginative act of communion which turns the poet's "I" and the reader's "you" into a convincing and relatively stable "we" is likewise called into question. But again, readers familiar with Bronk will say yes to this use of the pronoun, for it truly unites the individual who struggles and writes the poems with those who struggle and read them. For we all do struggle, and struggle precisely over the issue raised in this poem. Bronk's readers frequently observe that many of his poems are structured like logical arguments, in which certain premises are established and proven. But Bronk makes use of logic, of reason, and of ideas generally in order to demonstrate their inadequacy: as he says in "The Mind's Limitations Are Its Freedom," "What else but the mind / senses the final uselessness of the mind?" In "The Opposition," the poet's defense of rational discourse is undermined by the apparent rationality of the discourse itself. It is reasonable for us to desire for something to escape from sense because, after all, just what does it mean to live a "reasonable life"? Bronk desires a reasonable life and yet he says no to any claim for it, for he knows that our rational discourse (and our reasonable lives) "is more, is less—is other—than rational."

At issue in this poem (and here is another good example of Bronk's work seeking to know the ground of its knowing) is nothing less than the status of reason for modern human experience; thus Bronk is perfectly justified in his claim that "All the opposition there is in the world / is nothing much to this one." And here I cannot help but express my continued amazement at the scope and ambition of Bronk's project. Bronk tends to avoid grand claims for his work, though the manner in which he is always measuring his utterance against the cultural achievements of the past gradually becomes apparent to the careful reader. Still, his attitude is best summed up in "2+2 (=1?)":

Now I want to say oh, God yes
these impossible poems, crude and diverse:
what had you thought to say or didn't you think?
I guess I didn't nor planned them as a sequence. I took
them one at a time the way they came. Maybe they don't
add; we keep looking for whatever does.

The humility which drives Bronk's quest is one of the sources of his enduring strength. The engagement with the idea, which represents the singular occasion for each poem, may have eventuated in what we take as a sequence, an ongoing act of writing in which certain themes are relentlessly pursued. But, to borrow from the title of another poem, there is ignorant silence in the center of things, and it is his awareness of our diminished status in the face of this ignorant silence which leads Bronk to begin each poem as if it were the first occasion—and perhaps the last. "This nothing. This full silence. To not know." Yet the ignorant lust after knowledge, as another title goes. The poet has no choice but to bring to bear the full extent of his intelligence and craft upon silence and ignorance, knowing in advance the place to which he will come upon each occasion. From "The Ignorant Lust After Knowledge":

A light, this side of the hills toward Argyle,
flowed like fog through the hollows, rose to the depth
of the hills, illumined me. I faded in it
as the world faded in me, dissolved in the light.
No one to know and nothing knowable.

Is it too obvious to say that Bronk is also one of the loneliest of our poets? Even in those poems in which he makes gestures of love or friendship, such as "Colloquy On a Bed" or "The Tell" ("I want to tell my friends how beautiful / the world is . . ."), he speaks from the position of existential isolation to which somehow we are always relayed. This is not to say that we join him in isolation; rather, we are made privy to a voice speaking, perhaps to another but always to itself. Alone in its life, it rejoices and praises, rages and laments, or sometimes goes beyond all conventional emotional responses to become, as it were, the commentator upon its own inviolability. In "Life Supports,"

. . . Issue by issue the news
runs by, describing events and non-events,
reports sometimes of me, others I know.
Food, of course, often. Salty and sweet,
soluble, and other solutions at times
—corrective fluids needed to restore such balance
as may be lost. I am aware though I
not seem to be. Hard to believe the surge
of current through my angers, ecstasies
and frights sometimes at crises: a faulty tube,
power-outages, not long, but I cried
to be restored. The dials and switches wait.
No god comes near me. I am alone.

Each of us is alone in an individual life, each of us lives through life, and life lives through each of us. "Life Supports" and other poems from the series that bears that title insist upon the individual's isolation in the midst of life: it is our common fate because life is something radically other than the sum of living things. We are, as it were, attached to life as to a powerful, complex machine requiring constant care and adjustment. No god comes near us (in his agnosticism, Bronk can imagine no greater union); and our relations to ourselves, even in love, are impossible in their ephemerality, as in "The Errors of Order": "A friend kisses me and I respond. / There isn't a way; nevertheless . . ." And although the self maintains its fragile integrity and perhaps even its autonomy, in return it must live with the dreadful knowledge put bluntly at the end of "The False Corner": "Something is living which we know certainly. / It has little to do with man."

That we come away from Bronk's poetry in such an unsettled state is the sign of the peculiar satisfaction to be found in a wholehearted reading of his work. Generally speaking, modern poetry has not fared well because the lyric self, like all other avatars of the human subject, has been called into question in the most drastic terms. While Bronk fully acknowledges this crisis and confronts it head on (as in the strangely gentle "The Belief in the Self Abandoned" or the more urgent "Writing You"), he nevertheless finds the means to resist its most ravaging effects, aware of them but not determined by them. His work does not dissolve into the play of objects or of language; it never engages in sloganeering, in the exaggeratedly confessional, or—perhaps worst of all—in the merely anecdotal. Instead, we are provided with a poetry which speaks continually about "The Emptiness of Human Being":

No excuses: evasions are what we try:
form as adversary or, failing form,
other divisions, assertions by negatives.
We are the not this, not that.
The determined self makes be by partialness,
sets out his space, says here is truth,
is his, says less is all, defends, fades.

Theoretical statements about work such as this are obviated, in a sense, by the work itself, for no other poet has learned so well that "We are the not this, not that." This is why Bronk's poetry, unlike any other up until now, explicitly anticipates or includes within itself any critical assertion that can be made about it.

Yet for just this reason it demands much further discussion. For a long time, American poetry, with a few notable exceptions, has been a mediocre affair, but on this occasion I will not produce the usual catalog of explanations, with which the reader may be all too well acquainted. When a poet of Bronk's ability looms up in such a dismal landscape, offering poems of such sculpted beauty, with such a complex relation to tradition, one would like to think that he would become a center of serious attention. Fortunately, advocates of Bronk's work cannot claim that it was completely neglected by the official arbiters—*Life Supports*, did, after all, win the American Book Award—but I for one remain appalled at the continued failure to lend sufficient credence to its importance. As a teacher of modern literature, I am particularly scandalized by Bronk's absence from all the major anthologies, for in my own classes I have been struck by the way even relatively unsophisticated students quickly grasp Bronk's essential distinction among any number of other recent poets.

By now the reader will have noticed that I have mentioned no other poet, past or present, in this essay, nor have I invoked any literary critic or theorist. Discussions of literary value become increasingly frustrating in our present circumstances, and though I would never advocate a return to a vainly held belief in any one canon of taste, I must sadly acknowledge the inevitability of certain losses. As a consolation—because one of poetry's perennial functions is to offer hard-earned solace—here are excerpts from two more of Bronk's poems, "The Life" and "Not to Cry Out 'How Long, Oh Lord, How Long'":

I wonder why both Auden and Eliot
wanted papers burned or unrecorded?
They must have known how they were absent too
and how little it mattered. Does anybody care?
Let the little be known and let it be plain
life isn't about us; it's about
itself and that's what we try to write about:
the light it makes of us to see it by
and the iterate, pitiless deaths it needs to show.

• • •

What I mean to include is our helplessness and besides,
our confirmed intention. We mean it. What I have to feel
is both goodness and evil, which are strong but not the point.
We mean to be—whatever—what we mean to be.

(1988)

Helen Adam

I was enchanted—that is precisely the right word—by the poetry of Helen Adam from the moment I read "I Love My Love" in Donald Allen's famous New American Poetry *anthology. This was in 1973. At first I had difficulty finding more of her work, and it came as a wonderful surprise to see her poem "Troynovant Is Now No More a City" in the pages of the little magazine* Endymion, *edited by my friends David Katz and Linda Stern. Eventually I found her books, and then, in the summer of 1979, had lunch with her in her New York City apartment. I was one of the first critics to write at length on her poetry in the journal* Credences *and in my first book,* The Utopian Moment. *I then happily returned to it years later when Kristin Prevallet edited* The Helen Adam Reader.

I

Helen Adam and Romantic Desire

Helen Adam is a poet's poet, for it is in her own tribe that she has been most read and praised, despite her long history of public readings. She is probably best known for her appearance in Donald Allen's *The New American Poetry: 1945–1960*, that extraordinary anthology that was once read as a manifesto, but is now usually regarded as a historical document. In that collection, her long poem "I Love My Love" was included among the works of the San Francisco Renaissance poets, and her name was associated with such figures as Robert Duncan and Jack Spicer. Like them, she has always manifested a high degree of interest in the supernatural (indeed, it may be said to be her principle subject matter), but unlike them, she has merged this interest with an entirely traditional poetic sensibility. For her poems exist in their own right as thoroughly *new* poems, the best of which could serve as models of poetic integrity to more than one generation lost amidst a welter of styles and schools of verse.

Born in Scotland in 1909, Adam came to this country in 1939 with her mother and sister, having by the age of fourteen already established a reputation in her native land for the books she published under the name "the Elfin Pedlar." In 1953 she moved to San Francisco, where her impact upon an already thriving, highly eclectic literary community was soon felt. Robert Duncan writes that she

> opened the door to the full heritage of the forbidden romantics. Her ballads were the missing link to the tradition. How troublesome at first they were! They fascinated; they seemed entirely anachronistic. There was the mere lapse of time through which they had traveled. They were powerful; they should have been *wrong*. They were entirely concerned with event, with marvelous event; nowhere was the language shaded to hint at the poet's sensibility. In grasping the inspiration of Helen Adam, in admitting her genius, I was able to shake off at last the modern proprieties—originality, style, currency of language, sensibility, and integrity. I have a great appetite for approval from whatever source, and only the example of this poet who cares nothing for opinions but all for the life of the imagination, for the marvelous that is the grain of living poetry, saves me at times. And Helen Adam was right, passions may have voices in ballads and orders appear in fairy tales that were otherwise mute and garbled.

What Duncan immediately sensed about Helen Adam's attitude toward poetry was a conviction that he too was striving to achieve: that the poem was not a mere work of craft, an isolated linguistic structure upon which one could place a New Critical seal of approval; but part of a living, visionary tradition, an incantatory expression of transcendental desire, for which the poet was a vessel or medium. Thus, while Adam's formal precursors come from the oral tradition that is codified in the early nineteenth century by such poets as Burns and Scott, the more important influence upon her literary imagination is the High Romantic mode of Blake, Wordsworth, Coleridge, Shelley, and Keats, and that greatest of Romantic revisionists, W. B. Yeats. In the work of these poets, the simple oral forms and tragic or fantastic themes of the folk ballad are refined, imbued with a highly self-conscious sense of dialectical conflict, out of which comes magnificent lyric tension. The force of Romantic desire, of course, extends far beyond the ballad form. But when we place Helen Adam's poetry in juxtaposition to certain Romantic masterpieces—the *Songs of Innocence and Experience*, the *Lyrical Ballads*, *The Mask of Anarchy*, "La Belle Dame Sans Merci," or *Words for Music Perhaps*—it may be seen how much she has learned. The philosophical subtleties and transcendental passions of her precursors are often obscured by her outré subject matter and chant-like verse, but even these overt characteristics are themselves symptomatic of the poet's insistent visionary bent.

Helen Adam's visionary capacity, however, is most often of one particular kind, that of preternatural terror and unrestrained violence, both physical and psychic in nature. Invariably, Adam's ballads turn upon some act of cruelty and mayhem or of abandonment and despair. It would seem then that she departs from the heroic tradition in Romantic poetry, until one recalls that the original Romantic hero is Satan himself in *Paradise Lost*. Adam is firmly of the devil's party; the force of desire she expresses is thwarted desire, and the figures that people her poems are noble inasmuch as they are perverse. Their actions demonstrate how well the poet has learned a crucial Romantic lesson: that in the world of the imagination, desire, when it cannot achieve its object, will transform itself into a terrifying supernatural power, wanton in its destructiveness but magnificent in its lyrical expression. Unlike simple folk ballads, Adam's self-conscious pieces continually break into passionate apostrophes to desire, revealing the dialectical interplays of love and hate, calm and violence. The climactic stanzas of "Turn Again to Me," the title poem of her 1977 collection, demonstrates this important characteristic:

Those wild girls rage against the sea,
Their heads with hawthorne crowned.
Uprooted is their golden tree
Since Prince Brandaris drowned.
Oh! Lyonese, your Lords of Light
That furious loves command
Their chieftain cruises cold tonight,
And far off from the land.

Now only in the dreams of sleep
He'll dazzle Earthly eyes.

The callous creatures of the deep
Have found him where he lies.
The shadow of Leviathan
Floats o'er his hungry bed.
The nimble minnows nuzzle him.
The hunched crabs gnaw his head.

Oh! the tolling of the bells, sweet-heart,
The shining of the stars,
The great archangel Lucifer
Defeated in the wars.
And Prince Brandaris swept beneath
The slowly moving tide,
The shadow of Leviathan
His only love and bride.

In these lines, the speaker of the poem begs his sweetheart to turn from Brandaris, her ghostly lord, and accept his mortal love. Yet he himself is fascinated by the supernatural love of his rival, its insatiable, self-perpetuating power that outlasts death and change despite its outward appearance of defeat. The speaker's invocation of such power, contrary to his personal feelings, gives the poem its shattering tension, a sense of otherworldly possession that charges the traditional verse form and breaks the ballad's narrative flow. The nostalgia for a lost world of romance that seems at first to underlie the text quickly extends beyond itself to create an emotional atmosphere of far more vitality. Brandaris's destruction is equated with "The great archangel Lucifer / Defeated in the wars"; the proud self-love and heroic (albeit fallen) energy of both figures are one and the same. What we are finally left with, however, is an overriding sense of loss: the Romantic tragedy of unsatisfied desire has been enacted, and because desire now exists only as a vengeful ghost, we must try to "turn again" to the mundane and the mortal. Thus the ballad recreates the tradition of Romantic desire only to memorialize its compelling power.

The typical Romantic pattern for visionary poetry, in which the speaker departs from mundane experience, enters into the visionary state, and then returns to the everyday world bearing enlightenment or disappointment, is not, however, always followed in Adam's poems. Part of the poet's attraction for contemporary readers is her deliberate confusion of mundane and otherworldly experience, which involves distortions of time, space, and personal identity, all in an effort to prove, as we know from the hermetic tradition, that "The things below are as the things above." In accordance with her vision of dialectical conflict, akin to those of Blake and Yeats, Adam insists that the imaginary world and the world of ordinary circumstance impose themselves upon each other in a never-ending series of acts in which protagonists literally consume each other in passions of love and hate. Sexual possession by a supernatural lover is frequently equated with an act of devouring, an equation, as implied in "A Tale Best Forgotten," that is an eternal verity:

Hail most holy ANUBIS.

In a house by a river that lamented as it ran,
Lived a father, and his daughter, and the dog-headed man.
A father, and his daughter, and the dog-headed man!
It's a tale best forgotten, but before the tale began
From the house to the river limped the dog-headed man.
Blood swelled the river before the tale began.

In the garden, in the garden, while the river slowly ran,
Walked the daughter, and her lover, and the dog-headed man.
The daughter, and her lover, and the dog-headed man!
It's a tale best forgotten, but before the tale began
His daughter, by the river that reflected as it ran,
Fed the bones of her lover to the dog-headed man.

Dog Head he was fed before the tale began.

Here, we have come quite a distance from, say, "La Belle Dame Sans Merci," and yet the paradigm of the femme fatale remains remarkably consistent. One of the most intriguing aspects of Keats's great ballad is its subtly warped sense of time, which seems to cease in its linear movement when the knight encounters the seductress. When her victim enters into the trance in which the nature of his plight is revealed to him, we realize

that he is only part of an ongoing cycle, a rhythm of recurrence perpet-
uated by a malevolent force above and beyond human ken. The same is
true, but self-consciously articulated, in Helen Adam's poem. What has
occurred, what occurs, what will occur in the poem has all been pre-
ordained "before the tale began." Clearly, the lovers of this belle dame,
like Keats's knights, have been lured into a world governed by a mythic,
cyclical notion of time. This world, which corresponds to Freud's battle-
ground of Eros and Thanatos, is entirely self-perpetuating; like a self-
fulfilling prophecy it foreshadows its own completion ("Blood swelled
the river before the tale began") and in concluding declares that what has
been told are events that all precede the tale's actual telling ("Dog Head
he was fed before the tale began").

A further elaboration of the paradigm of the "belle dame" is the presence of the god whose desire allows for the continuance of the sacrificial
cycle. Keats's ballad, with its understated technique and partially veiled
eroticism, barely implies a motive for the ongoing acts of enchantment.
However, the images of fever, pallor, and starvation which abound in the
poem make the theme clear: love is death, and to indulge in the erotic is
to give oneself up to destructive delight. Adam again makes this a self-
conscious aspect of the poem: her seductress is part of an infernal family
whose lord is Anubis, the Egyptian god of death, whose presence in the
poem as a kind of shadow-figure is a constant reminder of the lover's fate.
Likewise, in Keats's poem, the knight, after having loved la belle dame,
must wander in a listless, somnambulistic state, destined, no doubt, to
join the other heroes whom the seductress has possessed. In "A Tale Best
Forgotten," possession by the rapacious desire of the god is more thorough: his priestess feeds her lovers to him, and the act of devouring love
is complete.

Having located the tradition out of which Helen Adam's work
emerges, we may still ask about its deeper truth. No poet is self-created:
Adam's poetry is not merely a rehash of certain Romantic tendencies,
but given her devotion to visionary experience, it is one of the purest,
the most rarefied product of Romanticism we have seen in recent times.
What knowledge, what gnosis, is to be gained by the endless rehearsal
of love, possession, and violence, that is Adam's most frequent theme?
The phantasmagoria of Romantic desire that the poems depict seems

doomed to repeat itself, but that vision of supernatural conflict is apparently celebrated despite the stasis and depravity it represents. The notion of *progress* therefore is absent from Adam's work, and the cycle of human life becomes an endless round of unfulfilled desire. Adam's long-time attraction to Buddhism certainly influences her view. In her essay "A Few Notes on the Uncanny in Narrative Verse," she criticizes James Thompson's anger against God as expressed in *The City of Dreadful Night*, noting that "The poet's rageful expression is a consequence of his belief in the Western idea that human beings are individuals. However, if the ancient Eastern notion that life is a cosmic game in which the Eternal plays at becoming all forms and creatures of Time is true (and I believe it is), then nothing, even the grimmest of human fate, is at all tragic."

Life then becomes a game; individuals lose their significance as such and become counters for the blithely uncaring Absolute. This is seen most clearly in those ballads in which two equal combatants struggle, each representing a satanic force of hate or an angelic power of love, but ironically in the service of a vision that scorns all dualisms. In "The Queen O' Crow Castle," Callastan, who walks with an angel, and the Queen, whose devil has slain seven previous husbands, spend a tempestuous wedding night while their supernatural guardians struggle above them. In "Crow Feathers Falling," a mugger discovers his victim to be as capable of violence as he, for each represents one pole in the dialectic of Yang and Ying, black crow and white dove. And in "Doll Song," the enchantress who makes two clay figures of Love and Hate, which slay the "careless" lads lured into her garden, becomes the victim of her own magical figures when she becomes obsessed with a young girl:

Love sprang to meet her gaunt and bold,
With hair and flesh of roaring gold.
And Hate, who bore a lime-tree rod,
Exultant through the garden trod.

They caught and tied her by her hair
Against a tree that blossomed fair.
Three times they kissed their mortal bride.
With barbs they pierced her hands and side.

The imagery of this poem leads us back to a crucial source of Adam's vision, William Blake's "The Mental Traveller":

And if the Babe is born a Boy
He's given to a Woman Old
Who nails him down upon a rock
Catches his shrieks in cups of gold

She binds iron thorns around his head
She pierces both his hands & feet
She cuts his heart out at his side
To make it feel both cold & heat

This is the beginning of a grotesque cycle of love and hate in which the life of the individual and the life of the age are deformed by the incessant demands of natural and social necessity. Desire, restrained by nature, and nature, exploited by humanity, consume each other in a world that to the Mental Traveller scarcely seems earthly. Blake clearly mourns this situation and struggles against it; Adam, at least in some of her most ambitious poems, chooses to endorse it. Blake, at the beginning of the nineteenth century, is intensely conscious of the human ability to make our own history, to free ourselves from the cycle of enslaving nature and liberate the creative force of desire. Adam, near the end of the twentieth century, seems to write from a post-historical world in which events confirm the cyclic, destructive power of human desire at its most rapacious. As she pointedly remarks in her essay on the uncanny in narrative verse, discussing Coleridge's Ancient Mariner, "His crime was symbolic of the evil race of man, the long, long history of hideous cruelty towards all the beautiful and innocent living creatures who share the planet with us. Personally I believe that the dark atomic dangers we now face, which may eventually destroy our world, are caused partly by a karmic residue from such cruelties." *The Rime of the Ancient Mariner* is yet another cyclical Romantic poem of repetitive psychic, if not cosmic, disaster. One can only imagine what Adam would say in response to the current climate crisis.

She learns this dark wisdom in part from a more recent figure, Blake's great disciple, W. B. Yeats, whose cyclic view of history and personality may be found not only in *A Vision* but in the many ballads of the latter part of his career. Commenting on the changes in the Romantic philosophy between Blake in the late eighteenth century, and Yeats and Robert Graves in the early twentieth, Harold Bloom, in *The Ringers in the Tower*, observes that "Both Yeats and Graves show us the nightmare cyclic world of Blake's *The Mental Traveller*, but what Blake tells us is mere unnecessary masochism Yeats and Graves affirm as imaginative truth." The seemingly endless destruction of desire, fruitless despite its self-perpetuation, is in Yeats a source of inspiration, a seemingly universal law which the poet must acknowledge and contemplate in order to express his historical vision. Ideologically, Yeats's vision of cyclic destruction and resurgence is the hypostatization of his political despair, a gyring movement, as in "The Second Coming," in which love, both in history and in the human personality, is forced into violent antithesis with barbarism and wanton rage. Nevertheless, his bitter wisdom is so thoroughly subsumed in his passionate rhetoric that it makes for wild, poignant poetry:

"Fair and foul are near of kin,
And fair needs foul," I cried.
"My friends are gone, but that's a truth
Nor grave nor bed denied,
Learned in bodily lowliness
And in the heart's pride.

"A woman can be proud and stiff
When on love intent;
But Love has pitched his mansion in
The place of excrement;
For nothing can be sole or whole
That has not been rent."

Yeats's Crazy Jane, spokeswoman for a Blakean dialectic, the very bitterness of which is a source of joy, recites a lesson that is subsequently learned by all the lovers in Helen Adam's poems. What Adam casts into the form of ghostly ballads is actually an extended meditation on the wreckage of love, the disastrous meetings of desire and its object that rule the course of human destiny. For Adam, as for Yeats, the failure of desire to fulfill itself betokens the calamitous fall of empires as well as the fall of an individual. "Troynovant Is Now No More a City," with its title taken from Thomas Dekker, sets the deceptive celebration of London as the New Troy in 1603 against the traditional figure of the ruined maid, who gives voice to her plight in a tone of sexual tension and impending madness:

The rainbow city of Troynovant
Rose up in a day and a night,
With its sky blue doors, with its sparkling floors,
With its towers of challenging height.
But towers and turrets balanced so neat
Fell down in a night and a day.
And my love won't give me a wedding ring
However hard I pray.

Doves pirouetted in Troynovant
Humming tops whispered bliss
When Golden Dan was my Fancy Man,
That a Queen might die to kiss.
Lie still, lie still, my lunatic babe,
While larks and nightingales chant.
You were got by the light of a meteorite,
In the streets of Troynovant.

Her seduction by a false lover deliberately parallels the New Troy's false grandeur, and Adam, in reading Dekker, is of course aware that London itself fell victim to the plague in 1603. Disastrous love and fallen pride bring woe to both the mighty and the insignificant; the history of the heart and the history of the nation are equally susceptible to the ravishes of what the maid calls "unendurable love." The pathos of her situation indicates the sympathy that Adam at times expresses for the victim of such desire, a sympathy that is the antithesis of the wanton pleasure that hovers over the carnage of so many of her other poems.

Because Adam portrays the struggle of Romantic desire in so many of its moments, it should come as no surprise that some of her poems express the wish for an end to all struggle, the cessation of desire in a kind of apocalyptic stillness to which only the most world-weary may attain.

The mystical calm that follows the most extreme passions may be noted, for example, in "Dirge for a Dazzling Star," based, as the poet tells us, on the opium dream of a young nineteenth-century clergyman:

"The Pole Star is dying,
The planets bend over it,
They lower it into
A bottomless grave."
The Pole Star is dead,
But shining, shining.
The Pole Star is shining
In a bottomless grave.

The Babes in the Wood
Are sleeping, sleeping.
The Babes in the Wood,
And the wolf at the breast.
The moon of late morning
Fadeth for sorrow
For sorrow she fadeth
Far down in the west.

Not a sound in the world
While the Pole Star was dying,
Not the cry of a child,
Nor the crash of a wave.
No sound over Earth
But sighing, sighing,
For the Pole Star alive
In a bottomless grave.

The languorous repetitions and syntactic turns of this poem are linguistically equivalent to a state of pure inwardness, the perfect repose of the poetic consciousness when all desire seems spent. Ironically, this is the point at which Yeats begins his career, turning completely from the storms of the outside world to bring to a culmination the most contemplative tendencies in the Romantic tradition:

We who still labour by the cromlech on the shore,
The grey cairn on the hill, when day sinks drowned in dew,
Being weary of the world's empires, bow down to you,
Master of the still stars and of the flaming door.

Why is it that Helen Adam assumes the philosophical stance of *The Rose* and *The Wind among the Reeds* when at the same time she celebrates the violent play of opposites into which her precursor's work will later pass? The answer, it seems to me, has a great deal to do with the situation in which current inheritors of Romanticism find themselves.

Romanticism, at one of its deepest levels, is concerned with the distance between desire and its object, between the apparent inadequacy or frustrations of the present and what is held out as a tantalizing possibility in the future. This tension can never be resolved. The poems of Helen Adam, written so purely in the tradition of Romantic desire, represent all the moments through which that tradition has passed. They recapitulate this tradition, which argues for its continued creative potential. Adam's personal belief in reincarnation therefore makes a great deal of sense, for as we have seen, many of her poems are themselves re-embodiments of Romantic masterpieces. One is almost tempted to claim that had Helen Adam not existed, Romanticism itself would have had to invent her. Actually, Adam and her poems teach us a more important lesson: Romantic desire as embodied in a poetic tradition, a tradition of forms, tropes, and gestures, is never superseded, never goes out of style. The magic at work in Helen Adam's poetry will lose its power only at that impossible moment she describes at the end of one of her most wistful poems, "Mune Rune":

And there shall be
No more moonlight.
And there shall be
No more moonlight.

And there shall be
No more opposites
Over a' the Earth.

(1985)

II

The Helen Adam Reader

When Helen Adam died, a ward of the state, in the Carlton Nursing Home in Brooklyn, NY, in 1993, it appeared that her work was heading toward oblivion. Most of her books, published originally by small presses, were out of print. Her uncanny performances of her compelling ballads had sometimes been recorded, but those too were inaccessible. The same was true of her musical, *San Francisco's Burning*, which had enjoyed successful runs in San Francisco and New York City, with music written by two different composers. Though she was a crucial member of the San Francisco Renaissance in the fifties, though she was a significant player in the downtown New York poetry scene of the sixties and seventies, though her ballad "I Love My Lovze" had been published in the groundbreaking Donald Allen anthology *The New American Poetry 1945–1960*, though her work had been praised by major poets of every school and style, and though she had granted important interviews and was the subject of a number of critical articles, she still may have seemed fundamentally eccentric, a figure destined to be a literary historical footnote: a sort of goth version of Baroness Else von Freytag-Loringhoven. Flamboyant in her dress, a weird combination of the Victorian and the bohemian in her demeanor, unwilling to hold any job except file clerk or bicycle messenger, a collector of magical stones (especially agates), statues of ancient Egyptian deities, costume jewelry, antique books, and thrift store gewgaws, Adam and her sister Pat (who sacrificed her own personal life to help Helen's dubious career) seem like characters out of the fairy tales which provide one of the most important building blocks of Adam's blithely anachronistic and utterly subversive romantic art. How can an age besotted with theory, an age in which writers speak of their stories and poems as "projects" preconceived as grant applications, an age in which the word "terror" is associated much more with politics than literature, come to terms with this woman, born in Scotland in 1909, the daughter of a Presbyterian minister (he was accidentally killed by a stray golf ball) who was writing poems by the age of six and who published her first book, *The Elfin Pedlar and Tales Told by Pixy Pool*, when she was fourteen? Even her close association with Robert Duncan, for whom Adam "opened the door to the full heritage of the forbidden romantics," seems perhaps only the oddest of Duncan's odd cultural tastes, the championing of a marginal talent merely for the sake of its marginality.

But no, Helen Adam has not disappeared. Like the most powerful and frightening of the figures in her ballads, who assume their greatest strength only after their (usually violent) demise, Helen Adam is back in all her spooky glory, and we have the indefatigable Kristin Prevallet to thank for her return. *The Helen Adam Reader* is the magnificent result of over ten years' worth of archival and editorial work, and it demonstrates conclusively how important a figure Helen Adam was—and will continue to be. Prevallet, who became aware of Adam's work the year Adam died, was a graduate student at SUNY–Buffalo, where the Helen Adam Archive (actually part of the Duncan Archive, since Helen and Pat stored their belongings in Duncan's basement when they moved to New York in 1964) is housed. Fascinated by Adam's collages, she decided to catalog the collection as her MA thesis. The Archive expanded significantly in 1997 with the addition of the contents of Adam's New York apartment, warehoused by the state after her death. This material was miraculously rediscovered by Jed Hershon, the son of Bob Hershon, Adam's friend and publisher, whose Hanging Loose Press had done a number of Adam's books. Thus, with access to a great range of Adam's books, manuscripts, artifacts, and belongings, Prevallet has produced a generous gathering of poems, lyric drama, fiction, correspondence, musical scores, illustrations, interviews, and commentary. The DVD which accompanies the *Reader* includes a selection of her hilariously creepy collages, music, and performance photos from *San Francisco's Burning*, the complete film *Daydream of Darkness*, which Adam made with William McNeil in 1963, and a 1980 videotape of Adam singing some of her favorite ballads in the wild clutter of her New York apartment. Prevallet's long introduction provides the most extensive biography of Adam to date, situating her in relation to the various literary traditions of Scotland and to the groups and schools of writers and artists with which she was associated in the United States. It also analyzes the various genres through which Adam presents her Blakean vision of cosmic passion and strife: the supernatural ballad tradition of Scotland and England, but also blues lyrics (which she studied with Allen Ginsberg), collage (her work may be compared to that of such West Coast artists as Wallace Berman and her close friend Jess), music hall performance (which she attended as a girl), and surrealistic film. As Prevallet observes, "Helen Adam was an original woman artist who blended a Victorian sensibility with a modern consciousness. The rhyme and meter of her ballads come from Scottish and English literary traditions and old-world schooling; the montage methods utilized in her collage and film work come from a post–World War II American culture and its experiments in breaking genre boundaries. This adaptation of old and new worlds mirrors her life story and the historical shifts—from Victorianism to postwar modernity—that framed it."

As Prevallet's remarks indicate, Adam's work in every genre crosses boundaries, undermines artistic proprieties, toys with audience expectations, and wreaks havoc with literary historical periodization. Writing ballads in the middle decades of the twentieth century meant challenging the divide between popular culture and high art, while at the same time reconnecting with a major tradition of romantic poetry which had *already* challenged that divide over 150 years before. Blake, Burns, Wordsworth, and Coleridge, in variously appropriating the folk ballad, had confronted the literary gatekeepers of Augustan proprieties; Adam, along with such colleagues as Duncan, Ginsberg, and Jack Spicer, likewise confronts New Critical proprieties (including, as Duncan put it, "originality, style, currency of language, sensibility and integrity") by insisting that the poet is a vessel for cosmic powers that transform language into lived event. In this respect, Adam's use of traditional rhyme and meter should be understood neither as cultural conservatism nor, conversely, as solidarity with some liberal idealization of "the folk." Rather, in Adam's practice, the traditional ballad form indicates a fundamental *indifference* to both political and aesthetic ideologies: what is made manifest in the form is nothing more or less than *desire* elevated to a cosmic principle. This is why the constant theme in Adam's poems is the transgressive nature of love. As Prevallet puts it, "Adam's ballads revel in taboo and tell tales of drama and passion, blood and vengeance. Love is not true until the flesh that inhibits desire is carnivorously devoured from skin to bone. . . . Partly because the stories she tells involve the triumph of eternal love over earthly desire, the characters in Adam's ballads always present a challenge to the mortal world and often seek out the fulfillment of their desires in spite of the social rules they have to break."

Adam's ballads move at a relentless pace: once the situation is presented and the rudimentary narrative line established, the language becomes charged with dreadful energy and events unfold with absolute fatality. Although the fates of individuals in the poems often leave us with a sense of cosmic justice—murderers are haunted to madness by the ghosts of their victims, wanton seducers fall prey to seemingly innocent young girls or boys—the poems just as often present a cyclical vision of desire in which human flesh and human spirit endlessly turn. From a psychoanalytic perspective, some of Adam's best poems, such as "The Queen o' Crow Castle," "The House o' the Mirror" or "Doll's Song," may appear to be exercises in a sadomasochistic repetition compulsion. But from what we may call a transcendental or cosmic perspective, the energy that pulses through the poems overwhelms not only any conventional morality but any individual psychic structures, however complexly mapped. In "Doll's Song," an enchantress makes two clay figures of Love and Hate, who slay the "careless lads" lured into her garden, but becomes the victim of her own magic when she becomes obsessed with a young girl:

Love sprang to meet her gaunt and bold,
With hair and flesh of roaring gold.
And Hate, who bore a lime-tree rod,
Exultant through the garden trod.

They caught and tied her by the hair
Against a tree that blossomed fair.
Three times they kissed their mortal bride.
With barbs they pierced her hands and sides.

...

She wanders with dishevelled hair
Beneath the trees that once were fair,
And gathers up, with hands half dead,
The fallen fruits that Love be fed.

Hate strikes her with his dancing rod
Until her blood be-stars the sod.

And when she starts beneath his blows
Love wreaths her brows with thorns of rose.

The ballad ends with another young girl going down to the river to make a set of dolls from the clay of the bank. When she returns with them to her bedroom,

The salamanders in the fire
Upon her hearthstone shriek in choir,
"The Dolls! The Dolls! Oh, mistress gay,
Beware the shapes of supple clay!

Behold they stand within your room,
Angels of agony and doom,
Risen alive from the abyss.
Oh! mistress gay, what game is this?

These are the Dolls named Love and Hate,
Fell images of mortal fate."
"Oh Hush," she sighs, "your foolish noise.
These are my toys, my charming toys."

As the admonitory voices in the fire declare, the force of desire results in a terrible game that rises from the abyss, but it is a game nonetheless. Beyond the pleasures and pains of the body, beyond the joys and sorrows of the heart, spirit cries to spirit in an endless dance. In "The House o' the Mirror" (one of the ballads Adam writes in Lallans, the Scottish dialect with which she experimented *after* she emigrated from Scotland and had moved to San Francisco), a mortal lover is obsessed not with his beloved, but with her reflection:

The ghaist that in the mirror gleams
Floating aloof, like one who dreams;
For her he rages, mad and blind,
And plunders a' my flesh tae find.

He dives in flame, and whirls me low
As if tae seize on drifting snow.
He shrieks because he canna clutch
What lies beyond the grief o' touch.

Aye! though we strauchle breast to breast,
And kiss sae hard we cry for rest,
And daur a' pleasures till they cloy,
We find nae peace, and little joy.

For still between us stirs the shade
That ne'er will lie beneath his plaid.
A' but my ghaist tae him I give.
My ghaist nae man may touch and live.

Here, the violence and exhaustion that seem to be inherent in normative heterosexual coupling is set against the female speaker's insistent spiritual autonomy, the "ghaist nae man may touch and live." In Adam's work, that spiritual autonomy asserts itself continually but is almost always undone in the universal dance of passion.

One of the many discoveries that *A Helen Adam Reader* offers is "In Harpy Land," a ballad that Adam illustrated with a set of collages. Adam's collages are perhaps even more subversive than her poetry; they make frequent use of images from women's fashion magazines of the fifties and sixties, juxtaposing elegant models and insouciant debutantes with grotesque animals, lurking gargoyles, and monstrous flowers. The speaker of "In Harpy Land" is betrothed to "the dreadful Harpy Queen / My promised bride in world unseen," an uncontainable force of pure appetite who rules a kingdom where "Heaven and Hell go hand in hand." In a verse which perfectly sums up Adam's vision, the lover of this gorgeous monstrosity declares that

Learning I lack, but this I know
All things exist, and change, and grow,
Only for her to overthrow.
She flits her wings
O'er battlefields of sumptuous red

In charnel pits her feasts are spread
She takes the outlawed to her bed,
And slaves, and kings.

Indeed, as in the Blakean dialectic of the Prolific and the Devourer (see *The Marriage of Heaven and Hell*), we learn in the last verse of the poem that

. . . I am warned that if I wait
Till trumpets sound at Heaven's Gate,
I'll see her where she sits in state
At God's right hand.

In the collage that accompanies the final two lines, God is a grinning, bearded Greek bust—more satyr or Silenus than Jehovah—and the Harpy Queen is a demure Victorian maid who resembles, perhaps, a young Helen Adam. I'm perfectly willing to read "In Harpy Land" as an allegory for Adam's relationship to her innocent, unschooled reader. So if you have not met her yet, let *A Helen Adam Reader* serve as your introduction to the Harpy Queen.

(2008)

Ronald Johnson

Ronald Johnson (1935–1998), who has given me the title of this book, remains a continual source of inspiration to me—and amazement. I wrote about him in both The Utopian Moment *and* On Mount Vision, *and I found his work so compelling that I celebrated the publication of two of his works with fairly extensive reviews. His connections to so-called "outsider art" led me to discuss his work in that context as well. He remains one of the most extraordinary visionary poets of our time.*

I

The Shrubberies

When Ronald Johnson died in 1998, he entrusted the manuscript of *The Shrubberies* to his literary executor, Peter O'Leary, directing him to "Prune the Shrubs!" As O'Leary explains in his afterword, the original manuscript "consists of 229 pages and perhaps 300 poems." Familiar with Johnson's severity in revising his books, O'Leary systematically pared the manuscript down to a volume of 134 poems. A responsible, sensitive, and above all, loving caretaker of Johnson's legacy, O'Leary now presents us with this last book, the joyous, bittersweet finale to the career of one of the great visionary poets of the second half of the twentieth century. More approachable than *ARK*, the "Walled Demesne" which remains the centerpiece of Johnson's poetry, *The Shrubberies*, as the name implies, is a more domestic production, not a stately pleasure dome but a public garden, a space in which the good citizens of Johnson's small-town American utopia can idle, contemplating flowers and stars. Eminently human in scope and unceasingly lyric in tone, the short poems of *The Shrubberies*, like the grander and more elaborate structures of *ARK*, still present what may be Johnson's most characteristic concern: the analogous unfoldings of the orders of being, from microscopic to macroscopic, which Whitman called *kosmos*. It is the Orphic task of the poet, through the visual and musical powers of language, to instruct us in the way of *kosmos*—but it is instruction that, as Wallace Stevens, a rather different heir of Whitman, put it, "must give pleasure." Johnson's last poems "invite the eye / invade an ear"—and it is through such invitations and invasions that we are made privy to what the poet calls "always my core dream / winding a garden / secret in every sense."

Although Johnson's overarching themes in *The Shrubberies* remain those of the visionary Romantics, his technique, as has also been the case in the past, owes a great deal to the modernists. His self-consciousness in regard to the play of eye and ear goes back to Pound, and to an even greater extent, Zukofsky's refining—miniaturizing—of Pound's lessons. In Zukofsky's codification, "The test of poetry is the range of pleasure it affords as sight, sound, and intellection." Particularly in his late work, such as the last movements of "A," the Catullus translations, and *80 Flowers*, Zukofsky pushes this tenet to the limit, challenging his readers to take visual, aural, and intellectual pleasure in increasingly condensed verbal forms. This poetry suggests, as Mark Scroggins writes in *Louis Zukofsky and the Poetry of Knowledge*, "the possibility of the word set free from meaning-determining context, liberated to interact with its neighbors in any or all of the combinations possible. The compression and foreshortening of syntax in *80 Flowers*, far from making the poems meaningless, open them up to a far broader range of potential meanings and connotations." While not as daunting (or obsessively formalist) as *80 Flowers*, *The Shrubberies* employs similar syntactic strategies, and is equally invested in the horticulturalist's art. Johnson, however, gives us not individual flowers, but Wordsworthian "spots of time," captured and focused moments involving elements of the whole garden. Here is one such moment:

catalpa with skirt
of fluted ivory bloom

oblivious to dandelion
globe to reach stars

robin intent succulent
& loam-pulsing worm

In Johnson's work, nature is to be experienced synchronically: at any single moment, an infinite set of events is occurring, some few of which may be perceived and rendered into poetic language. In this poem, each couplet constitutes one such event; the awareness of the poet composes the whole with maximum verbal economy and musicality. The catalpa is "oblivious" to the dandelion; the robin, intent on the worm, is likewise oblivious to both the catalpa and the dandelion nearby: a scene from what Johnson in another poem calls the "Theater of the Actual." Note the internal rhymes in "robin intent succulent," as the two syllables of "intent" are pulled toward the "in" of robin and the "ent" of succulent. "Succulent" itself carries at least a double charge: is it a noun indicating a plant under which the bird searches for the worm, or an adjective describing how the bird regards his anticipated meal? Overall, this poem achieves the goal which Johnson sets for himself in *The Shrubberies'* opening lyric:

mostly circadian rhythms
"and words to jointly knit"
a series of circumlocutions
eye in the eye-of-things
mirror cascade of asphodel
yet delight in spectacle

In biology, circadian rhythms control those natural events with a twenty-four-hour periodicity. Loosely put, then, in these poems Johnson seeks to convey the daily rhythms of nature, to put nature on a human scale. With his "eye in the eye-of-things," the poet jointly knits "a series of circumlocutions," a speaking around the event, not to be evasive but to indicate that all events constitute a single Event, an endless repetition of Itself. As Johnson says in *ARK* 34, "*Spire on the Death of L.Z.*,"

this is paradise
this is
happening
on the surface of a bubble
time and again

Likewise, in *The Shrubberies*, we hear the

buzz of the flies
in the honeysuckle
far flung Utopia
stretched to limits

For Johnson, who invokes Leibniz's monads in *ARK*, this is truly the best of all possible worlds: each moment in the garden is equally as utopian as the next, "stretched to limits" as far as one can imagine. "[N]o fall, no / folderol" declares the poet, at the end of a Dickinson-like piece on Christ, the serpent, and the Garden of Eden. Did we ever truly fall? As Hugh Kenner recognized when the first volume of *ARK* appeared in 1980, Johnson is primarily a religious poet, yet the origin of his religious experience remains difficult to locate: Is it a religion of immanence or transcendence? Or is the question, posed to such a sensibility, beside the point? How serious, I wonder, is a poem like "No Picnic"?

beyond some lillied Elysium
bordered by snowdrops
are Dejeuners sur l'Herbe
after a dip in the Jordan
all else is illusion

"For at least half of the time he was writing these poems," O'Leary notes, "RJ was in ill health, increasingly aware that he was going to die." Writing in the shadow of death, does Johnson consider this life to be an illusion, and the afterlife to be an eternal Dejeuner sur l'Herbe? If so, life beyond the Jordan actually resembles the world as Johnson celebrated it for much of his career. Then again, life has also been "No Picnic": as O'Leary reminds us, the work Johnson composed prior to *The Shrubberies* was his darkest, the remarkable "Blocks to Be Arranged in a Pyramid," written in memory of those who died of AIDS and available, at this writing, only as a poster-sized broadside. In *The Shrubberies*, Johnson writes sadly of his "accelerated commune with beyond / scattered many buddies' ashes / all swept in waltz of death." Yet equally moving—and quite surprising

222

for such relatively impersonal poet—are the few erotic poems in this last book. What lover would not appreciate the following:

sunlight thru slat
onto rumpled bed
lie kindly our kin
oft, oft, softly
skin to like skin

Or in a darker, Whitmanian mode:

uncut pale-caramel cock
one among many such

lightning crack earth
away on horizon sway

O radiant saraband!
companion along the way

I suspect that this poem is as much about the erotic lure of death as it is about sex, as the "cock" in the first couplet gives way to the orgasmic "lightning crack" in the second. Coming from dry and dusty Kansas, Johnson equates lightning with potentially fatal prairie fires, as in the Zukofsky Spire quoted above, "when the wind's bright horses / hooves break earth in thunder" to reveal "Lord Hades, whom we all will meet / crackling up / like a wall of prairie fire / in a somersault silver." Likewise, in what O'Leary designates as Johnson's "Last Poem" in The Shrubberies, "lightning's eternal return / flipped the ecliptic," as the annihilating and life-bringing bolt of energy intersects the celestial path of earth's solar orbit. This too may be a "radiant saraband," and if so, then the "companion along the way" may be Lord Hades himself.

Johnson's last poems bespeak, as even two lines might indicate, a friendly intimacy with cosmic matters that comes from a lifetime of gazing upon and contemplating the natural world. A run of these brief pieces, written, as it were, sub species aeternitas, foregrounds plants or animals against the immensity of the open heavens; the effect, paradoxically is both comforting and sublime:

sweep and sleep of ravens
west in extremis sunset

see a windowed expanse
let in light of galaxies

The dark birds of death, posed against the setting sun, are harbingers of a dawn that is not of the sun, but of the galaxies. In another poem, the stars are seen in miniature, captured in a fountain amidst a blooming landscape:

landscape with pomegranates
tubs of lemons at each corner
all in bloom and bearing fruit
of course a leaping fountain
at center, turning suns

And here, the dimensions of flowers and stars share a common border:

beyond, a Province of wheat
and streams to grind the grain
fields framed by scarlet poppies
and bluest bachelor-buttons
and borderline to the stars

There is, obviously, a great deal more to be said about Johnson's synthesis of Romantic and Objectivist poetics under the general rubric of *vision*, a vision that begins with the inner eye but extends outward to the furthest reaches of the material universe. Meanwhile, let's take pleasure in the garden walks and grand vistas of *The Shrubberies*, keeping in mind that even at the end, Johnson continued to exhort himself in terms that summed up precisely his most enduring poetic powers:

stroke unlimited amethyst
pencil in exact bumblebees,
among bronze lacquer cacti
so rampart senses incensed

lift sentient to the skies
again and again and again

It is as good a credo as I have heard a poet offer in a long time.

(2001)

II

The New *ARK*

In the afterword to his long poem *ARK*, Ronald Johnson names the poets whose "shipwrecks" lay before him as he wrote: Ezra Pound, William Carlos Williams, Louis Zukofsky, Charles Olson. But Johnson, with typical insouciance, tells us he was "undeterred." As he explains, "If my confreres wanted to write a work with all history in its maw, I wished, from the beginning, to start all over again, attempting to know nothing but a will to create, and matter at hand. William Blake would be a guiding spirit. . . ." I suspect that Blake is invoked not only for his absolute freshness of vision, but because of his famous declaration, which he puts in the mouth of Los in *Jerusalem*: "I must Create a System. or be enslav'd by another Mans / I will not Reason & Compare: my business is to Create." It is a paradox that no reader of *ARK* can avoid: like Blake, Johnson feels his business is to create, which means tapping into a perpetual stream of invention. But for Johnson, invention also means a careful engagement with the past, and especially with the tradition of the American long poem beginning with Whitman—not necessarily an anxiety of influence (on the surface, Johnson appears to be one of the least anxious of recent poets) but surely an opening to influence, to "the Voices" that call to him not only from beyond, but from behind. And again like Blake, Johnson looks somewhat uneasily behind him at his precursors (note that he democratically equalizes them all by calling them "confreres"), while at the same time he gazes at a remote horizon toward which one moves only through pure, self-inspired energy and the unbounded spirit of delight. In Johnson's masterpiece, the result of this magical tension, or as he puts it in *ARK* 72, this "legerdemain in the Elaboratory," is an astounding panoply of forms coming from a *laboratory* where the poet conducts his experiments in verbal *elaboration*. And now, once more, these forms are here for us to behold, but with some significant differences. What the poet calls, in *ARK* 81, his "good ship *Praxis*" has been refurbished and launched again into the readerly sea.

The new edition of *ARK* is lovingly edited by Johnson's literary executor, the poet and critic Peter O'Leary, beautifully designed and produced by Jeff Clark of the Quemadura bookmaking studio, and published by Flood Editions. Flood has also given us Johnson's late work, *The Shrubberies*, as well as a new edition of *Radi Os*, Johnson's visionary poem composed by "writing through" Books I–IV of *Paradise Lost*. Johnson worked on *ARK* for twenty years, beginning in 1970 and completing the final section on New Year's Eve, 1990. Over that time, his blueprint changed relatively little and was realized with extraordinary determination. The poem is in three books with a total of ninety-nine sections. Thirty-three Beams make up The Foundations, thirty-three Spires rise above them, and thirty-three Arches constitute the surrounding Ramparts. Time as well as space is structured, since the first book moves from sunrise to noon, the second from noon to sunset, the third through the "night of the soul" until the great "Lift Off" of the following dawn, with which the poem concludes. *ARK* was originally published by Living Batch Press in a paperback edition in 1996, its front cover decorated with a photo of the Watts Towers, one of the sculptural environments made by "outsider" artists which are emblematic of Johnson's aesthetic. The formal inventiveness of the poem (parts of which had appeared in separate volumes beginning in 1980) could certainly be seen in the Living Batch edition, but as a devoted reader of Johnson, I always thought that the visual aspects of the poem and its self-consciousness as constructed artifact could have been better served. Still, it was wonderful to have it, and it went out of print all too soon.

The new edition, therefore, is all the more important. Its white cloth cover, with the title stamped in black in two fonts (A and R in a serif font, K in sans serif), bears a black slip cover on the rear with the fonts reversed (A in sans serif, R and K in serif). Below is a quote from Guy Davenport, one of Johnson's earliest and most perceptive readers. If one holds the volume in one's hands before opening it, the overall effect is a sort of auspicious restraint: this, declares the object, is a *book*, to be embraced in its materiality, but it is also a *scripture*, so be prepared to plumb the depths and climb the heights. As Davenport notes, "It is for those who can see visions, and for those who know how to look well and be taught that they can see them." Readers familiar with the first edition will be surprised when they do open the volume: the font is a clean, Art Deco–like sans-serif font, and the poem seems to have a great deal more room to breathe. O'Leary notes that "Previous editions of the poem vary the leading to reflect single- and double-spacing in Johnson's typescript. However, for greater legibility, this edition adopts a basic leading that is uniform." This may sound like a mere technicality of book design, but with a work like *ARK*, by an author who also writes concrete poetry and who insists early in the work that "The eye may be said to be sun in other form," it is anything but. What we can now *see* in the new edition is, indeed, the power and scope of the poem's visual design. I would not go so far as to say that *ARK* is entirely a concrete poem (parts of it certainly are), but the visualization of an ideal architecture is fundamental to Johnson's conception and method of composition. By standardizing the leading in the poem, the new edition resolves the complicated ideas and unfortunate misconceptions that a number of mid-twentieth-century poets have about typewriters, scoring poetry, and the visual space on the page, matters which become even more troublesome when the work goes from typescript to print. Most importantly, in the new *ARK*, Johnson's stanza structures stand forth with far greater clarity and integrity. In a thread on Facebook (12 Nov. 2013) in which a number of Johnson enthusiasts were discussing the new edition, the poet and critic Ben Friedlander made an illuminating comparison between earlier editions of the poem and the new one: "But those always felt to me like books containing a poem that imagined itself to be architecture, whereas this one feels like the architecture of a poem in the form of a book."

But what exactly does this mean? After all, when Johnson tells us that as an "architecture, *ARK* is fitted together with shards of language, in a kind of cement of music," he is being metaphorical. Yes, the placement of various arrangements of words in a given section of *ARK* (for instance, the concrete passages in Beams 5, 27, and 29) could be said to resemble, or function like, the broken pieces of tiles and bottles that Simon Rodia stuccoed to the surfaces of the Watts Towers. Likewise, Johnson's verbal music is masterful, and could be understood as cementing the words of the poem, though it may be more accurate to say that the words produce the music, and not the other way around. I choose a passage from *ARK* 73, more or less at random:

Sound they about us:
dusks' every thrust athrob together
at syrinx split infinities

rained down in daily radiance, no
never did hoedown jamboree
so strum flesh harp

rung out but harbinger of
believe, believe, be Live above!
& bluegrass all about

globe consuming itself, say
brain by spinal Chord
to pierce new universe thrice on

As is true of Louis Zukofsky, Johnson's late style foregrounds a dense play of vowels and consonants, a "music" that signifies in and of itself, and perhaps to a greater extent than any one thing or idea signified. Meaning in poetry of this sort is overdetermined, though in an initial reading, one may sometimes find the determination of any meaning quite challenging. In other words, the pleasures Johnson has to offer are difficult pleasures, despite, or perhaps because of, their intense verbal sensuality. In the passage quoted above, Johnson typically conflates sight and sound. It is dusk (recall that the third book of the poem goes from sunset to dawn) and the poet is reminded of how the setting sun's light "rained down in daily radiance." Yet the light is also experienced as a "thrust athrob together / at syrinx split infinities." Syrinx is the nymph who is transformed into a reed when pursued by the aroused Pan. From the reed, the god makes his panpipes, creating music out of his thwarted desire, a throbbing music of "split infinities." In a typically folksy gesture, Johnson compares Pan's music to a "hoedown jamboree," and it is then implicitly contrasted in the phrase "so strum flesh harp" to the harp music of Apollo, Pan's great rival, and the god of the sun. Pan's music is the sound of natural desire; Apollo's is that of spiritual transcendence—"believe, believe, be Live above!" Such cosmic tensions lead to the "globe consuming itself, say / brain by spinal Chord / to pierce new universe thrice on." The material globe or the human brain is consumed by the "spinal Chord," a typical

Johnsonian pun. In *ARK*, meaning—and spirit—move continually from immanence to transcendence and back again, and language—both music and vision—is its instrument.

As I hope I have demonstrated, with this one brief example, the polysemic language of *ARK* opens itself at all points to extended commentary, commentary that calls for a finely tuned ear, a sensitive eye, and a breadth of cultural knowledge that includes myth, music (Ives is crucial), the visual arts (*ARK* 75 is drawn from the letters of Vincent van Gogh), and, of course, literature. Be that as it may, the poem wears its cloak of allusions lightly; it is invitingly, some might say naively, democratic, celebrating, in the critic Eric Selinger's words, an "exuberant Americana"; and it has the charm one would expect of a poem seeking "To do as Adam did"—that is, to be an original namer—and to "build a Garden of the brain." Selinger writes of Johnson's "utopian patriotism," and as I have argued on a number of previous occasions, there are few recent poets more imbued with a utopian sensibility. Utopian thought always depends upon a vision of primal origins: it seeks to reestablish an unfallen state of things, a return to the Garden and, as Johnson puts it, "the body of light," even as it imagines the new form of a perfected world that never has been. The poet tells us that the controlling myth in *ARK* is that of Orpheus and Euridice, "the blessed argument between poet and muse," codified when Johnson read Elizabeth Sewell's *The Orphic Voice: Poetry and Natural History* (1960). But I have always believed that in addition to Orpheus, the doomed cosmic singer, Johnson's poem is also determined by another myth to which he frequently alludes, the kabbalistic myth of Adam Kadmon, the cosmic man whose body is the universe, and whose fall anticipates that of the biblical Adam. Or as Johnson puts it in Beam 10, the shortest section of *ARK*, "*daimon* diamond Monad I / Adam Kadmon in the sky." Blake seeks to restore the wholeness of this figure in England's green and pleasant land; Whitman makes it into the celebratory centerpiece of his American identity; Johnson gladly inherits the task.

Johnson's prelapsarian inclinations, simultaneously redemptive and utopian, not only link him to the tradition of the long visionary poem, but, as I mentioned above, to various self-taught makers of fantastic, visionary sculptural environments. The works of such figures as Simon Rodia, le Facteur Cheval, Raymond Isidore, and James Hampton serve as formal and thematic models for the enormous verbal construction that is

ARK. As Johnson explains in the afterword, a turning point in the composition of the poem "was a visit to Le Facteur Cheval's *Le Palais Idéal*
in Hautrives, France. Cheval claimed that on his postman's rounds he
kicked a stone one day, then suddenly conceived the idea of building a
palace 'like a dream.' In one moment of vision he was Everyman who
attempts creative quest." Likewise, consider Johnson's passage in Beam 28
of *ARK* on James Hampton's masterpiece, *The Throne of the Third Heaven
of the Nations Millenium General Assembly*, a dazzling assemblage of junk
furniture and tinsel which Hampton constructed over many years in a
garage in Washington, DC. (It is now in the Smithsonian Institution.)
In the midst of Johnson's encomium for Hampton, the poet simply tells
us that "He did not call himself an artist," a sentence which, as I see it,
betrays a powerful longing on Johnson's part to achieve a state of original
innocence, free from what we ordinarily think of as the aesthetic, which
he perceives in figures like Hampton, and for which he in turn aspires in
his poem.

But Johnson, despite his sympathies with the outsiders who created
these works, is not a naïve or self-educated visionary; he *is* an artist, and
a highly educated, sophisticated one at that. And it is at this point that
readers of *ARK* will want to turn and reflect upon the function of such a
work, "steeped in makeshift" and yet "Exact as Ezekiel" in the articulation
of its spiritual wonders. Granted, those wonders are verbal objects, and
the spirit is almost always immanent. But as the poet moves us steadily
toward the transcendence of "Lift Off," we gradually realize that the "Elysian elision" of this poem has designs upon us that are other than, or at
least additional to, the aesthetic designs of, for lack of a better term, normative poetry (as in "normative religion"). *ARK* is what its author tells us
Eden is: a "glossolalia of light." Listen. Behold. Read.

(2014)

III

"He did not call himself an artist": Johnson's Outsider Aesthetic

Ronald Johnson's relationship to outsider art has long been recognized as
crucial to our understanding of his poetry. In interviews and other statements, the poet often affirms his connections with the self-taught mak-

ers of fantastic, visionary sculptural environments. The works of such figures as Simon Rodia, le Facteur Cheval, Raymond Isidore, and James Hampton serve as formal and thematic models for the enormous verbal construction that is *ARK*. Following Johnson's cues, critics have carefully investigated this dimension of *ARK*, interpreting the poem, to use Eric Selinger's term (borrowed from John Beardsley), as a "Garden of Revelation," or alternately, according to Rachel DuPlessis, as "a continuous practice that declares itself in the continuing production of wonderful objects." This remark responds to Johnson's passage in Beam 28 of *ARK* on James Hampton's masterpiece, *The Throne of the Third Heaven of the Nations Millennium General Assembly*, a dazzling assemblage of junk furniture and tinsel which Hampton, who worked as a janitor, constructed over many years in a garage in Washington, DC. Comparisons of such works to *ARK* shed a great deal of light on the poem, but also have the potential to complicate our reading. Here is Johnson's description of Hampton's work in Beam 28:

> Hampton's gleaming throne—made of tinfoil, old lightbulbs—his orbs and crowns and altars, the throne room he prepared for the hosts of heaven, now have been placed on public view in gallery 3-D of the National Collection of Fine Arts. He did not call himself an artist. . . . What strikes one first is radiance. Cardboard forms, sheathed in shining gold and silver foil, conjure a rich, ecstatic vision of cherubs, golden orbs, seven-pointed stars, temples, angels' wings. The cherubs have no faces, the columns are not fluted, the butterfly-shaped wings are not attached to bodies. Nothing is explicit. The eye is swept along by symmetries and rhythms and an ever-present gleam. Imagine what it was like to slide back that heavy warehouse door and see first it glittering inside!

For my purposes, the key sentence is "He did not call himself an artist." This is often the case with outsider artists, many of whom feel themselves to be summoned to the act of creation by some sort of religious crisis or moment of divine revelation. As Selinger puts it in his essay on *ARK* as Garden of Revelation, "The contrast Johnson subsequently notes between the 'heavy warehouse door' of Hampton's garage and the 'glittering inside' enact in concrete terms the tension between who Hampton was to the social world around him and who he was to himself: not an artist, but a saint, making his D.C. neighborhood ready for the Second Coming. . . . To the makers of Gardens of Revelation, then, the vision that tells one to build supplies a saving knowledge, one that turns old chairs, wine bottles, and cardboard into gold."

Hampton sees himself as a saint, not an artist, and presumably Johnson understands this—though it is worth noting that in the passage from Beam 28, what the poet stresses are the aesthetic rather than the religious qualities of Hampton's work, described in careful and admiring detail. As I noted above, whatever the similarities between Johnson's poem and Hampton's visionary environment, we must still acknowledge that Johnson *does* see himself as an artist, and a highly sophisticated, very self-conscious late modernist artist at that. Despite his sympathies with Hampton and the other outsiders he invokes, Johnson is not a naive or self-educated visionary, and if he sees himself as bringing us "saving knowledge," it is not of the same order as Hampton's saving knowledge. Rather, as DuPlessis puts it, "Johnson articulates folk or untutored artists as perfect equals, if not more necessary mentors and models than untold numbers of normally and normatively celebrated artists." Why are these untutored artists even more necessary mentors and models than normatively celebrated artists—in this case, celebrated poets such as Pound, Olson, or Zukofsky, whom Johnson acknowledges as important influences on *ARK*? My sense—indeed, the thesis of this essay—is that when Johnson observes how Hampton "did not call himself an artist," he betrays a powerful longing to achieve a state of original innocence which he perceives in figures like Hampton, but which he knows he cannot claim. The gates of Eden, of the garden of revelation, are closed to the poet. The great poem he composes is the gorgeous compensation for the loss of belief that Hampton and his like still hold.

It is important to note that the title of Beam 28, where the description of Hampton's throne room appears, is "The Book of Orpheus," and the story of Orpheus and Eurydice, as Johnson tells us on a number of occasions, is his "central myth." They give us "the blessed argument between poet and muse, man and his anima." Having read Elizabeth Sewell's *The Orphic Voice: Poetry and Natural History*, Johnson tells us in his essay "Hurrah for Euphony" that "I knew I wanted to be of that order of writer she talked about. I'd met my myth: Orpheus and Eurydice, and that proved honeyed terrain." Joined together, Orpheus and Eurydice represent an impossible cosmic wholeness. Having lost Eurydice, Orpheus too compensates through his art. This is why, I believe, Johnson suddenly invokes Hampton's work midway through Beam 28. The poem begins with the "Voices" ordering the poet "TO GO INTO THE WORDS TO EXPAND THEM," and proceeds with a whacky, Rimbaud-like play of letters that whirls its way to a declaration that "Y is space. X, time." An instant later, these building blocks of the Orphic poem yield to the revelation that is Hampton's *Throne of the Third Heaven of the Nations Millennium General Assembly*.

Here, I would ask readers of *ARK* to turn and reflect upon the function of Johnson's great poem, "steeped in makeshift" and yet "Exact as Ezekiel" in the articulation of its visionary wonders. Granted, these wonders are verbal objects, and their spirit is almost always immanent. But as the poet moves us steadily through its ninety-nine sections toward the transcendence of "Lift Off," we gradually realize that the "Elysian elision" of *ARK* has designs upon us that are other than, or at least additional to, the aesthetic designs of, for lack of a better term, normative poetry (as in "normative religion"). Can we say that these designs resemble those of works by outsider artists? If we assume that such is the case, the questions I would pose are these: What happens when an outsider aesthetic (if "aesthetic" is even the correct term) is appropriated by a poet like Johnson? What is it about the creative impulse behind much outsider art that so appeals to Johnson, and how does it affect the composition of a poem like *ARK*? How does the sensibility of the outsider artist—a sensibility which I believe Johnson both does and does not share—help us understand this poem?

I take Johnson very seriously when he declares in the afterword to *ARK* that, unlike his modernist "confreres" who "wanted to write a work with all history in its maw, I wished, from the beginning, to start all over again, attempting to know nothing but a will to create, and matter at hand." In and of itself, this wish is highly reminiscent of the moments of origin variously described by outsider artists when they are called to their work, given only "a will to create, and matter at hand." Here I turn to the art criticism of Roger Cardinal, one of the most important experts on the subject, whose book *Outsider Art* (1972) virtually defined the field. Over twenty years later, after a great deal of debate over the concept of outsider art (how it relates to folk art, to the art of the mentally ill, to popular art, and so on), Cardinal attempts to clarify the term in an essay called "Toward an Outsider Aesthetic." Cardinal notes that "Traditionally, the Outsider has been described as producing his or her work in response to some unusually strong internal impulse, spontaneous and unprogrammed, and . . . having no specifically artistic character. Such an impulse might be equated simply with the urge to articulate a pressing idea, feeling or corpus of experience. There is evidence that old age is common precondition for the creative outburst . . . it may be that a personal trauma is a frequent catalyst." Most importantly, Cardinal insists that "the critical definition of the creative Outsider is that *he or she should be possessed of an expressive impulse and should then externalize that impulse in an unmonitored way which defies conventional art-historical contextualization.*"

How might these ideas be helpful in understanding the creative impulse behind *ARK*, and the strong identification its author has with the outsider aesthetic? Despite some similarities, what we may call the sociologies of the art and poetry worlds are certainly different. Likewise, there are gradations and variations of the outsider status, just as there are gradations in regard to the related concept of the "self-taught" artist, which, as Cardinal argues, "is now a dead letter; our technological society has reached a point where it is unthinkable that anyone should reach maturity without extensive exposure to images transmitted by the educational system and the media." Of course, anyone familiar with Johnson's biography knows that this cannot apply: the Columbia-educated poet steeped himself in literary studies, was mentored in the ways of poetry publishing by Jonathan Williams, and sought the company of many contemporaries from whom he obviously learned a great deal about the craft. By the time he began *ARK* in 1970, he had published a number of major books with both small and mainstream presses. The innocence or naiveté which we associate with outsider artists (accurately or not) does not have a place among the facts of Johnson's career. Then again, consider Beam 2 of *ARK*, where we find the following:

> *The circumambient!*
> *in balanced dissent*
> *enlightenment—on abysm bent.*

Angels caged

in what I see,
externity in gauged
antiphony.

A lineaged clarity.

(Mid-age. Brought to my knee.)
1935–70

The altitude
unglued

A god in a cloud

aloud.

Exactitude the flood.

What Peter O'Leary, the editor of *ARK* and Johnson's literary executor, calls in his author's note "the Dantean formula" certainly applies here, with the poet in midlife brought to his knee by revelation, though the detail seems more out of Blake than Dante. "Circumambient" means surrounding, encompassing, and it would appear that in these lines, Johnson finds himself surrounded—and flooded—by an excess of supernatural presence. He is in "balanced dissent" or "gauged / antiphony," poised between heaven and the abyss. He sees "Angels caged" and hears "a god in a cloud / aloud." He experiences "altitude / unglued" and is called upon to record this experience with "Exactitude." There are very few moments in recent poetry when a supernatural summons to visionary expression is so definitely articulated (though there are intimations of this moment in Johnson's earlier *Book of the Green Man*). Yet it is also worth noting that this is "A lineaged clarity": if the poet is about to assume the prophetic mantle, he knows that it has been worn by others before.

"*I KNEW THEN THAT I HAD COME TO A PLACE*" Johnson declares immediately afterward, in the opening line of Beam 3. In the scene before him, the poet bears witness with a renewed urgency. He experiences "mind over (under, behind, ahead) matter." And in a "WAKING DREAM," he testifies that

> "At the same time I saw myself in him, reflected as in a mirror, and it seemed to me that I was looking at myself through his eyes. But another feeling told me there was nothing in front of me but the blue sky and that within me a window opened . . ."

> *through which The Voices called each to each*

> *: How to explain :*

> *the blind design,*

> *or make it sane behind its shine?*

> *How to inquire*

> *within*

> *the fire?*

This passage, with its collage-like mix of verse and prose, is typical of The Foundations, the first part of *ARK*. The prose, which fits so perfectly with the paradigm of the visionary outsider experiencing a transcendental calling, is actually taken from *A New Model of the Universe* (1931) by the occultist P. D. Ouspensky (1878–1947). It appears in the chapter on the Tarot, which includes Ouspensky's metaphysical reflections on each card in the Major Arcana; the lines which Johnson excerpts come from the section on Card 1, The Juggler, and it is the figure of the Juggler, which is to say, a magician, to whom the speaker refers. He sees himself in the Juggler's eyes, yet this uncanny doubling is also perceived to be an illusion, and there is actually nothing before the speaker but blue sky. It is worth noting that Johnson leaves out the rest of the sentence after "a window opened," which reads "through which I saw unearthly things and heard unearthly words." Instead, he segues into his own nursery rhyme-like verse as "The Voices" articulate the challenge of the poet's Orphic task.

This moment of midlife vision does indeed indicate, as Cardinal would put it, that Johnson is possessed of an expressive impulse and externalizes that impulse in at least a somewhat "*unmonitored way which defies conventional art-historical* [or rather, in this case, literary-historical] *contextualization.*" Somewhat, but not entirely: in Johnson's case, it is a moment of vision and a call to create that is both old and new, and I strongly suspect that whatever else "The Voices" may be, they consist in part of echoes of his poetic precursors. Thus, he is both inside and outside an expressive tradition of prophetic, cosmological poetry. It is a poetry of immediate, exacting responsiveness, a making that is a verbal equivalent to Rodia's Watts Towers, which, as Johnson describes in the afterword to *ARK*, "is fitted together with shards of language, in a kind of cement of music"—in other words, as we previously noted, what he conceives of as "a will to create, and matter at hand."

At the risk of making too much of this phrase, "matter at hand" suggests a number of ideas to me that may help us further parse the relationship of *ARK* to the outsider sensibility. Matter as in materials, the letters, the words, the way in which they build up rhythms, cast images, and suggest meaning. But matter also as in the sense of the substance of a discourse, suffused with deep intent, in the way that we may speak of the "matter" of *Paradise Lost* or the *Divine Comedy*. And here we have recourse to another art critic, Randall Morris, who, like Cardinal, has done extensive research and curatorial work with outsider art. In "Charles A. A. Dellschau: Enigma in Plain Sight," an essay on the books of airship images by Charles A. A. Dellschau (whose work Johnson would have adored had he been able to see it), Morris notes that one of the most important aspects of work by self-taught artists "pertains to the ancient because there is little differentiation made between art and life. It serves a function. It is ephemerally utilitarian, not made for the white cube of the art world but made to fulfill the intricate intentionality of its makers. . . . Are there aesthetics involved? Of course there are. But its identity as art spills way outside the lines of our narrow Western conceptions of what art is. . . . Dellschau had a reason for making his work. That it became art in the process of his inventing it is something that is really only of interest to us. This is almost a universality in the field of *art brut* and self-taught artists."

In *ARK*, Johnson is writing very much in this spirit, except, perhaps, for the notion of *ephemeral* utility, since, like Rodia or the Facteur Cheval, he is constructing an architecture, something built to last. But certainly the functionality of making, of inventing a spiritually charged, useful thing which becomes art in the process of its invention, is very apropos. In *On Mount Vision*, I argue that Johnson's linguistic materials, including the religious symbols and terminology which he appropriates, can be understood in terms of what the religious studies scholar Steven M. Wasserstrom calls in *Religion After Religion* the "tautegorical sublime." According to Wasserstrom, imaginal forms achieve this status when they are "Released from a need to deliver religious phenomena to a meaning outside themselves.... The documentary remainder of religious history, the symbolic heritage of the past—angels, *sefirot*, hierophanies—could now successfully resist condescending 'explanations' which read them against their original spirit. They are now allowed to be themselves; they are themselves meaning; they mean themselves. These traditional symbols demand to be read in their own terms." In our present context, I would note that the "stuff" of religious discourses which Johnson employs, like the thrones and cherubs which Hampton creates out of aluminum foil and light bulbs in his ecstatic environment, "mean themselves": they bear a cultural history, of course, but they also have a direct quality of manifestation, the immediacy of a vision.

For instance, in *ARK* 49, Johnson writes of "Poems plain / as Presbyterian pews, / tarrying angels / page, on page / sat in great hymnal." Likewise, in *ARK* 65, he declares "here, rhyme may be / anywhere / stubborn timber / splinter off the very orb." Quite simply, words, charged as they may be with traditional symbolic meaning, are also material, and language is something with which one builds. What results may be as plain as Presbyterian pews or as gorgeously abstract as Hampton's throne room, but what counts is that the poem, in coming into being, is a lived thing. Johnson's father managed a lumberyard, and Johnson spent time in his childhood helping out there. The idea of a built thing charged with meaning through its building, of angels tarrying around hymnals in plainly built pews, comes naturally to him. Did he think of himself as an artist? Yes, to be sure. His father was a carpenter, but his mother was a dancer: "I think that those are my main characters" he tells Peter O'Leary at the end of their long interview. But to these early models of creativity, we must add artists like Simon Rodia, and, in music, Charles Ives. Comparing both Rodia and Ives with himself, he notes that "Ives is not that different from the Watts Towers. He was like me—he knew a lot about music, but he wanted to appear a naïf, to get back to where you don't know anything about art. And then you construct something."

It is in the forgetting and then the making that we can locate *ARK*, in the desire for lost innocence, the resumption of creative naiveté, and the descent of the spirit. In this respect, Johnson is very much like one of his early masters, William Blake: one falls from innocence into experience, but through experience, one may also harbor the hope of returning to innocence again. We see this in the last lines of *ARK* 34, "Spire on the Death of L.Z.," Johnson's elegy for Louis Zukofsky, the first of The Spires, and for me one of the greatest sections of the poem:

> to say then head wedded nail and hammer to the
> work of vision
> of the word
> at hand
> that is paradise,
> this is called spine of white cypress
> roughly cylindrical
> based
> on the principle
> of the intervals between cuckoos
> and molecules, and molecules
> reechoing:
> these are the carpets of
> protoplast, this
> the hall of crystcycling waltz
> down carbon atom
> this, red clay
> grassland
> where the cloud steeds clatter out wide stars
> this is

Here again we note the phrase "at hand": "wedded nail and hammer to the / work of vision / of the word / at hand / that is paradise." The poet *builds* his work of vision as would a carpenter; he uses whatever language he finds available, just as many outsider artists scavenge their materials, making a paradise out of odds and ends. And as in so much of *ARK*, we are simultaneously positioned in both the macrocosm and the microcosm, in "the intervals between cuckoos / and molecules," with "intervals" meaning both a time between but also, as in music, a difference in pitch between notes. Thus the molecules are "reechoing," and thus we find ourselves in "the hall of crystcycling waltz," an architectural space, a musical composition, and what I also take to be a pun on "chrysalis," the transformative stage between caterpillar and butterfly. But this microcosmic site (or sight) opens into "red clay / grassland / where the cloud steeds clatter out wide stars": in other words, the poet's home state of Kansas, where the clouds sweeping over the prairie are like horses, and the night sky opens wide with stars. The poem ends (or perhaps, simply stops, since we are left hanging) with "this is": we may assume that the glimpses of eternity vouchsafed the poet are intermittent but still ongoing. Johnson (and Zukofsky, who is never directly invoked in the poem itself) are taken up into a cosmic motion, a dance that is also a building, in a perpetual cycle of mythic transformation which constitutes an experience of "paradise."

In his classic treatment of myth as bricolage in *The Savage Mind*, Claude Lévi-Strauss writes "Like 'bricolage' on the technical plane, mythical reflection can reach brilliant unforeseen results on the intellectual plane. Conversely, attention has often been drawn to the mytho-poetical nature of 'bricolage' on the plane of so-called 'raw' or 'naive' art, in architectural follies like the villa of Cheval the postman or the stage sets of Georges Méliès." Almost by definition, the outsiders who serve as Johnson's models (including, as Lévi-Strauss mentions, le Facteur Cheval) are *bricoleurs*. *Bricoleurs*, whether they are myth-makers, artists, or simple handymen, address themselves "to a collection of oddments left over from human endeavours, that is, only a sub-set of the culture." In *ARK* 90, Arches XXIV, Johnson uses the portmanteau word "*scrapture*," gathering together "scrap," "scripture," and "rapture," to describe a text such as *ARK* itself. Out of scrap, outsider artists produce scriptures which lead them to rapture. Johnson, deeply schooled though he is, follows their lead from experience to innocence to produce an epic myth, a mythic epic for our time.

(2014, 2019)

Michael Palmer

I have been reading and writing about the poetry of Michael Palmer for my entire critical career. I wrote "The Case of Michael Palmer" because I was simultaneously fascinated and frustrated by my first encounters with it; writing that essay, which I still regard as a breakthrough for me, helped me understand and appreciate it—and sense the new possibilities for lyric poetry in our time. As his oeuvre grew, I followed it, happily serving as a commentator. There is a long chapter on the tension between the spiritual and the secular in his work in my book On Mount Vision; the second part of this chapter, originally a conference paper, followed that. I returned to his work just recently in a review of his Little Elegies for Sister Satan for my poetry review blog, Restless Messengers.

I

The Case of Michael Palmer

> What I mean is words
> Turn mysteriously against those who use them
> —JACK SPICER, *THE HEADS OF THE TOWN UP TO THE AETHER*

In 1969, Michael Palmer, born in New York City in 1943 and educated at Harvard, moved to San Francisco. The San Francisco Renaissance was already becoming a chapter in literary history, but in making his move, an heir to some of its most important figures had symbolically come home. Eight years later, at the end of a long, uneven book of poems called *Without Music*, Palmer offered this:

THE MEADOW
for Robert Duncan

Resembling a meadow
'folded in all thought'
a lamp is lit only vaguely remembered
for its form, an elephant
of pale blue porcelain
with trunk curved upward
lighting a room a gift
toward a featureless room
whose walls are lined with children's books
whose readers are unable to read

Even without the dedication or specific allusions to "Often I Am Permitted to Return to a Meadow," the *topos* of the poem would be clear. As in Duncan's work, the "featureless room / whose walls are lined with children's books," which is also the interior "meadow" of mental life, is the source of poetic activity. Following Freud, Duncan always returns to earliest childhood, when language was still a magical "disturbance of words within words" under the protection of the maternal "Lady." His return to this "place of first permission" is consistently empowering. But Palmer finds Duncan's formula problematic, despite his obvious admiration: the "readers are unable to read." Like Jack Spicer, Duncan's persistent critic, Palmer is always aware of the ambiguities of the sign, the troublesome surplus of meaning: though he wishes to celebrate Duncan's "polysemous" vision of poetry, he also knows, with Spicer, that writing is "a game of blind man's bluff played among ghosts." As Palmer's work has grown in its theoretical sophistication, the play between Duncan's cabalistic "orders" of language and Spicer's disruptive, self-referential ghosts has become more and more apparent, manifesting itself in various formal, semiological, and epistemological spheres. Depth and surface, secretive interior and leveled exterior, create extraordinary linguistic tensions in Palmer's poetry, and it remains to be seen just how well the poems themselves bear up as products of and subjects to those tensions.

The final poem in *Notes for Echo Lake* is in some ways paradigmatic of Palmer's entire recent enterprise. It reads as follows:

SO THE DARK FIGURE

So the dark figure falls
backward, arms out and
eyes wide, through the purple

door to another
world. No hint had
been given him

that he would be called
upon and taken
into this painting.

Although this particular text is probably more conventional than much of Palmer's work, it provides a useful springboard for a discussion of all that is most valuable and all that is most vexing in *Notes for Echo Lake* and the subsequent volume, *First Figure*. The backward fall of the dark, unknowing figure into another world is a gesture that signifies the sudden entrance into the text as cabalistic mystery and—perhaps—the equally abrupt departure out of mystery onto a purely self-referential textual surface. Palmer's reader likewise falls into another world, and that is certainly what the poet intends: as he says in an interview, "It is a kind of poetry that insists that the reader is an active part of the meaning, that the reader completes the circuit." However, unlike his discourse, which shows every sign of pleading for a freedom from fixed interpretation which it may not require or even deserve, Palmer's reader, in the presence of his discourse, is instantly alerted to more remote, subterranean demands for commentary—which is an activity that the poet may not have intended of his reader in his disingenuously open description of his work. "Comments would the text confound" implies this latterday George Herbert, in all his fragmented urgency—not in the service of any higher truth, but for the sake of semiotic *plaisir*, which is perhaps the modern equivalent of textual mystery. The reader, skidding about on endless planes of language, politely demurs and does not fall but dives through the purple door.

1.

> All such writing is an assault on the frontiers; if Zionism had not inter-
> vened, it might easily have developed into a new secret doctrine, a Kab-
> balah. There are intimations of this. Though of course it would require
> genius of an unimaginable kind to strike root again in the old centuries,
> or create the old centuries anew and not spend itself withal, but only then
> begin to flower forth.
>
> —FRANZ KAFKA, *DIARIES*

In an interview Palmer gave after the publication of *Notes for Echo Lake*,
the word *mystery* occurs with notable frequency. He speaks of "the mysteries of reference embedded in the poem," "the mystery of how words
refer," "a mystery of what the narrative is, something that often shimmers at the ends of the page." Palmer's texts are apparently designed to
produce polysemous meaning, but they also are seemingly intended to
arrest what is conventionally considered "meaning" entirely: that is, they
are intended to produce mystery, the most important requirement of any
secret or hermetic doctrine. Palmer comes by such attitudes honestly, for
as an heir to the poetics of Duncan and Spicer (who in turn adopted the
esoteric concerns of such poets as Blake and Yeats), he understands the
compelling power of a poetry invested with the aura of secrecy. Duncan's
"Lasting Sentence" and Spicer's "ghosts of the poems" call for readers
as initiates, exclusive inner circles as devoted to textual rituals (and dis-
putes) as medieval kabbalistic communities or the Order of the Golden
Dawn. "Because, to him who ponders well, / My rhymes more than their
rhyming tell": these lines of Yeats's have perhaps been all too eagerly
chosen as a motto for more than one generation of San Francisco poets,
who, despite their public insistence on open form, have delighted in the
notion of a hermetic readership. As Gerald L. Bruns writes in *Inventions*,
his study of writing and interpretation among the ancients, "The concept
of secrecy is perhaps the principal way in which the ancients responded
to the primary hermeneutical question: What do you do when the text
you are studying doesn't make sense? Answer: you are now in the presence of the book's most sacred portion: you have come upon one of its
secrets, and must now begin to ponder in earnest—to search the scriptures. The concept of secrecy was also a way of engaging a second question: Who can say what Scripture says? (Who, in other words, is privy to
the mind of God?)"

But Michael Palmer is neither an ancient writer nor a religious one, and though he claims in an interview to have neither a "romance of the text" nor a "romance of the code," we must still inquire into the obsessive lacunae, the gaps in meaning upon which so much of the total effect of his poetry depends. It could be said that Palmer writes his poems out of the linguistic equivalent of negative space, strategically placing his words around privileged silences toward which the code can only gesture. Later I shall discuss the degradation of these gestures into a set of mere literary conventions, but at present it is sufficient to note their inevitable importance to a hermetic writer when scripture in itself supplants deity, leaving him with endlessly deferred meaning. For better or worse, Palmer, like the earlier poets with whom we have identified him, yearns to be a kabbalist; he even cites Gershom Scholem on the relationship between language and the *sefirot*, the successive emanations of God in Kabbalah. But the idea of Kabbalah surely changes when the Absolute is decentered and textual authority is dispersed. Traditionally, kabbalistic attitudes toward scripture emphasize the essential secrecy of the text. As Lawrence Fine observes, "the Torah must not be read on the simple or obvious level of meaning; it must be read with the knowledge of a kabbalist who possesses the hermeneutical keys with which to unlock its *inner* truths." Probably the most frequently cited passage of the Zohar (3:152a) refers to the literal text of the Torah as the jar in which the wine of inner meaning is kept, and Scholem, in *On the Kabbalah and Its Symbolism*, demonstrates that the Torah, in its infinite linguistic potential, may be known as an organism that is coextensive with God, pre-existing Creation. Based partly on the linguistic indeterminacy and free play of midrashic interpretation, kabbalistic reading focuses upon the endless complexities of divine life that are not only symbolized in numerous hermeneutical procedures but may actually be *entered* through these procedures. God, in short, is a Book, a literary world to which the reader has access through the constant refinement of his textual skills. As Moshe Idel declares in his essay "Infinities of Torah in Kabbalah," "Torah is either pushed in the direction of revealed Divinity and sometimes even identified with It; or, attracted in the opposite direction, Torah becomes an instrument by which is achieved the union of man's intellect with God. The status of the Torah as an independent entity—such as we find in the talmudic-midrashic literature—standing between man and God and separated from both, vanishes."

While it is clear that neither the congruence of text and Divinity nor the instrumentality of the text in achieving union with the Divine applies to contemporary poetry such as Palmer's, it can be said that this poetry manifests elaborate signs of the decay or negation of such notions. Considered from this perspective, Palmer's work may be read as an immense exercise in nostalgia. For example, "A Dream Called 'The House of Jews'" broodingly expresses the poet's frustrated desire to join that mythical group of initiates that the *Zohar* calls "the Comrades":

Many gathered many friends maybe everyone
Many now and then may have entered
The ivory teeth fell from her mouth
The typewriter keys
Many fell then at the entrance
Many held them
Many fell forward and aware
Various friends gathered at the entrance
Some held back
The room contains a question
Many said now before then this then that
The room contains a question to be named
He said I will tell the book the dream the words tell me
The room is not the place or the name

This poem is based on the "Pre-Face" to Jerome Rothenberg's anthology *A Big Jewish Book: Poems & Other Visions of the Jews from Tribal Times to the Present*, in which Rothenberg recounts a dream which, in effect, empowers him and grants him permission to assemble his book. As in Rothenberg's text, the "friends" who appear in this poem (related to the dark figure we observed earlier) seek to gain entrance into the "room" or hermetic chamber of textual ritual. They are literally "people of the book," though given Palmer's fascination with secrecy, some are held back, their verbal ability denied. These vague, anxious images of restraint are linked to the lines "The ivory teeth fell from her mouth / The typewriter keys," as oral and written communication is forcefully disrupted. Those who manage to enter encounter not an answer but a question, a source of continual commentary ("Many said now before then this then that"). And although the book, the sign of authority, seems to be present ("*I will tell the book the dream the words tell me*"), indicating the continuity of a textual tradition belonging to an initiated community of readers, the last line of the poem is couched in the negative, again indicating dispersal, deferment, and frustration.

As is indicated by this poem, Palmer's nostalgia, as well as his anxiety, is nowhere more evident than in his omnipresent references to books, words, grammar, and so forth. These should not be misconstrued as self-reflexive language games (although these too are to be found in Palmer's work), but rather understood as the hollow vessels that long ago were filled with a rich tradition of textuality: a tradition which, unlike literature today, affected all the spheres of cultural and social production. Typically, Palmer's frustration over the loss of such authority results in a determined show of nonmeaning, self-induced linguistic vacuities offered under the rubric of "Sign that empties itself at each instance of meaning, and how else to reinvent attention." Through such allegedly subversive strategies, "infinities of Torah" are rendered void; midrash as an interpretive mode is maintained, but there is nothing left to interpret. Yet in Palmer's less programmatic moments, traces of older mysteries are revealed:

> The letters of the words of our legs and arms. In the garden he dreamt he saw four bearded men and listened to them discussing metaphor. They are standing at the points of the compass. They are standing at the points of the compass and saying nothing. They are sitting in the shade of a flowering tree. She is holding the child's body out toward the camera. She is standing before the mirror and asking. She is offering and asking. He-she is asking me a question I can't quite hear. Evenings they would walk along the shore of the lake.

This passage enacts what Walter Benjamin would call the Fall of the language-mind; it does indeed empty itself of meaning, but in doing so it discloses and confirms the meaning from which it seeks to escape. The first phrase ("The letters of the words of our legs and arms") reminds us, as Moshe Idel notes, that kabbalists "conceive Torah as inscribed on God's 'limbs,' thereby minimizing the difference between it and God." From the inmost truth of the text, we descend to a Zoharic dream of four rabbis "discussing metaphor"; that is, engaging a midrashic consideration of poetry while in the *pardes ha-Torah*, the garden paradise of the Torah. As

Gershom Scholem explains, "Moses de Leon [the probable author of the *Zohar*] employed this highly suggestive term, so rich in shades of meaning, as a cipher for the four levels of interpretation. Each consonant of the word PaRDeS denotes one of the levels: P stands for *peshat*, the literal meaning, R for *remez*, the allegorical meaning, D for *derasha*, the Talmudic and Aggadic interpretation, S for *sod*, the mystical meaning. The *pardes* into which the four ancient scholars entered thus came to denote speculations concerning the true meaning of the Torah on all four levels."

Yet for Palmer, despite the apparent omnipresence of textual authority ("They are standing at the points of the compass"), the truth of interpretation is impossible: they are "saying nothing." The flowering tree beneath which they sit is the tree of knowledge, traditionally associated with the Shekhinah, the fallen female presence of God who has accompanied the Jews into exile. In the next downward turn of Palmer's text, she is transformed into the grieving mother in the news photo (probably the famous picture of the Vietnamese peasant woman holding her dead child); thus the meaninglessness of discourse is confirmed by the chaos of contemporary history. Finally, the self-reflexive narcissism that pervades *Echo Lake* takes control: the mirror and the lake preside over minute narrative fragments of unfulfilled desire, failed communication, and tedious routine. From infinities of linguistic potential we have come to a complete breakdown in the basic modes of discourse, as pronouns blur and questions go unanswered. Palmer's text adumbrates this process but gives little indication of any attempt to transcend it. As he writes soon after, "In silence he would mark time listening for whispered words."

Despite the important fact that this passage enacts the fall of language or desecration of the text with which Palmer is so concerned, it actually differs somewhat from most of the "bookish" references scattered throughout this poetry. More often, the process of emptying the sign has taken place before the poem's inscription; the words have become little more than husks or shells. Consider "Dear M" (the second of three poems with that title):

Look this figure half-hidden is not a book
This mirror-house is not the book
This photograph conceals a book
I tripped over the flower in the porcelain cup

This shoulder-talk was never a book
She offered a single syllable
This slowness is the book
This spiral is a mark

This mark is no part of it
She rolled over and spoke
I can see from here through something broken
This turning is not a book

This turning from is nothing
The owl is lost within the tree
I tripped over the voice in the porcelain cup
These moths are visitors or were

They are so tired of the book
The pages tell us so . . .

Playing with the essential binary opposition of absence and presence, Palmer dodges about a splintered domestic *topos*, invoking the book by negating it. The fascination with secrecy is maintained, but to little avail; in the broken world, the plenitude of the text consistently eludes the poet. The Talmud says: "Turn it and turn it again, for everything is in it." Palmer replies: "This turning is not a book // This turning from is nothing." The result is a semiotic exhaustion that correlates to and mingles with apparent sexual exhaustion ("This shoulder-talk was never a book / She offered a single syllable"). Ironically, such exhaustion is itself derived from the book ("They are so tired of the book / The pages tell us so"); authorial autonomy and erotic fulfillment seem equally impossible when the poet is haunted by the text as absence, a palpable lacuna. The poem ends on much the same note: "The coral benches and tables are empty / The rooftops were painted a useless red / We collected the letters in perfect error / and hurried to unlearn them."

They are lines that Kafka would have appreciated: like the interpretation leading to the conclusion that the parable is uninterpretable, the letters are collected "in perfect error" (and, of course, one wants to read "in perfect order") only so that they may be unlearned. The contrast with rabbinical tradition is again useful. As Joseph Dan explains in his essay

"Midrash and the Dawn of Kabbalah," "In Rabbinic Judaism it is almost impossible to use a biblical verse as a final proof in a religious controversy; every verse can be and was interpreted in fully legitimate ways to support conflicting arguments." As is often observed, it was believed that any commentary that might ever arise already existed at Sinai. The boundaries of truth are thus established by the sacred canon; within those boundaries, however, interpretation is free, open, and, indeed, infinite. When such boundaries are removed, as in the case of a contemporary intertextual writer like Palmer, the process of textual production is completely reversed. Despite the desire for authority, all that can be produced is "perfect error," and the poetry celebrates its infinite capacity for such error over and over again.

"The Theory of the Flower," from *First Figure*, is one of the clearest examples of this state of affairs. Arguably, the principle behind the workings of this poem, as in much of Spicer's work, is that of disruption or interference. The poet repeatedly attempts to identify his text with the tradition of the book but is interrupted by other fragments of discourse that are at odds with this crucial impulse. These disruptions range from the portentous ("The islands will be a grave for their children / after they are done") to the surreal ("How strange / The winged figure in tuxedo is bending from the waist") to the pornographic ("'Now kiss her cunt' / 'Now take his cock in your hand'"). Juxtaposed against this we find that "This is Paradise, a mildewed book / left too long in the house // Now say the words you had meant to / Now say the words such words mean." Because the doctrine of Paradise, once contained within the book, is now mildewed, left too long in the house (the House of Jews?), the original words can no longer be pronounced or interpreted; they amount to nothing more than the language of the rest of the poem. Thus "This is the paradise of emptiness / and this the blank picture in a book." As the poem ends, we fall out of mystery, as the desperate hope of poetry as secret truth is abandoned: "It isn't true but must be believed // and the leaves of the sound of such belief / form a paradise // (pronounced otherwise) / from which we fall toward a window." The already absent or unbelievable authority from which is engendered the paradise of the book ("the leaves of the sound of such belief") is acknowledged at the moment of final departure. The window we fall toward, unlike the purple door, leads us as far from mystery as we can possibly go.

2.

> ... One man could not understand me because I was saying simple things; it
> seemed to him that nothing was being said. I was saying: there is a mountain,
> there is a lake
>
> —GEORGE OPPEN, "ROUTE"

The language of secrecy is the language of depth. Below the surface of
the text, truth glistens and winks, suggesting a plenitude of meaning
that consistently eludes the seeker, who remains mocked and thwarted
by its absence. Shelley understood: "If the abysm / Could vomit forth
its secrets. . . . But a voice / Is wanting, the deep truth is imageless."
Romanticism marks the first occasion that the dichotomy of surface and
depth becomes a self-conscious poetic concern. In *Prometheus Unbound*,
Demogorgon rises from the abyss but remains unknowable; imageless,
he acts and departs. But even at its most refined, poetry depends upon
images; and we understand him all too well when Yeats admits after a
lifetime of labor that his images emerged from no place more mysterious
than "the foul rag-and-bone shop of the heart." Perhaps poetry should
remain on the surface after all.

What happens when the poet chooses to remain on the surface? First
this:

Pink confused with white
flowers and flowers reversed
take and spill the shaded flame
darting it back
into the lamp's horn
   —William Carlos Williams, "The Pot of Flowers"

And then this:

No changes of support—only
Patches of gray, here where sunlight fell.
The house seems heavier
Now that they have gone away.

In fact it emptied in record time.
When the flat table used to result
A match recedes, slowly, into the night.
The academy of the future is
Opening its doors and willing
The fruitless sunlight streams into domes
The chairs piled high with books and papers.
  —John Ashbery, "Last Month"

The language of the surface, we discover, is the surface of language. Language that refers consistently to an exteriorized reality will inevitably begin to refer to itself; it will see itself as that exterior to which the poet has become so devoted. From Williams's search for a discourse that can be immediately commensurate with the world of things, we move to Ashbery's dissolution of that world into an endless plane of leveled discourse. The epiphany in "Self-Portrait in a Convex Mirror," more charged with pathos than any other point in Ashbery's poetry (hence its fame), adumbrates these circumstances with terrible accuracy:

But your eyes proclaim
That everything is surface. The surface is what's there
And nothing can exist except what's there.
. . . .
And just as there are no words for the surface, that is,
No words to say what it really is, that it is not
Superficial but a visible core, then there is
No way out of the problem of pathos vs. experience. You will stay on, restive,
    serene in
Your gesture which is neither embrace nor warning
But which holds something of both in pure
Affirmation that doesn't affirm anything.

By denying mystery (or interiority) to poetic discourse, Ashbery also forecloses on any poetry that seeks to render exterior surfaces as well. Poetry becomes what he calls "the action of leveling"; before our eyes, all that is secret, all that is apparent, is transformed into text.

What I have been describing in rather abbreviated terms of poetic history is the origin of the contemporary desire to "process" language, which may be considered a corollary to the vast theoretical assault on the human subject that has taken place in all the liberal arts. As Palmer neatly puts it, "For me this represents virtually a linguistic model—an abolition of pure subjectivity." Poetry, the traditional domain of the lyric "I" and its affective discourse, has been especially vulnerable to such an assault; in mid-twentieth-century American poetry, the two most significant arenas for this struggle are the works of Charles Olson and Jack Spicer. Ashbery, less tendentious than these others of Palmer's precursors, provides a more easygoing and homogenized kind of poetry: compared to Olson's histrionic assertions and Spicer's agonized theological debates, the degree zero, almost textureless writing which Ashbery frequently produces seems to leave no question of the subject's disappearance. In his kabbalistic reading of "Self-Portrait in a Convex Mirror," Harold Bloom argues that Ashbery is a poet of the sublime, but it appears that what Palmer inherits from Ashbery is not a matter of late-romantic textual mysticism but of endlessly reproducible, synthetic discourse. Consider these lines from Palmer's sequence "Echo":

which in a dry season might
begin or might precede its
beginning with a list
of truths self-evident: these
clouds (these crowds) you
now see are permanent
and fixed; the arboreal splendor, the
meadows and chalk cliffs
are artificial, devised
of wired concrete and paint
by a developer in the forties
and therefore beautiful . . .

Proceeding in much the same manner for nearly two more pages, this set of non sequiturs is just one of many examples from Palmer's work of a technologized poetry from which the subject or human center has been systematically expunged. The disruptive voices of "The Theory of the Flower" take complete control; no lingering whisper remains to hint of some lost paradise of signification. At such moments as this, Palmer's poetry shares a great deal with Ashbery's cheerful ruthlessness, what he calls in "Grand Galop" the "already all-but-illegible scrub forest of graffiti on the shithouse wall" which supplants the lyric expressivity of the autonomous self. As Palmer declares, speaking in a typically technical metaphor about the way he perceives the composition of his work, "Various *selves*, aspects of a heightened attention, did it in a certain way, but not your *self*. You are that paradox, both sender and receiver, and as such you modify the sound, transmit the highs and lows effectively or not, and thus alter the signal in a dramatic fashion."

What remains so intriguingly contradictory about this stance is that the resulting poetry bears the mark of a unified, carefully articulated style or manner, which, despite the poet's avowed intentions, argues for the presence of a decidedly autonomous, even willful author: the reports of his dispersal, disappearance, or death are quite premature. In short, much of both Ashbery's and Palmer's work is engineered poetry demonstrating a far smaller degree of indeterminacy than one would originally suspect. Ashbery admits as much in the opening passage of his "The New Spirit":

> *I thought that if I could put it all down, that would be one way. And next the thought came to me that to leave all out, would be another, and truer, way.*
>
> > *clean washed sea*
> > *The flowers were.*
>
> *These are examples of leaving out. But, forget as we will, something soon comes to stand in their place. Not the truth, perhaps, but—yourself. It is you who made this, therefore you are true. But the truth has passed on to divide all.*

Because the self endures whether one puts it all down or leaves all out, what results in either case is a set of gestures that have become quite familiar to Ashbery's readers. We have already observed Palmer's use of ellipsis coupled with the subtle insertion of gnomic phrases, a technique which, however appropriate to his yearning for the lost authority of the book, ultimately limits his expressivity in a way that a more continuous mode of discourse might not. This willful self-defeat, with its attendant tropes or gestures, is a salient quality in both poets, in contrast to the occasional pathos of direct utterance struggling for the sublime.

Furthermore, Palmer, like Ashbery, seems incapable of resisting the temptation to "explain" the procedure of the poem as it unfolds on the page. "Lies of the Poem," with its Ashbery-like title, ends as follows:

Sound decays
and then there is the story

and then the features are erased
The addition of one more chair

and the arrangement is complete
Here another festival

to which no one is invited
and where expectation plays no part

How do the lies of the poem come to be? The primal word "decays," leaving a human narrative, which the poet then strategically erases. The notion of deliberate "arrangement" jars against the supposed result, the festival (poem) to which no reader is invited and "where expectation plays no part"—the biggest lies of all. This is artifice disguised as indeterminacy, the disappearance of the subject as hoax; and we must be extremely cautious when the poet says in "Prelude" that

. . . The days
yet propose themselves
as self-evident, everything there
everything here
and you are reading
in a way natural to theater
a set of instructions
that alters itself automatically

In Palmer's work, all that appears self-evident is actually proposed, and because of its very theatricality, reading can be considered neither natural nor automatic—a fact that the seemingly random grace of Palmer's measured cadences often hides.

Thus the requisite conditions for the "automatic writing" that Palmer yearns to produce can never be achieved. Whether the poet is visited by ghosts or makes himself into a transmitter of linguistic signals, the presence of the subject remains inscribed upon the text. Jack Spicer learns this the hard way. At the height of his power, in *A Textbook of Poetry*, he is able to observe that "The poet thinks continually of strategies, of how he can win out against the poem." But by the end of his career, it is apparent that those strategies are merely holding measures; the more forceful the repression of the subject, the more vengeful its return. As he writes in his last book, "The poem begins to mirror itself. / The identity of the poet gets more obvious." The further poetry moves toward an egoless state of self-reflexive dictation, the more clearly defined becomes the space that the poet was compelled to vacate—compelled, of course, by none other than himself. In the end, we always discover ourselves in the poems we write. And perhaps this is what Palmer really means in "This Time," one of the five charming poems in *First Figure* written for his daughter:

One time I turned blue all over

then got clear as glass
This really happened

but not to me
Once I couldn't see

for a while
so I listened lying down

Another time I looked out the window
and saw myself at the window

across the street
This time it was me

3.

> This is lesson three
> where the fiddler is made real
> —MICHAEL PALMER, "AS A REAL HOUSE"

The case of Michael Palmer is crucial to our evaluation of contemporary poetry. As I have argued, Palmer's work represents the confluence of two poetic tendencies, both of which affect but also transcend matters of style and school: on the one hand, the desire to transform poetry into a quasireligious secret doctrine or language of mystery, complete with reader-initiates; on the other hand, the desire to level all possible modes of poetic discourse, so that a synthetic language of otherness supplants and disperses the human subject altogether. The fact that these tendencies are logically incompatible is also significant: they are, after all, necessary critical fictions through which we can discuss the peculiar linguistic tensions so readily apprehensible in a reading of Palmer's work. We apprehend these tensions because, as Terry Eagleton observes in *Criticism and Ideology*, "every text can be seen as a 'problem' to which a 'solution' is to be found; and the process of the text is the process of problem-solving." As in the case of all important writers, the "problem" in Palmer's work encompasses both form and content. A formidably intelligent stylist, Palmer offers such a provocative play of signs that content appears alternately buried or erased. Again, Eagleton: "Literature is a peculiar mode of linguistic organization which, by a particular 'disturbance' of conventional modes of signification, so foregrounds certain modes of sense-making as to allow us to perceive the ideology in which they inhere. Such foregrounding is at once constructed artifice and experiential enticement swallowing the reader into a play of signs which is seductive in proportion to its 'unnaturalness.'" For Palmer, this seductive unnaturalness results because the poem must always resist "meaning" but at the same time display the semiotic trappings by which meaning is ordinarily construed. This attitude constitutes what could be called Palmer's aesthetic ideology, and he has indeed presented a political rationale for his poetic practice: "There has been a radical disjuncture between what is proper behavior and improper behavior in American poetry, and in this age of Reagan it seems solidified. There is a psychology of reaction in the arts, or at least in literature, which reaffirms the old values which were never really values in the first place."

It seems to me that Palmer is here falling into the trap of confusing aesthetic stance and political belief: one can remain completely out of sympathy with conservative political policies without having to endorse the aesthetic program represented by poetry such as his. Ironically, Palmer, who makes reference to Eagleton in his notebooks, elsewhere more carefully observes that "Poetry seems to inform politically (this being a poetry that does transmit material of some immediate as well as enduring freshness) beyond its aspect as opinion or stance. Thus a Baudelaire, Pound, Eliot et al. may render a societal picture of transcendent accuracy." Here Palmer invokes the old Marxist notion that a writer with a conservative ideology can still render a historically accurate view of social relations. The same, of course, could be true of a "textual leftist" like Palmer, though a case could also be made that such self-consciously deconstructive writing as his merely duplicates, in literary terms, the dazzling fluidity of the commodity form in postindustrial capitalism. Perhaps it is best to say that art—and here Palmer is a perfect contemporary example—usually displays qualities of both reification and critique in relation to a dominant ideology.

But politics aside, Palmer is a far more conventional author than the typical reader of modern poetry would usually suspect. All poets inherit, reproduce, and refine a set of gestures, techniques, and attitudes. When these become ascertainable, as with Palmer, we can say that a conventional kind of poetry has come into being, such as Cavalier poetry of the seventeenth century, or much more recently, the poetry of the "scenic style" identified by Charles Altieri. Also, Palmer is becoming more conventional on the simple level of subject matter, as a sequence of poems for a young daughter would indicate. *First Figure* is a less tendentious volume than *Notes for Echo Lake*, too; it is much less a "Book" in the sense used by Edmond Jabès or, closer to home, Robert Duncan—though perhaps this is only to observe how Palmer may be shifting from one set of conventions to another. In a revealing notebook passage, he muses on these issues:

> The question, unapproachable, of whether the book following *Notes* should aim toward eliminating the "holes" in Notes, or should aim

toward being a book of holes. . . . The simple fact is that one must not aim, or if one does, it is the deflection that makes the work. And yet from someplace there must be (for me) a wholeness to the work itself, i.e., no random agglomeration which is what we have already, everywhere . . .

It may not be entirely possible to judge *First Figure* in these terms, but it is certain that Palmer moves toward the first option rather than the second, thus acting upon his need for "a wholeness to the work itself." What is so impressive about his poetic intelligence here is that he understands the need to balance that desire for wholeness against the equally formative concept of "deflection," that moment when the ego (if not the subject) does lose its grip, allowing other voices to enter the text.

It is difficult, however, for an ambitious poet like Palmer to achieve such balance in today's intellectual climate. Although he wisely condemns the idea of an avant-garde as "a military term which has lost its meaning," Palmer is still susceptible to what may amount to one of the biggest avant-garde poetic red herrings of the century, dating back at least as far as Eliot's call for the "continual extinction of personality" and Yeats's experience of dictation in writing *A Vision*. The idea that the poet should somehow seek to bypass the self can certainly be salutary, especially in light of the worst excesses of the confessionals or of those poets in the seventies whose work becomes, as Altieri puts it, "a psychological hot tub." Poststructuralist theory provides even more philosophical, linguistic, and psychological weight to this argument, and Palmer's work bears every mark of his theoretical sophistication. But it is just at this point that our most far-reaching problem becomes clear.

Beyond the question of the subject—which, whether viewed as an essence or a function, seems to me to be both inescapable and indispensable in the production of poetry—lies the problem of poetic sophistication in itself. One test of a poem's significance is the manner in which it renders itself as sustained form, in relation to what the poet, his contemporary readers, and finally his future readers deem to be the most emotionally or intellectually moving ideas and experiences of the time. The result may be as deceptively simple as the *Songs of Innocence and of Experience* or as obviously complex as *The Waste Land*. It could hardly be said that Palmer has shirked this challenge. However, whether the architectonics of poetry can support Palmer's investigative concerns remains to be seen.

The boundaries of poetry could presumably be expanded indefinitely, accommodating whatever forms such a writer achieves: as Wallace Stevens says (and Palmer quotes him), "All poetry is experimental poetry." It took years for such modernists as Stevens, Pound, Williams, and H.D. to find their audiences; indeed, we can go back to the Romantics as we seek a poetry that posits a gap of difficulty between itself and its readers as part of its self-definition. That gap comes into being most often as a result of the urgency of the poet's utterance; as Yeats observes of Blake, "There have been men who loved the future like a mistress, and the future mixed her breath into their breath and shook her hair about them, and hid them from the understanding of their times. William Blake was one of these men, and if he spoke confusedly and obscurely it was because he spoke of things for whose speaking he could find no models in the world he knew." In Palmer's work, there is little evidence of such circumstances: instead, as his various notebook entries and commentaries on his poetry suggest, a methodical intelligence honed on abstraction produces texts that defy understanding while simultaneously allowing us to perceive the reasons for our incomprehension. This claim to our attention represents a cultural impasse, and an enterprise of this sort runs the serious risk of collapsing beneath its own theoretical weight.

That it has yet to do so indicates the tenacity of the speaking subject, a specter with a human shape appearing and disappearing, as in the paintings of Palmer's friend Irving Petlin, amid what Palmer himself calls "endless semiotic activity." This situation, finally, marks Palmer's poetry as worthy of continued attention. Those who would dismiss the subject in his work as a vestigial presence (as he does occasionally) fail to recognize the utopian potential that nostalgia for the subject always signifies. A poststructuralist like Foucault posits his discursive utopia upon the death of the authorial subject. As he writes in "What Is an Author," "All discourses, whatever their status, form, value, and whatever the treatment to which they will be subjected, would then develop in the anonymity of a murmur." By contrast, Olivier Revault d'Allonnes, in a critique of poststructuralism, argues that "these philosophers, claiming to be modern, proclaimed the death of the subject and the end of humanism, thus accomplishing the final murder that the dominant ideology itself dare not perpetrate. By disposing of the last rights of the subject in a world which repents of having given the subject too many as it is, one becomes not merely the accomplice but a constituent element of the system." The same could be sympathetically addressed to Palmer, who clearly wishes to avoid becoming "a constituent element of the system." Indeed, one could turn Revault d'Allonnes's injunction directly upon the poet and his project: "It is the only point on which one must never compromise or waver: the right to inwardness. The duty of inwardness." Whether Palmer has surrendered that right completely remains to be seen. Surely his case would be impossible in any other time but our own: he is an important poet who is almost entirely unreadable.

(1988)

II

From C to D: Michael Palmer from the Eighties to the Nineties (and Beyond)

In 1988, I published an essay in *Contemporary Literature* called "The Case of Michael Palmer," which focuses on *Notes for Echo Lake* (1981) and *First Figure* (1984). In that essay, I characterize Palmer's situation as "the confluence of two poetic tendencies, both of which affect but also transcend matters of style and school: on the one hand, the desire to transform poetry into a quasi-religious secret doctrine or language of mystery, complete with reader-initiates; on the other hand, the desire to level all possible modes of poetic discourse, so that a synthetic language of otherness supplants and disperses the human subject altogether." Palmer's work, then, is hermetic, dreamlike, portentous, ritualistic, and *mysterious*, a kind of postmodern kabbalism based on a withdrawal or distantiation of meaning, as in the Lurianic notion of *tzimtzum*. Yet it is also obsessed with codes, signification, the connections and disruptions between words and things in the contemporary world of the simulacrum, an endless play of signs through which all modes of discourse and experience are leveled and, as it were, *profaned*. These two dimensions are made to coincide through the extraordinary resonance and musicality of Palmer's writing: rhythm, stanza structure, diction, voicing, and tone all contribute to a well-defined style. Indeed, however much he may have been grouped with other experimentalists, by the mid-eighties, there is no mistaking a Michael Palmer poem.

In recent years, however, the highly inventive semiological play that characterizes Palmer's work through the late eighties (and which aligns that work to some extent with that of the Language poets) gives way to an equally inventive, equally philosophical engagement with agencies of desire, meaning, truth, and what Palmer calls in his essay on Robert Duncan, "the dimension of Spirit, with that troublesome, rebarbative capital letter." The turning point is Palmer's last volume of the eighties, *Sun* (1988). The major works in *Sun*, the *Baudelaire Series* and the two title poems, bring certain radically skeptical—and radically secular— tendencies in Palmer's poetry to their highest pitch, producing, in effect, a crisis in the work which clears a space for a new kind of poetic investigation that continues into the present. It is no accident that after publishing the three brilliant volumes in the eighties that culminate in *Sun*, it would take Palmer seven years to bring out his next book, *At Passages* (1995). In those years, Palmer's work changes dramatically: it becomes more intimate, more overtly lyrical, more expressly affective, and increasingly concerned with matters of inwardness and of spirit. Although the subject remains decentered and the representational qualities of language continue to be interrogated, the mysteries of signification which have always concerned the poet become reconfigured into what is called in the poem "Under the Perseids," "the b—the buzz—of blessing."

I have just stated that *Sun* represents a crisis in Palmer's work. What sort of crisis? As I understand it, *Sun* confronts a contemporary world where things begin to lose their uniqueness and identity, and where interconnectedness becomes totalizing, leaving less and less space for difference. How does the poet respond when particularity is lost, and what appear to be various levels of identity are revealed to be homogenous and monological? This is what occurs under the historical conditions of modernity and then postmodernity, conditions which Palmer addresses with increasing seriousness on the political level, on the cultural level, and on the level of the individual psyche. "The concept of progress," writes Walter Benjamin in *The Arcades Project*, "must be grounded in the idea of catastrophe. That things are 'status quo' *is* the catastrophe." This catastrophe, or crisis, is both represented and addressed in *Sun*. The poetry in this volume both enacts a catastrophic loss of "Spirit" and criticizes those forces of "progress" which lead to its destruction, making the book a crisis in Palmer's own "progress" as well.

In order to demonstrate the changes in Palmer's work that I have just sketched, I will address two relatively short sets of poems which, to my knowledge, have not been much discussed: the two sequences called *C* in *Sun* and the *Six Hermetic Songs* for Robert Duncan in *At Passages*. Complicating the issue of a transformation in Palmer's poetry of this period is the fact of Duncan's death in 1988. The loss of this great friend and mentor could well have led the younger poet further into "the dimension of Spirit." In any case, we will examine what happens when the poet moves from the "mute flooded paper" of verbal reflexivity articulated in *C* to the "night-songs and bridges // and prisms" of the *Six Hermetic Songs*, exemplary of his more recent work.

The two sequences called *C* are strategically located in *Sun* between the *Baudelaire Series* and the title poems. The first is subtitled *("called Poem of the End")* and the second is subtitled *("Paper universe of primes")*. Each sequence consists of four poems; each poem is seven lines long. They are spare, minimalist, and more formulaic than any of the other poems in *Sun*; they are also the most obviously elliptical poems in the volume. In this respect, they look back to an earlier phase in Palmer's work, when ellipsis served as a master-trope. That phase is ending for the most part in *Sun*, where much of the poetry, however enigmatic, reaches toward more complete utterance in terms of syntax and rhetoric. The *C* sequences, by contrast, are both about and enact arrested communication. In these poems, speech and writing are either forgotten and or barely remembered, scarcely recovered. Stripped down almost to the point of mere self-referentiality, they are lacking in the kind of literary and cultural allusions that Palmer deploys so extravagantly in the rest of the volume. This is a different sort of reflexivity, much closer to a degree zero sort of writing. The vehicle of the discourse, the medium of the writing itself, intrudes and blocks expression; each poem seems to defend against its own utterance, and the result is a rhetorical act of repression which leaves only the slightest lyrical trace.

Furthermore, the fate of the writing is entirely predetermined. The first poem in the first sequence reads as follows:

called Poem of the End
four evenings in a row
now with a bridge in the distance

I came upon by chance
called Poem of the End
blue seven like this
hazed: nothing but the printed lines

The poet comes upon the poem by chance, and it begins by presenting itself as "the End." The "four evenings in a row" correspond to the
four poems of the sequence, which likewise constitute "the End." The
poem in its entirety is a "blue seven like this / hazed: nothing but the
printed lines." This establishes a pattern that will be repeated in the three
following poems. In the second, we are told that "You can't make a mis-
take because you understand nothing," and the poem ends with two
paratactical lines, "pushing them away // is typed." In the third, regarding
the text, the speaker observes "I began a few days ago / to give a direct
answer," which is "like not calling out the window / something else I
wanted to say"; then, in italics, perhaps indicating another voice, the last
line appears "*Here, instead of a letter.*" Finally, in the fourth poem, we get
the following:

It's called Poem of the End
I found it beside me where I slept
and called it Poem of the End
whose name was crossed out
I found it in a letter
and recalled writing from it
in broken sevens like this

To what does this all add up, other than to the elegance of "broken
sevens"? The references to printed and typed lines, to not calling out the
window, to a crossed-out name, and most importantly, to letters (a standard figure in Palmer's work) from which the poem is taken, or which
the poem replaces, all indicate that this "Poem of the End" is ultimately
about its own inability to move past its inception and say what it means
to say. In other words, in its end is its beginning, and in its beginning is
its end. Unlike Eliot's "East Coker," however, Palmer's sequence is not a
meditation on one's spiritual fate, but rather, on the fate of writing and of
self-expression. As is the case of so much of Palmer's poetry through the

eighties, the two *C* sequences are works that continually and rigorously
undermine themselves, calling the premises of their own utterance into
question as soon as they are established. They are yet another instance of
what I have identified elsewhere as a poetry that "presses for the end," a
tendency that I find in, among other figures, the work of Creeley and of
Spicer, two of Palmer's important precursors. Poems which follow this
path may be understood in terms of the kabbalistic notion of *tzimtzum*,
or contraction, which I mentioned earlier. As they leap almost immediately toward closure, they simultaneously withdraw into themselves, for
in their self-thwarted desire for expression, they find that they cannot
sustain themselves as utterance. The poem contracts, and upon emanat-
ing outward, the vessel of its linguistic expression immediately shatters.

Thus, in the second *C* sequence, there are repeated instances of mir-
roring and self-negation. The first poem ends by referring to "both speaking / not speaking." The second, likewise, ends with a quote: "'Now you
cannot speak / and now . . .'" The ellipsis after the second "now" implies
that the whole phrase is "and now you can." In the third, "a dog sings
songs / asking nothing / we cannot speak." And the last, in its entirety,
consists of

stages
of what was not
the speaking say
in day's word for night
'mute as stalks'
('moths')
are figured there

In effect, all the poems in the *C* sequences are "stages // of what was
not": that is indeed what the speaking say. As Paul Mann observes in
his magisterial work *The Theory-Death of the Avant-Garde* (a book that
was written nearly at the same time as *Sun* and sometimes reads like a
ghostly commentary on it), "what dies is not the need or desire to produce new, advanced, adversarial work but the discursive space in which
that impulse is permitted and permits itself to operate."

In Palmer's case, however, the closing of the discursive space represented by *Sun*, including the two *C* sequences, is not a permanent con-

dition, and the desire to produce "new, advanced, adversarial work" is renewed in the writing of the poems that are gathered in *At Passages*. In the *Six Hermetic Poems* for Robert Duncan, we can see the distinctive change in Palmer's work as he moves from the late eighties to the mid-nineties. Here, Patrick Pritchett precedes me; his remarks on this set of poems in his review of Palmer's later collection, *Threads*, are extremely insightful. As Pritchett observes, "With its prayers of intercession and spells for safeguarding the soul's passage through the underworld, Palmer models his own funerary chants for Duncan after *The Egyptian Book of the Dead*, guiding the older poet into the afterlife of language. . . . This ritualistic language sets the scene for the six sections to follow, each of which charts a stage on the soul's journey through the hazards and judgments of the underworld in its progress back toward day." The search for ancient wisdom in this "afterlife of language" connects the references to the *Book of the Dead* with the title of the sequence: the songs are hermetic in the sense of secretive, sealed up or hidden away, but also hermetic as in the Hermetic tradition, founded upon the mythic figure of the quasidivine Egyptian sage Hermes Trismegistus, traditionally thought of as the author of the *Corpus Hermeticum* and other Gnostic texts. For Palmer, as Pritchett notes, Duncan is "a guardian of ancient and esoteric knowledge"; he is, arguably, a modern Hermes, and one, I would suggest, whose death would have serious implications for the younger poet often seen as his heir.

Here I have recourse to Peter O'Leary's account in *Gnostic Contagion* of Duncan's teaching in the Poetics Program of New College in San Francisco, which began in 1980 and continued even after Duncan was struck with kidney disease in 1984, the illness that would lead to his death in 1988. Palmer was an instructor in the Program, and he later provided O'Leary with important insights into the extraordinarily high-pitched, stressful, nearly hysterical atmosphere in the Program, brought on in part by the extreme demands that Duncan, in his great erudition and in the excesses of his inspired condition, placed on all those around him. Students and faculty alike were struck with numerous ailments, and though Palmer tells us that he himself was not made ill, he "made a very distinct effort to monitor the emotional state of the program's students in the aftermath." In other words, as O'Leary understands, Palmer's role became therapeutic; he attended upon or offered service to these students, who were suffering both physically and psychically from their exposure to Duncan's uncanny "gnostic contagion."

How then is Palmer to properly mourn and elegize Duncan, especially in the aftermath of such a catastrophic period? As a counterpoint to the soul's journey which Pritchett identifies in the sequence, I would like to suggest that in the *Six Hermetic Songs*, Palmer builds a tomb, a house, a sort of sacred space in which the dead poet may reside, but also, given his dangerous powers, may be contained. The songs, therefore, are both elegies and apotropaic magic spells. Arguably, the house that these songs seek to build has already been constructed, for it was originally built by Duncan himself out of the poems that he has written. Thus it becomes Palmer's task to "measure" the dimensions of the house and guide Duncan there; in doing so, Palmer will assume a hermetic status like that of his mentor, for one role traditionally ascribed to Hermes is that of psychopomp, who guides the soul to its resting place. "How did we measure" is the first line of the first poem, and measure, as Pritchett demonstrates, indicates the measure of the poem itself, what is referred to in the fifth poem as "the fever of tongues / the metron, with wandering eye." (A metron is the smallest unit in Greek poetic meter, equivalent to the foot in English versification.) We are, then, with tongues and eyes, taking the measurement of a house of song. "Go there" says Palmer to Duncan at the end of the first song.

But there are difficulties. The second song reads as follows:

You can bring down a house with a sound.
Not to understand this.
But we builded it.
Not with periods (the
sentence) or any sense of design—
sight or sound.
Builded it while blind.
Rain came in.
Noises not ours.
Steps called walls.
Model of a house.
Work we had done before.
In-

harmonics as when
as children
still writing,
writed, written
interrupted, begun.

This song is concerned with the tension between unwilled poetic *inspiration*, poetic possession or frenzy, and deliberate poetic *craft*, poetic making or measure. A possessed poet, especially a Gnostic poet like Duncan, can "bring down a house with a sound." Duncan's house in what Pritchett rightly calls "the afterlife of language" cannot be built through measure or craft alone; building it requires an acknowledgment of and an acquiescence to powers of poetic inspiration beyond "any sense of design." This is why it must be built blind, in a state of possession, so that it is open to the elements and equally open to "Noises not ours." The music that raises these walls is "In- / harmonics," and the poet who makes this music must be like a child, "still writing, / writed, written / interrupted, begun." The poet engaged in such work—work, Palmer tells Duncan, "we had done before"—both writes and is written, experiencing interruptions from the outside (as Jack Spicer would say), that actually carry the building on.

So the building can be built, and the poet can dwell there, however uneasily. The fourth song, which is one of the most haunting and hypnotic of all of Palmer's lyrics, shows us around:

There were nine grand pianos in my father's house
one a water object in my head
and one a ship of glass
one an eye on the end of a branch
and one a paint-pot spilling red
There were live fandangos in the father's house
so that sleepers might sleep within the dance
and set their images to rest
Please tell me if you can
Did it snow pure snow in some father's house
and did the children chant Whether me this
then Whether me that

There was a winding stair in this father's house
climbing or falling no one would say
There were notebooks and nightbooks
and voices enclosed in a ring of bone
They were crying Wait Don't Wait
There were travelers standing at the gate

Exegesis in the case of a poem such as this strikes me as entirely insuf-
ficient if not downright impertinent, so much does it depend upon its
incantatory meters, its lexical theme and variations, and its ravishing
sonic effects. I would note, however, that the first line alludes to the
mansion of the Wittgenstein family where Ludwig Wittgenstein, who
has had a profound influence on Palmer's poetic investigations, grew up.
The pianos in the mansion of the poem, however, are not pianos in the
real sense but surreal objects in the poet's head, which leads me to spec-
ulate that the mansion, the poem, and the poet's head may in the end all
be one and the same. The poem is suffused with references to the arts: "a
paint-pot spilling red," "live fandangos," "notebooks and nightbooks": it
is a house in which the imagination may find expression in any number
of modes. But the house is troubled and vexed by ambivalences: whether
or not there is "pure snow" there, the children chant "Whether me this /
then Whether me that" (note the pun on weather, which changes all the
time and is never pure); on the winding stair, there is no telling if one is
climbing or falling; and the mysterious voices cry "Wait Don't Wait." Little is resolved here, at what is called in the fifth song this "zero of streets
and of windows." But for this reader, one thing at least is certain: like the
travelers at the gate, we arrive finally, as is declared in the sixth and last of
these "night-songs," at "the doorways of our disappearing." The *Six Her-*
metic Songs themselves are such doorways, through which both Palmer
and Duncan may disappear. Palmer as psychopomp completes his task
and vanishes, and as for Duncan, if I may rely on Pritchett one more time,
the "final image is of the poet composing himself with his familiar ink-
pot in the resurrected life, writing beyond the ending."

So we have gone, as I promised, from C to D, from a poem of the end to
a writing beyond the ending. What does this mean for our understanding
of Palmer's poetry at this period? Again and again as we move through
Sun and *At Passages*, we encounter instances of what Duncan calls "pri-

mary trouble," the feeling of crisis that occurs when "the word no longer protects, transforming the threat of an overwhelming knowledge into the power of an imagined reality." Although he never fully abandons the mirrors, negations, contradictions, and code switching that characterize his work in the eighties, Palmer in the nineties and beyond cannot avoid the possibility, as he writes in "Under the Perseids," that "the b—the buzz—of blessing / might have been all knowledge." The hesitance of the stuttered "b" moving to "buzz" and then "blessing" reveals a great deal: in the buzz of endless discourse to which we are continually exposed, might we also hear a blessing? Does that buzz constitute a blessing in itself—or does it interfere with the reception of the blessing? Does that blessing constitute in turn the entirety of "knowledge"? Secular knowledge, the mastery of techné or science? Or knowledge as gnosis, Duncan's "overwhelming knowledge" that entails the imaginative leap of spiritual transformation? There are, of course, no definite answers to such questions, which is precisely the point that Palmer's enigmatic poems make again and again.

(2012)

III

Review of *Little Elegies for Sister Satan*

A new book of poetry by Michael Palmer is always an important event. Palmer is generally seen as an "experimental" poet; the citation when he won the Wallace Stevens Award from the Academy of American Poets calls him "the foremost experimental poet of his generation, and perhaps of the last several generations." I totally concur with this description—indeed, let me state quite plainly that I regard Palmer as one of our greatest living poets—but I also want to note that as Wallace Stevens himself tells us (and as Palmer knows well), "All poetry is experimental poetry." I take this to mean that all poetry is engaged in a process of discovery; it is seeking to uncover something new, to reveal through the medium of language what we never knew, or perhaps what we only intuited but could not yet put into words. Why, I wonder, is Palmer seen as an "experimental" poet, if it is a term that in one sense is intrinsic to poetry itself? Labels tend to adhere to artists even when they may no longer be completely accurate. As I hope to explain regarding *Little Elegies for Sister Satan*, Palmer's poetry is central to our poetic concerns, not only because of its experimentalism, but because of its roots deep in the wellsprings of the lyric tradition. What Palmer tells us about his friend and mentor Robert Duncan applies equally to himself: "Duncan felt the need to assert the force of heretical opinion, which in turn for him was grounded in the authority of timeless heretical *gnosis*. The poem was to stand as a 'grand collage,' a constellation of myriad myths and voices from an eternal counter-tradition, as well as of impulses, accidents and intrusions, disciplined and informed by an attention to the poem's ratios or measures. Into its field, 'where sympathies and aversions mingle,' closed and open forms, harmonies and disharmonies, the mythic and the mundane, the hieratic and the demotic, were to be equally welcomed." This vision of poetry as "an eternal counter-tradition" looms large in Palmer's new book.

Palmer is also often characterized as a "difficult" poet. He has spent a lifetime producing a challenging, radically defamiliarizing body of work of uncanny beauty and grandeur. But again, what is "difficult" poetry? In his magisterial essay "On Difficulty," George Steiner posits four different types of difficulty. As he summarizes, "*Contingent* difficulties aim to be looked up; *modal* difficulties challenge the inevitable parochialism of honest empathy; *tactical* difficulties endeavor to deepen our apprehension by dislocating and goading to new life the supine energies of words and grammar." Palmer's work fits all three of these categories, but most importantly, it also fulfills Steiner's fourth category, that of *ontological* difficulties, "which confront us with blank questions about the nature of human speech, about the status of significance, about the necessity and purpose of the construct which we have, with more or less rough and ready consensus, come to perceive as a poem." Presumably then, we may come to *Little Elegies for Sister Satan* anticipating challenges to our poetic expectations, language that baffles us and stops us in our tracks, novel forms and modes of discourse. Above all else, we can anticipate what Steiner calls "the status of signification" to be called into question.

Let me note at this point that I have written extensively about Palmer's work on several previous occasions, most recently in *On Mount Vision* (2010). In regard to the matter of Palmer's signifying practices, I observe that "the highly inventive semiological play that characterizes his work through the late eighties . . . has given way in recent years to an equally inventive, equally philosophical engagement with agencies of desire, meaning, truth, and yes [quoting from one of his interviews], 'Spirit, with that troublesome, rebarbative capital letter.'" Hence we see a body of work that in some respects moves from an aggressively experimental stance to one in which the experimental aspects of the work are increasingly subsumed in what may appear to be more traditional lyricism. Palmer's poetry in the twenty-first century continues along this trajectory. Writing at a relatively steady pace (*Little Elegies* is his fifth collection since 2000), Palmer has produced a body of work of increasingly refined musicality, achieving a surface style that is all *luxe, calm, et volupté*. Below this surface, however, many of the same themes he has always engaged produce an inescapable verbal—and ontological—turbulence. *Little Elegies for Sister Satan* registers this turbulence in a poetry of grace, pathos, and surprising wit.

Little Elegies consists of three sections: the title series, World Enough, and Midnights. Seriality has always been fundamental to Palmer's method of composition. The individual lyric poems in each series maintain relative autonomy; they stand as discrete entities yet resonate with, and sometimes speak directly to, the others in the series. Additionally, the concept of the Book, with its roots in such diverse writers as Mallarmé, Jabès, Derrida, and Spicer, creates an overarching structure, so that again, a more or less subtle resonance informs the totality of the work. Increasingly prominent in this new book, however, is the sense of the poem turning upon itself, of a self-conscious making (*poesis*) through unmaking. As Palmer writes in "Elegies: First Commentary," "Many things bring me to a state of near paralysis, as when the demands of form, its counterlogical certitudes, begin to take hold, without so much as a word." The notion of poetic form as a kind of "counterlogic" has been at work in Palmer's oeuvre from the beginning, but here, "the demands of form" point toward silence, a silence that is both antithetical and fundamental to the writing of the poem. Thus in "Pillows of Stone," "We ask the words to do their work / but they have nothing to tell." If language speaks us, as the structuralists believe, then what will become of us— what will become of poetry—when words no longer do their work? Perhaps, as at the end of "Solunar Tablets," we have reached the point where "the poem-road below / of silences and stones // comes to a final turn."

But Palmer understands, like Beckett before him, that coming to the end of the road, the terrifying possibility of language collapsing upon itself, is not necessarily a bad thing, for this situation compels writers to return to the roots of their art. The result in Beckett is a bleak comedy staged at the edge of the abyss. The result in Palmer (though he too, as we shall see, has a quirky sense of humor) is a rhapsodic, fluid lyricism that is always unsettled by the impossibility of the visions it conjures:

I saw a house of ink-dark glass
and Minerva's Owl flying backwards

towards that city with a future
never to be. It's there we learned
those countless lessons about falling,
night falling, and the inner sky, it
too falling, and the masters of Doo-Wop,

Techno and Ska,
of tone row and dice throw,
and angel-winged messengers
of Utopia, their showers of light
and open-tuned guitars, the Green

Dancer in her flesh-clinging mist,
Flora and Kiki and Mme. X.,
glistening Ava, fading Echo
and, silently, the Anti-Icarus
falling among concrete cliffs,

his welcoming arms outstretched.
City of conjurors and crumbling gates,
mute buskers and alphabets aflame—
    —"Seventh Elegy"

In the "house of ink-dark glass" that is the poem (as in *The Promises of Glass*, Palmer's collection published in 2000, at the cusp of the new century), Minerva's Owl flies backwards. Palmer alludes to Hegel's famous aphorism from the *Philosophy of Right*, "The owl of Minerva spreads its wings only with the falling of dusk," meaning that philosophy, or more generally, wisdom, comes into being only at the end of an era. Palmer's owl flies backwards, into the past, leading us "towards that city with a future / never to be." There is no going forward; the city has no future, and it is there, understandably, that "we learned / those countless lessons about falling." What follows this Gnostic insight is another of the catalogs of strange figures, slightly out of place cultural references, and surreal, disquieting images which Palmer has given us in some of his most haunting poems since his book *At Passages* (1995), if not before. Without unpacking all of these references, I cannot help wondering whether the "angel-winged messengers / of Utopia" can deliver their messages in this "City of conjurors and crumbling gates, / mute buskers and alphabets aflame." Would it avail them to do so in a city with no future?

The figure to whom these prophetic words are addressed is the enigmatic "Sister Satan." At the risk of narrativizing what is essentially a sequence of lyric poems, the poet first encounters her in opening lines of the "First Elegy":

Singing is prohibited in this café.
Torture is permitted in this café.

I'll have a double, thank you.
in ¾ time, Sister,

may I call you Sister, you
almond-eyed, unsmiling,

in this ever-changing light
that cloaks the feral world?

"Feral": gone wild, no longer domesticated. The world in which the poet finds himself in the company of Sister Satan, the world, or the vision of reality, which she represents, is not evil per se, but perhaps beyond good and evil, outside of accepted ethical norms. Torture is permitted, and indeed, the poem goes on to name "Hiroshima, Nagasaki, Abu Ghraib, // Oradour, Terezín, Deir Yassin, / Vel d'Hive, Vorkuta, Magadan"—all more or less famous sites of inhuman cruelty, terrible suffering, and genocide—

but seen as "that waltz, that dance." Modern history with all its horrors is ironically portrayed in aesthetic terms: "All the beautiful names, // Sister, the infinite names, / roll off the tongue // innumerable as the stars / that frolic in the sea."

Palmer has interrogated the dialectic of art and politics throughout his career (see, for example, the "Adorno poem" in the *Baudelaire Series*), but in the poet's relationship to this "Sister," I sense an unprecedented pathos. Given Palmer's attitude toward the notion of self-expression and poetic voice, I must put this cautiously, but there is an intimate, personal note here that sorrowfully links the poet and Sister Satan as together they face the horrors of our "ensorcelled earth." It is a bond that comes into being through loss, as Palmer explains with rueful irony:

They ask me now at readings
about the strange creatures

suddenly turning up in my work—
you, Sister Satan, among others—

and I try patiently to explain
that as my truest friends in this life

begin one by one to vanish
I must find new ones, equally strange.
    —"At Readings"

This bond becomes both more loving and more frightening through a device which Palmer has used before, but rarely with as much foreboding and poignance: the rhetorical question. Here is one of any number of examples, from the "Fifth Elegy":

How many languages, how many limbs,
are scattered along the roads
of this earth? How many sounds
meeting their anti-sounds?
How many books burning

to light the way?
How many pure believers
to shatter the icons
of the pure believers
while the ensorcelled earth spins

on a turtle's back?

The questions which the poet asks of his "ghost sister" ("Sixth Elegy") or which they ask together, adumbrate the terrible contradictions of our contemporary politics. By the "Ninth Elegy," the poet watches "the crazed sister / as she hurls / wine glasses and dinner plates / from her apartment window." And in the "Tenth Elegy," "Sister Satan declares, When poetry reinvents itself without words, I will be first in line to listen." Again, we approach the point at which poetry yields to silence, as implied in Adorno's famous dictum (now bordering on cliché) that to write poetry after Auschwitz is barbaric. Like Celan's work before his, Palmer's poetry is both a refutation of Adorno and an acknowledgment that his dictum must be taken into account.

Thus we are led back to the making and unmaking in this book, the "sounds / meeting their anti-sounds" from which come Palmer's unique lyricism. As the passages I've quoted indicate, Palmer's sense of *measure* is remarkably subtle. Stanza structure, repetition, enjambment, occasional rhyme—from poem to poem, all work to produce a sustained rhythm that still registers every perturbation of thought, every surprising shift in affect. And in poem after poem of great integrity, the poem deconstructs itself:

Never beg for mercy
from the poem,
since it can offer none.

Do not ask
what language it speaks
since the answer is none.

Remember that the light and the dark
are the same,
if you can,

if you can,
that the I
and the Thou are the same,

the above and the below,
the far and the near.
Embrace the words you cannot hear.
    —"Tbilisi Thoughts"

In words one cannot hear, in a language that does not exist, the poem asserts a terrifying, liberating unity. Creation unmakes itself, the existential distance between Buber's I and Thou collapses, and the poem reminds us of the ancient hermetic truth of the Emerald Tablet, "As above, so below." Note Palmer's use of the imperative here, which may be regarded as the converse of his use of the interrogative. The poem questions, the poem demands: both are rhetorical means which Palmer deploys to simultaneously dethrone and reinstate the power of lyric utterance.

The portentous tone of many of the poems in *Little Elegies for Sister Satan* is leavened by other, mostly shorter pieces, that demonstrate Palmer's rarely noted wit. A mordant ironist regardless of the mode in which he writes, Palmer is not what one would think of as a humorous poet (though if you want a laugh, however bitter, read his "Falling Down in America" in *The Laughter of the Sphinx*). What are we to make, then, of "Midnights: A lifetime":

It took me a lifetime
of midnights
to realize
that the signifier and signified
are just a bunch of jive.

When Palmer gathered his three groundbreaking books of the eighties, *Notes for Echo Lake*, *First Figure*, and *Sun*, into a single volume, he called it *Codes Appearing*. Like the Language poets with whom he was associated during that period, a (post-)structuralist understanding of signifying practices and linguistic codes was crucial to Palmer's writing practices, and it is safe to say that such understanding remains a subsumed influence in his more recent poetry. Is Palmer turning away from the high theory he embraced when he was becoming well known? Was he jiving us back then? Or now? I don't really know the answer, but I will point out that every line of this seemingly off-the-cuff poem is bound together with slant rhyme: lifetime, midnights, realize, signified, jive, all with a long "i." This is what Pound calls "the tone leading of vowels," passed on to Duncan and from Duncan to Palmer. The jive of signifier and signified never ends.

This kind of play is especially prevalent in the *Midnights* section of *Little Elegies*. Floating in and out of these poems is Han Shan, the legendary ninth-century Chinese poet, the laughing Master of Cold Mountain. "If you // can't improve / upon // the silence / of deep night," Han Shan tells the poet, "then please / just shut // the fuck / up" ("Midnights: Crazy Han Shan"). And even more to the point: "As I scribble / these 'Midnights' / in the dark, / wise Han / Shan advises, / Above all, / don't get them right!" ("Midnights: Wise Han Shan"). A marvelous carelessness obtains here, a wild permission that may be found in late work of this kind. As Palmer writes in "Midnights: Moments," the last poem in the book, "So it is that we spend our moments or midnights fashioning a language from that which cannot be said." Palmer has devoted his entire career to fashioning such a language. He has transformed the unsayable into high art.

(2021)

Nathaniel Mackey

Starting with his first book, Eroding Witness *(1985), and continuing to the recent three-volume* Double Trio *(2021), Nathaniel Mackey has come to be recognized as one of our most important poets. His intertwined serial poems* Song of the Andoumboulou *and "mu" constitute what the great scholar of Sufism, Henri Corbin, would call a "visionary recital" of enormous proportions. Balanced between the spiritual, the musical, and the political, Mackey's poetry is a Gnostic revelation of the highest order. I have been writing about his poetry for many years. My central study of his work, focusing on his relationship to shamanism, is found in* On Mount Vision. *Here I present two other essays, along with my introduction to the "blog symposium" I organized to celebrate the appearance of* Double Trio.

I

Nathaniel Mackey: Poetry Terminable and Interminable

> Freud's aetiology informs the gnosticism of a poetics of illness in that Freud was always looking for a repressed emotional catastrophe that organized the neuroses of his patients. In the clinical process of working through neuroses by way of the transference, Freud sought not to rid his patients of their complexes but to make them something his patients could live with, without undue anxiety. As important as the "myth" of catastrophe, admission, and healing is in the Freudian milieu, so too is the analysis— the interpretation—of this myth. It is perhaps analysis that is Freud's most ingenious legacy. Analysis allows the patient to enter into an Initiatic condition, in which he or she finds a potential for self-regeneration.... The point is not merely that analysis facilitates this creative state; analysis in fact *creates* it. Analysis—whether the psychoanalysis of H.D., the poetic metaanalysis of Duncan in his correspondence with H.D., or the poetic-analytical paraphrase of Mackey's poetry—is a deeply creative act.
>
> —PETER O'LEARY, *GNOSTIC CONTAGION*

1.

Gnostic Contagion, Peter O'Leary's groundbreaking study of Robert Duncan (which includes a crucial chapter on the poetry of Nathaniel Mackey), is a book to which I return frequently. My first reading of it inspired me to write *On Mount Vision*; it gave me the necessary theoretical tools for my own exploration of sacred traditions and modern poetry, and just as importantly, it gave me *permission*, in a precisely Duncanian sense, to write the kind of literary criticism (part close reading, part psychoanalysis, part historicism, and 100 percent mystical commentary) toward which I had been unconsciously moving for many years. O'Leary's interpretation of Duncan, with H.D. placed before him, and Mackey following him, draws freely on psychoanalysis, myth criticism, ethnography, and comparative religious studies, in order to produce a theory of poetic illness and cure that is both structured by Gnosticism and is in itself an instance of gnosis. In this regard, I am reminded of what Lévi-Strauss observes in "The Structural Study of Myth": "we define the myth as consisting of all its versions; or to put it otherwise, a myth remains the same as long as it is felt as such. A striking example is offered by the fact that our interpretation may take into account the Freudian use of the Oedipus myth and is certainly applicable to it. . . . not only Sophocles, but Freud himself, should be included among the recorded versions of the Oedipus myth on a par with earlier or seemingly more 'authentic' versions." O'Leary, an ecstatic visionary poet in the tradition of Duncan and Mackey, does not only give us an analysis of the Gnostic myth as treated by the poets in his study, but also, as in the case of Freud and Oedipus, gives us a new version of that myth. O'Leary's gnosis extends through the poets he treats, and through his own poetry, but also, as my epigraph from *Gnostic Contagion* indicates, to Freud himself.

In regard to poetics, the most important question posed by O'Leary is "Does the poem heal?" At the risk of oversimplifying the matter, we may say that poetry is a disease and the poem is the cure. This notion is at the heart of O'Leary's reading of H.D., Duncan, and Mackey, as well as his understanding of poetry as intimately related to both shamanism and psychoanalysis. Following O'Leary's cues, my chapter on Mackey in *On Mount Vision* focuses on Mackey as a shaman, a cured sick man (or a revived dead man) whose magical powers and initiation into gnosis are represented in his poetry through the endless spiritual travels of the band of pilgrims described in the twinned serial poems, *Song of the Andoumboulou* and "*Mu*." Seriality in poetry is predicated on finding verbal structures which successfully embody *ongoingness*—the writing keeps going, keeps moving, much like Mackey's restless band. In the course of the poems, we encounter an endless set of psychic crises and psychic resolutions, endless traumas, endless cures. For Mackey, serial form, as he notes in the preface to *Splay Anthem*, produces "the draft unassured extension knows itself to be. Provisional, ongoing, the serial poem moves forward and backward both, repeatedly 'back / at / some beginning,' repeatedly circling or cycling back, doing so with such adamance as to call forward and backward into question . . ." Seriality involves "recursive form, a net of echoes." This recursive form in turn is related to "ongoing myth, an impulse toward signature, self-elaboration, finding and losing itself. The word for this is *ythm* (clipped rhythm, anagrammatic myth)." The endless language play that Mackey calls *ythm* is what the work is *about*, as much as it is about the search for hermetic knowledge, the endless reaching for erotic fulfillment, the historical and political struggle against forces of injustice, the longing for a utopian place at the far horizon that is also a return to a lost, original paradise. One of the many ironies in Mackey's work is that however much it constitutes what he calls a "discrepant engagement," it is also one of the most seamless bodies of contemporary poetry, where form is never more than an extension of content, but content is never more than an extension of form.

O'Leary refers to Mackey's relation to Duncan as a "poetic-analytical paraphrase," but we can also say that in and of itself, Mackey's poetry is a mythopoeic self-analysis, both inspired by and dependent upon the interminability of the serial form. Freud famously analyzed himself by attending closely to his dreams and simultaneously inventing a technique of dream interpretation that became a cornerstone for the psychoanalytic method. For him, the dream is a fulfillment of a wish, however cunningly disguised by the censorious functions of the mind. It addresses real desires, but those desire are encrypted, and must be uncovered through the analyst's knowledge of the dreamwork. But for Mackey, the dream "is a way of challenging reality, a sense in which to dream is not to dream but to replace waking with realization, an ongoing process of testing or contesting reality, subjecting it to change or a demand for change." This statement aligns with a more contemporary psychoanalytic understanding of dreaming, in which dreams are seen, according to Benjamin and Thomas Ogden, as "the expression of multiple forms of thinking in which we struggle and experiment with a plethora of ways of gaining a sense of truth of our lived experience, of who we are in relation to other people, and of the knowable and unknowable world."

Mackey's poetry presents us with a sustained and endlessly unfolding dream-state. In the introduction to *Splay Anthem*, he cites Géza Róheim's *The Eternal Ones of the Dream*, in which the Aranda of Australia "actively seek to remain in the dream, to be in more than one place at a time." *Altjeringa*, the revelatory dreamtime of the Australian tribes, is, as Mackey mentions, of great significance to Duncan in *The H.D. Book*. In chapter 6, "Rites of Participation," Duncan synthesizes Roheim's psychoanalytic anthropology with Gertrude Stein's "Composition as Explanation" and Gershom Scholem's *Major Trends in Jewish Mysticism*, in order to present a vision of the magically totalizing power of the mythic imagination, especially as it manifests itself in dream. For Duncan, "What we experience in dreaming is not a content of ourselves but the track of an inner composition of ourselves. . . . The endless repetitions of rituals and wanderings and hunting as the pattern of life for the Australian is a living inside the Composition." Likewise, in Mackey's serial poems, however nightmarish the circumstances he describes may become, the desire remains to move through and beyond those circumstances, to continually move forward in dreamtime toward the unreachable utopian horizon signified by that mythic place or condition the poet calls "*mu*." The poems, in Duncan's terms, constitute "the track of an inner composition of ourselves." Each episode, however resolved (or not), takes on the quality of an initiatory ritual, one more in an endless sequence offering up its own particular take on gnosis. Arguably, this has become more explicit in Mackey's poetry of the last decade. One thinks of the violence and sociopolitical disasters described in "Nub," the last section of *Splay Anthem*, and throughout the more recent volume, *Nod House*. Yet even the title—Nod as in the Land of Nod, dreamland—indicates the need and the desire to keep dreaming, and to keep interpreting the dream.

2.

Poetry, religion, anthropology, and psychoanalysis all intersect at the point labeled "myth." The epigraph to "Song of the Andoumboulou: 79" is an extraordinary quotation from the nineteenth-century philologist Max Müller: "Mythology is inevitable, it is natural, it is an inherent necessity of language . . . it is, in fact, the dark shadow which language throws on thought, and which can never disappear till language becomes altogether commensurate with thought, which it never will." It makes a great deal of sense that Mackey would find this quote useful. As Duncan, his mentor, once said in *A Little Endarkenment*, "So I immediately turn away if someone says, 'I'm going to spiritually improve you, here's a little enlightenment.' I say, 'No, no, I'll take a little endarkenment and in my poetry you find me.'" Like Duncan, Mackey prefers endarkenment, and his dark gnosis can only be found in and through the poetry itself. Thus, in "Song of the Andoumboulou: 79," "It wasn't religion we were / feeling"; rather, "What we felt / could've been said to be myth / but we said ythm, first would / be last we thought . . ." Mackey recognizes that his poetry is not religious per se, however much it borrows from various religious traditions. But it is unquestionably mythic (or *ythmic*), and indeed, in his case, it could even be said that poetry, every bit as much as myth, is the dark shadow, the endarkenment, that language throws on thought. Both poetry and myth come into being because language can never be commensurate with thought. Indeed, from a psychoanalytic perspective, thought itself can never be commensurate with thought; there remains an unbridgeable divide between our conscious mental operations and the unconscious.

Poetry, myth, and dream—all of which are languages, systems of signification—provide some access to the unconscious, but only through interpretation. In "Song of the Andoumboulou: 79," we encounter the following scenario:

> No sooner did we think than what
> we thought faded, wordless what we
>   thought we saw . . . A new member
>   known
>   as Huff joined our group. Strange
> Brother he was known as by some . . .

Without language, thought fades. But "Huff / pointed into the blur, claimed he'd / come from it." Like a shaman (or an analyst), Huff guides the group into the blur of the unconscious and, in effect, makes it comprehensible. Feeling is given structure and significance; it becomes organized, and in effect, speaks:

> In Huff's domain we saw waves
> come in, swells an emotional debit,
> > light's
> > dilated slide . . . Symphonic sway,
> more feeling than any of us could've
> > said we felt . . .

Huff, we learn, "wore wingtips, argyle socks. / He had a way of dancing standing / still." This dancing through the blur leads the group to pose the most basic of psychic questions of themselves: "Were we dead or / yet to be born we couldn't say . . ." The poet makes a point of noting that "It wasn't that / Huff had wings on his feet. Wingtips / were a type of shoe. Huff's way had / it both ways." In other words, Huff both is and is not an avatar of Hermes, the messenger god, leading the soul through the realms of being by the power of his hermeneutics. Part con artist, part sage, Huff leads the group to discover "the underside rising, soon- / come counsel of souls in absentia." Bringing knowledge up from the depths, Huff prepares the way so that the previously absent voices within may speak. "As a child," the poet tells us, "his first words had been / 'other side', some inkling even / then he'd come from elsewhere." Huff's origins are appropriately mythic; he comes from the "other side" and it is to the other side that he takes us. At the end of the poem, the group appears to be in a library where in "the upper stacks one found a / book entitled *My Friend Huff.*" The title sounds like a children's-book version of a volume from the *Corpus Hermeticum.* Huff is a friend, a mysterious guide promising gnosis. In reading his book, "Blur blended with lamplight."

3.

What counsel might the "souls in absentia" bring to us? Fundamental to *Song of the Andoumboulou*, as Mackey explains on a number of occasions, are the Dogon funeral rites which include the singing of the original song, intended to propitiate "the dead who have not yet been properly laid to rest by their surviving kin." The Andoumboulou themselves are, as he tell us in an interview with O'Leary, "an earlier form of human beings who were flawed and failed to maintain themselves . . . an earlier draft of human being that didn't work out." Mackey surmises that the Andoumboulou are invoked at a Dogon funeral because it is "a ritual that is marking death and mortality, the failure of human life to sustain itself indefinitely, because they are figures of frailty and failure. Mortality is a reminder of frailty and failure. But the song is also a song of the spirit of the person who has died and is moving on to another realm. It's a song of lament and rebirth." Access to this other realm, the realm of the dead, is crucial to shamanic healing, and that access may come to the shaman in dream: "Dream too is a school of ancestors, one of the altered states in which the dead reappear, one of such states the we in these pages [of *Splay Anthem*] pursue." Without the performance of the proper rites, the ancestors who would school us in our dreams remain troublesome, restless ghosts. In the case of the Dogon, the dead enter the beer that the elders drink, who then wander the streets abusing members of the community, declaring "The dead are dying of thirst." As is so often the case in poetry and ritual, we find illness, diagnosis, and cure.

In his great essay "Therapeutic Action in Psychoanalysis," Hans Loewald, describing the therapeutic power of the transference neurosis in the analytic process, explains that this power is

> due to the blood of recognition, which the patient's unconscious is given to taste so that the old ghosts may reawaken to life. Those who know ghosts tell us that they long to be released from their ghost life and led to rest as ancestors. As ancestors they live forth in the present generation, while as ghosts they are compelled to haunt the present with their shadow life. Transference is pathological insofar as the unconscious is a crowd of ghosts, and this is the beginning of the transference neurosis in analysis: ghosts of the unconscious, imprisoned by defenses but haunting the patient in the dark of his defenses and symptoms, are allowed to taste blood, are let loose. In the daylight of analysis the ghosts of the unconscious are laid and led to rest as ancestors whose power is taken over and transformed into the newer intensity of present life . . .

At this crucial moment in Loewald's essay, it is revealing that, as is so often the case in psychoanalytic writing, the author turns to myth and literature (in this case, the episode in Book XI of the *Odyssey*, in which Odysseus descends into the underworld) in order to describe psychic phenomena. The mythic bond between psychoanalysis and poetry, including Mackey's poetry, is to be seen in Loewald's assertion that the ghosts "long to be released from their ghost life and led to rest as ancestors": a longing that leads in turn to ritualized action occurring again and again in Mackey's work. It seems to me that if the poem can heal—both the poet and the reader—then that healing involves an awareness of "the newer intensity of present life." Such recognition is there even in *Nod House*, Mackey's darkest book, as in the poem "Lone Coast Periplus": "Wished for remedy, dreamt-of / return, / awake less alive than asleep it seemed / of late, each the other's dream had only / dreaming . . ."

4.

Let us return to the matter of seriality in Mackey's poetry. The continuous and ceaselessly provisional nature of the writing, its salient quality of "unassured extension," indicates that seriality is far more than a technique, though it certainly entails a mastery of technique. Mackey's poetry registers an exceptionally high level of self-consciousness in regard to form. In the preface to *Splay Anthem*, he notes how "statement backtracks or breaks off, ellipses abound, assertion and retraction volley, assertion and supplementation: addition, subtraction, revision, conundrum, nuance, amendment, tweak"—to which I would add his use of call and response, anagrams, multilinguistic (or sometimes, *pseudo*-multilinguistic) puns, repetitions, reversals, sliding transformations of phrases, words, syllables, even single vowels and consonants, as well as a precise compositional use of the page space, the stanza, the enjambed line, to achieve a highly syncopated recursive rhythm and cadence that is all his own. If, as I noted earlier, seriality seeks to embody ongoingness, seriality achieves this end through the total mobilization of technique.

But what exactly are we talking about when we talk about technique?

"A technique, after all, is a means devised by someone to get what they want. It makes wanting make sense. A technique is not supposed to have an unconscious. The [poet's] technique should tell us what the

[poet] wants, and what the [poet] wants from [poetry]." As the reader can no doubt tell, this is a fake quote. In the original, from Adam Phillips's introduction to *Wild Analysis*, a retranslation of Freud's papers on technique, the word "poet" is actually "analyst" and "poetry" is actually "psychoanalysis." Be that as it may, I think Phillips's remark can shed a great deal of light on *The Song of the Andoumboulou* and "*Mu*." For if Mackey is, as I believe, one of our most important "technicians of the sacred," then the technique he develops in his poetry certainly "makes wanting make sense": it structures desire—for healing, for wholeness, for greater psychic knowledge in a broken world—and in so doing, it does indeed reveal itself to have an unconscious, an unconscious that is endlessly tapped as the poems unfold. Later in his introduction (and this is the real quotation), Phillips observes that "If the unconscious is amenable to technique—and the whole practice, if not the theorizing of psychoanalysis depends upon it being so—this, in itself, would change our sense of what the unconscious is like. The idea of technique implies that someone knows what they are doing. After the invention of psychoanalysis, the idea of knowing what you are doing, the idea of a person as an agent of intentions that are transparent to himself, never quite makes sense."

As much as I concur with Phillips's perspective here, I must also point out that poets, in effect, have always known that the idea of a person as an agent of intentions that are transparent to himself never quite makes sense—one thinks of Keats's "negative capability" or Rimbaud's "je est un autre." This psychopoetic awareness has predicated a range of compositional procedures, which is to say that in poetry, there is no doubt that the unconscious is amenable to technique. Mackey's serial poetry, given all that its form entails, is one of our best contemporary instances of this enduring truth. Technically speaking, Mackey knows what he's doing, but what he's doing entails a deep working with and within the unconscious, an intentionality that thwarts intention. This becomes even more the case if we consider recent, post-Freudian revisions of the unconscious. Drawing on Wilfred Bion's theories, Thomas and Benjamin Ogden describe the unconscious less as a structure or place of repressed drives and desires, and more as an aspect of mind in which "the individual *simultaneously* views his experience from the standpoint of rational, cause-and-effect reasoning *and* from the vantage point of omnipotent, magical causation . . . from the perspective of an impatient need to find the safety of closures, conclusions, judgments and understandings, *and* from the perspective of an equally forceful need to dissolve closures in order to open up the possibility of fresh understandings. . . ."

This is an apt description of the kind of poetic thinking that is to be found in Mackey's serial poems. There is a certain calm, seemingly rational expository tone in many passages, produced by such phrases as "It was . . . ," "It wasn't . . . ," "Insofar as . . . ," "Notwithstanding . . . ," etc.—as if the poet were presenting a logical, cause-and-effect explanation for what is happening to the group at any given moment. And yet what *is* happening is irrational, magical, the stuff of dreams. Likewise, the poet will often seek longingly for "the safety of closures, conclusions, judgments and understandings," even as closure continuously dissolves in the never-ending, episodic pilgrimage, the insistent journeying that constitutes the very substance of the work. This, as Mackey declares in "Song of the Andoumboulou: 75," is "A dream of endlessness, what could be said / to've / just begun, muttered while asleep / letting / go."

5.

"Here I have the feeling," writes Freud in "Analysis Terminable and Interminable," "that I ought to be embarrassed about making all these ponderous observations, since what I am saying has been known for a long time and is self-evident. We have really always behaved as though we knew all this; it is just that our theoretical account has neglected to give the same weight to the aspect of the 'economy' of the psyche as we have to its dynamic and its local aspects. So that my excuse is that I am drawing attention to this neglect." Once again, I am tempted to make a substitution, replacing "psyche" with "Mackey's poetry," or perhaps simply, "poetry." By this I mean a number of things. One of the reasons Mackey's poetry has received the attention it has, not only in terms of awards, but in terms of devoted study, especially by other poets, is that it accords so fully with both ancient and modern poetic and psychic paradigms. Even readers who may know little about Gnosticism, shamanism, psychoanalysis, anthropology, ethnomusicology, etc., sense this in the work, and recognize the way that it takes them into a dream that is saturated with mystery, beauty, suffering, desire—and an ineluctable sense of the real. At any given point in the work, in any one poem, we see this in the text's "dynamic and its local aspects." But given the comprehensive and syncretic nature of this poetry, its participation in what Duncan famously calls the "symposium of the whole" (however Mackey's contributions to this symposium may "creak" against each other), we also feel that some theoretical attention must be paid to the "economy" of the work.

It is my understanding of this "economy" that I have tried to engage in this essay, specifically its interminable quality, bound as it is to dream and myth, psychic illness and psychic cure. Throughout *Nod House*, there is the recurring motif of a lost or hidden album that comes to light. "Song of the Andoumboulou: 66" begins

> *In an obscure bin or in an under-*
> *ground vault they found it, The*
> > *Namoratunga Double Xtet*
> > > *Plays for Lovers, the album*
> > > *they'd been dreaming of . . .*

Much later in the volume, in "Sound and Severance," "The book bit its tail and became a / disc." The result is "Antiphonal spin toward what tore / loose, / prolegomena, epilogue and prologue / both . . . The book as it turned acoustic became / a disc, *The Namoratunga Nextet / Live at the Nod House*." The book biting its tail invokes the image of Ouroboros, the serpent biting its tail, ancient figure of eternity and of the eternal return. The interminable text, the book that has no end, is also, magically, a circular "disc," a recording of a music that has no end. That music, played by the "Namoratunga Double Xtet," is for lovers; hence it doubleness, made eternally for two in the endlessness of erotic desire. But the band is also the "Namoratunga Nextet," always playing what's next, what's moving on into the future. And where is it playing? Live at the Nod House. Live in the dream.

(2015)

II

Mythos, Quest Romance, and Mackey's "Wandering 'We'"

1.

At the "Mackey Sessions," recently hosted by Duke University to honor Nathaniel Mackey on the occasion of his seventieth birthday, two workshops were held, the first on Mackey and music, the second on Mackey and myth. These topics broadly define the directions that a great deal of Mackey scholarship has taken since critics began to delve into the work. Guided in part by the author's own literary, musical, and cultural concerns as laid out in his essay collections, and by his editorial and curatorial efforts in his journal *Hambone*, this scholarship has examined the complex web of influences and filiations which Mackey has woven over many years. It has also considered the political implications of his visionary poetics (especially, but not exclusively, in regard to African-American history and the history of the African diaspora); it has explored the performative aspects of his art; and it has sought to define the religious and spiritual dimensions of his projects, which are increasingly immersed in various cross-cultural mystical and esoteric belief systems. Mackey's work constitutes a "discrepant engagement" with the literary, cultural, and spiritual traditions to which he belongs: at once deeply respectful and highly innovative, Mackey's poetry, fiction, essays, and performances are, as he puts it in the preface to *Blue Fasa*, "a mix of rapport and alterity." The importance of the work, especially the poetry, lies in its "recursive reach": its forward motion, its movement into the future, depends upon its repetition, its constant rediscovery and revisiting of the past.

Mackey has given a great deal of thought to these conditions over many years; they are fundamental to the "whatsaying" that unfolds in his poetry, but also to the unfolding itself, the process of serial form that is the poem's making. He understands seriality, as he notes in the preface to *Splay Anthem*, to be "recursive form, a net of echoes." This recursivity in turn is related to "ongoing myth, an impulse toward signature, self-elaboration, finding and losing itself. The word for this is *ythm* (clipped rhythm, anagrammatic myth)." The endless linguistic play that Mackey calls *ythm* is what the work is *about*, as much as it is about the mythic search for hermetic knowledge, the endless reaching for erotic fulfillment, the historical and political struggle against forces of injustice, the longing for a utopian place at the far horizon that is also a return to a lost, original paradise.

Given these foundational concepts, all of which point to the importance of myth in Mackey's poetry, but also to the need to continually redefine it, I would like to propose two models for thinking about the work. Neither of them is entirely original; both are at least implied in earlier Mackey scholarship, and even more so, in his own poems, essays, prefaces, and occasional remarks. They are intended to help us understand (as Mackey himself understands) the increasing coalescence of space and person, the constant invention of names and places, in *Song of the Andoumboulou* and "*mu*"—the perpetual (re)creation and proliferation of the figures he calls in *Blue Fasa* "Would-be refugees from history ... the wandering 'we' of this if not every long song, this if not every long poem, especially this if not every serial poem, this extended lyric, dream [that] would usher in a new history." My two models for what is happening in the work are *mythos* and *quest romance*, both of which have long literary histories, before they become entangled in Mackey's serial poems. In some respects, they will take us rather far from the ways in which critics have usually read Mackey, but I also think we will find them to be hauntingly familiar.

2.

In his essay "The Poet As Native," Jerome Rothenberg observes that:

> Mythology always carries with it an element of automythology. Mythology as automythology (experience as *mythos*) reaches its extremes in the self-projections and world-creations of tribal shamans and certain post-tribal mystics, and perhaps equally so in the work of contemporary poets/artists as mythmakers, narrating the world and their experience of it as a story. The poet's and artist's telling is an instance of any person's need to do the same but with a continuing demand for a heightened self-consciousness and, often, a quirkiness and openness to change that casts doubt on its own projections.

If I understand this passage correctly, Rothenberg is saying that there is an impulse in all of us to transform personal experience into mythos, that mythos may be understood as both "self-projection" and "world-creation," so that the self, in the process of imaginative reflection upon its experience, transforms that experience into a world. This world, as we shall see, is made of a set or arrangement of episodes, small narratives which in juxtaposition create a comprehensive (but not totalized) mythos. The shamans in tribal cultures, the mystics in premodern cultures, and the poets in modern culture all draw from their experiences to narrate their worlds, but it is given to them to be especially self-conscious of the process, leading to doubt, to an instability both linguistic and psychic, what Rothenberg calls "a quirkiness and openness to change that casts doubt on its own projections."

This is fundamental to our understanding of myth in Mackey's work: it is a doing and an undoing. From "Song" 85:

> *Came now to another crossroads.*
> *Stick people stood awaiting us, to*
> *   the left, straight ahead, to the right.*
> *   What was that song you sang,*
> *   they*
> *   asked, spoke without sound sound's*
> *   immanence, not without song but*
> *only one song, the one song summon-*
> *   ing song's eclipse . . . The one song*
> *   sang*
> *   song's inconsequence, crooned it*
> *   could not've been otherwise, song*
> *   song's own lament . . . The one*
> *   song sang song's irrelevance, we*
> *   were*
> *exhausted, we looked straight ahead,*
> *   left,*
> *right.*

In this strange episode, the stick people want to know the song, but the song brings forth "song's eclipse," "song's inconsequence," "song's own lament." The mythic impulse is simultaneously expressed and impeded; Mackey tells us as much in the preface to *Splay Anthem*, when he writes that both of his series are "shaded or shadowed by rut, the condition they seek to undo or come to new terms with." This is what Jean-Luc Nancy calls, in a phrase that is also the title of his essay, "myth interrupted." As Nancy observes, "The phrase 'myth is a myth' harbors *simultaneously* and *in the same thought* a disabused irony ('foundation is a fiction') and an onto-poetico-logical affirmation ('fiction is a foundation'). This is why myth is interrupted. It is interrupted by its myth." This interrupted status is especially pertinent to myth in the condition of modernity (or postmodernity): "This is what constitutes the interruption: *'myth' is cut off from its own meaning, on its own meaning, by its own meaning*. If it even still has a proper meaning."

How might this puzzling, paradoxical, but nevertheless insightful formulation help us understand Mackey's mythopoesis? The mythic impulse in Mackey's work seeks to secure meaning, even as it undercuts meaning. It seeks, to use the title of Robert Duncan's great essay, "The Truth and Life of Myth," but understands, perhaps more deeply than Duncan, what Nancy means when he declares, in his double-voiced discourse, that "myth is a myth." In his chapter on Mackey in *Gnostic Contagion*, Peter O'Leary notes the corrosive difference between Mackey's and Duncan's versions of their Gnosticism, their desire for occult knowledge which both inspires and betrays them: "Unlike Duncan, who bore the gnostic contagion in his body, where its devouring knowledge flowered into a cancer of poetry he tended to, Mackey bears the alien spore into a land of ghosts, a realm simultaneous with the sunlight world in which he dwells. In this world, invisible vampiric beings suck the life Mackey offers them, even as he starves his own malady of words." The condition which O'Leary describes and attributes to Mackey's poetry is that of Nancy's myth "*cut off from its own meaning*." Mackey himself recognized this situation long ago, when he chose the Dogon myth of the "disgruntled dead" to begin *Song of the Andoumboulou*. He recounts their condition years later in the preface to *Splay Anthem*: "These are the dead who have not yet been properly laid to rest by their surviving kin, those for whom the requisite rites have not yet been performed, the required altars not yet built, the attendant libations not yet poured." The myth of these disgruntled dead is the myth of myth unmade, out of which, in the sideways, crabbed movements of the twinned serial poems, comes Mackey's mythos.

But what exactly is a *mythos*?

Rothenberg, as we have seen, relates the term to "self-projection" and "world-creation," though on the simplest level, the word is a synonym for *myth* or *mythology*. The *OED* also gives us a definition specific to literary criticism: "The general structuring of events presented in a text, esp. interpreted with regard to certain archetypal themes or patterns." Related to this, "a traditional or recurrent narrative theme or plot structure" or more simply, "theme, plot." Mackey, and before him Robert Duncan, are keenly aware of this concept. Both poets draw from Jane Harrison's *Themis* (1912), a fundamental early work in the field of myth studies; Duncan places a passage from it at the beginning of "The Truth and Life of Myth" while Mackey uses part of the same passage as an epigraph to "Outlantish," the second part of *School of Udhra*; he reminds us of it again in the preface to *Splay Anthem*. In Duncan's quote, Harrison in turn cites Aristotle: "*by myth I mean the arrangement of the incidents.*" Surely Mackey's serial poems are just that: an endless arranging and rearranging of incidents, charged with a primal power that is also entirely responsive to the conditions of the present moment.

Returning to the *OED*, another meaning of *mythos* is "A body of interconnected myths or stories, esp. those belonging to a particular religious or cultural tradition. More generally: an ideology, a set of beliefs (personal or collective)." Put somewhat differently, this is "a pattern of beliefs expressing often symbolically the characteristic or prevalent attitudes in a group or culture" or "the pattern of basic values and historical experiences of a people, characteristically transmitted through the arts." A *mythos*, then, suggests not only a structuring or patterning of events—events which recapitulate or reenact primal or archetypal incidents—but also of beliefs. Indeed, event and belief are so deeply intertwined in the mythic sensibility that at the root, they cannot be distinguished, especially not in any type of artistic representation. Here, I think again of Jean-Luc Nancy and the magnificent opening to his essay, which is itself a recitation, a reenactment, of the myth of the myth-teller and his audience: "He is his own hero, and they, by turns, are the heroes of the tale and the ones who have the right to hear it and the duty to learn it. . . . It names things unknown, beings never seen. But those who have gathered together understand everything, in listening they understand themselves and the world, and they understand why it was necessary for them to come together, and why it was necessary that this be recounted to them." In this respect, the speaker of *The Song of the Andoumboulou* and of "*Mu*" is his own hero, but insofar as he is also subsumed into a "we" and speaks in the first-person plural as part of a collective or community, he is also among those who are gathered together to hear him: "We the migrating they we / instigated, those in whose / name we went . . ."

Yet there is one more definition of *mythos*, extending beyond a pattern of belief or the historical experiences of a people, which darkens our consideration: "a deliberately fostered cult." Indeed, there is something weirdly cultic in Mackey's work, or if not in the work itself, then in the *reading* of the work. In my chapter on Mackey's poetry in *On Mount Vision*, I argue that its Gnostic vision leads to the creation of a "reader-initiate," since both reading and writing are *esoteric* activities:

> Historically, such esoterism, requiring initiation upon a path toward gnosis, has met with resistance, whether in Islam, Christianity, or Judaism, none of which regard themselves, normatively, as initiatory religions. Analogously, we do not ordinarily think of reading poetry as requiring initiation, though it could be argued that exposing students to the deep reading of poetry is precisely that—an initiatory test which most students resist, and therefore fail. In its cross-culturality, Mackey's poetry seems remarkably democratic, and it surely serves as an explicit rebuke to any form of identity politics. . . . But to go as far as Mackey wants us to go in our reading of him is a different matter. What holds his diverse interests together and produces [to use René Girard's term] . . . the unity of all rites? To answer that question requires . . . a willingness to endure the trials that the poems both witness and become. Shamanism in tribal, oral culture; exegetical mysticism in religious, literate culture; poetry in modern, secular culture: all call equally for initiation leading to gnosis.

Does this imply that deep readers of Mackey are members of a cult? If this notion strikes us as bizarre, let us recall that the poetic or literary creation of a mythos, by virtue of the fact that it *is* poetic, entails a self-awareness or automythic quality on the part of both poet and reader which makes and unmakes settled beliefs, or, if you will, ideology. In Marxist terms, we may say that in the hands of a maker, mythos does not, ultimately, reduce to mere false consciousness. By virtue of its turbulence, an indeterminacy or instability that is both linguistic and psychic in nature is constantly produced. Mythos involves the construction of an interrupted narrative; as Nancy puts it, "A name has been given to this voice of interruption: literature."

The problem of ideology, or of cultic thinking, that is inherent in the concept of a mythos (a problem which Nancy addresses at length in "Myth Interrupted") may be considered in relation to Mackey's work through an unusual comparison. In his recent *Thick and Dazzling Darkness: Religious Poetry in a Secular Age*, Peter O'Leary notes that "Mackey's series have proliferated a wild, idiosyncratic, nearly nonsensical set of locations and personas whose variegated names remain steadfastly opaque, even to devoted readers: Ahtt, Nath, N'Ahtt, ythm, Ba, B'Us, Ouab'da, Ouadada, B'Dot, B'Leg, Ra, Stra, C'rib, C'ahtt, Zar, Qu'ahttet, Lag, Nub, Atet, B'Hest, B'Head, the Late Night Lounge, Lone Coast, Dread Lake, Outlantish, Southern California, Los Angeles." This sentence also bears a crucial footnote: "Listing these names prompts another comparison: Mackey's personal mythology bears curious resemblance to that of H. P. Lovecraft's Cthulhu mythos, which likewise relies on a negative epistemology and whose stories portray characters who intuit, sometimes unwittingly, that horrible nature of the suprareality surrounding them, in which the veneer of 'normal' reality hides the hideous truth of alien realities inhabited by unspeakable beings—with names such as Yog-Sothoth, Shub-Niggurath, and Nyarlothotep—too much for any humans to bear without going irredeemably mad."

In some respects, O'Leary's comparison of Mackey to Lovecraft is rather perverse, given Lovecraft's notorious racism and xenophobia. These attitudes do not merely compose a set of personal beliefs; rather, they function as an aesthetic as well as a political ideology, structuring all his writing from within. Hence the paranoia in regard to the alien that permeates Lovecraft's stories, determining both his plot structures and the psychology of his characters, especially his hapless, victimized narrators. One cannot imagine a set of values more remote from those of Nathaniel Mackey, whose resolute cross-culturality and encyclopedic knowledge of world music, literature, and mystical traditions constitute, as I noted above, a forthright critique of tribalism and identity politics of any sort.

Yet in a number of respects, O'Leary's comparison is not only provocative, but quite accurate. He applies the term "negative epistemology" to both the Cthulhu mythos and to what we might call Mackey's Andoumboulou mythos, meaning that "the hidden truth discovered in Mackey's poetry is, overwhelmingly, disastrous, disintegrating, disabling, and catastrophic." "Negative epistemology," which may be associated with the Gnosticism of both authors, points to the limits of human knowledge: that is, in both Lovecraft and Mackey, the more we know, the more mysterious, unknowable, and increasingly unbearable the conditions of our knowing become. We know that we do not know, and we know that what we do not know is by its nature unthinkable. In Lovecraft's case, what we do not know is horrible, monstrous, and fully capable of driving us, as O'Leary puts it, "irredeemably mad." As Lovecraft declares in the famous opening lines of "The Call of Cthulhu,"

> The most merciful thing in the world, I think, is the inability of the human mind to correlate all its contents. We live on a placid island of ignorance in the midst of black seas of infinity, and it was not meant that we should voyage far. The sciences, each straining in its own direction, have hitherto harmed us little; but some day the piecing together of dissociated knowledge will open up such terrifying vistas of reality, and of our frightful position therein, that we shall either go mad from the revelation or flee from the deadly light into the peace and safety of a new dark age.

As for Mackey, what we do not know is neither horrible nor maddening (though as O'Leary claims, it may well be disastrous and catastrophic). It is, however, every bit as transformative. Even in approaching it, on the endless journey that is Mackey's poetry, we are changed in strange ways. In the poem "Moment's Gnosis," from *Blue Fasa*, the titular moment of knowing is actually a

> *Not to*
> *know moment or no sooner*

know than not, moment's know-

> *ing nothing if not vanquishment,*
> > *relin-*
> *quishment they called it instead . . .*
As if instead we stood around in
> *circles, hunched over, heavily ex-*
> *haling, let go, moment more the*
> > *less*
> *could be made of it, we grimaced,*
arms out, had at by bliss, misgiving,
> > *more*
> *than any one feeling . . .*

What exactly is going on here? What Mackey names at the beginning of the poem a "philosophic posse" seems to be seeking gnosis, secret or hidden knowledge, engaged in some sort of strange exercise or ritual involving both relinquishment and bliss. This leads in turn to an awareness of "galactic light's late arrival" which "was gone by the time we heard / it." Thus "we"—Mackey's posse, his pilgrims, his travelers, but also his readers—constantly reach a point of knowing, of gnosis, that instantaneously recedes or disappears. The quest for knowledge in both Lovecraft and Mackey is indeed an elaborate exercise in negativity, a continuous veiling and unveiling of what cannot, and perhaps should not, come to light. This quest is comparable to Freud's analysis of the *heimlich* and the *unheimlich* in "The 'Uncanny'": "In general we are reminded that the word *heimlich* is not unambiguous, but belongs to two sets of ideas, which, without being contradictory, are yet very different: on the one hand, it means that which is familiar and agreeable, and on the other, what is concealed and kept out of sight. . . . everything is *unheimlich* that ought to have remained secret and hidden but has come to light." Both Mackey and Lovecraft are fundamentally writers of the uncanny.

The construction of a literary mythos around this void or absent core produces the seductive allure and cultic devotion which is certainly associated with Lovecraft's stories, and which seems to be developing, on an admittedly smaller scale, in regard to Mackey's writing as well. What reading an author of this sort leads us to recognize is our deep-seated fascination with mystery, mystery that expresses itself, as O'Leary puts it, through "a wild, idiosyncratic, nearly nonsensical set of locations and personas." Mackey's own term for this is not "nonsense" but "nonsonance," a fundamental quality of being in his world, and a fundamental quality of being, mysteriously, other than oneself. We hear it in music and in poetry; it unfolds before us in narrative, which always resonates (or perhaps, in an interrupted fashion, "nonsonates") with myth. If, as we have seen, a mythos is a body of interconnected myths or stories, or an arrangement of incidents that come to be charged with cultural or religious significance, then these arrangements, these interconnected episodes, serve to explain who we are to ourselves, reciprocally revealing our own and their own significance. But a mythos in this sense also furthers the mystery of ourselves. In two of Lovecraft's most elaborate narratives, "The Shadow Over Innsmouth" and "The Shadow Out of Time" (the similarity in the titles is not accidental), the plots move inexorably to the discovery that the protagonist is the very thing he has dreaded, or as Mark Fisher puts it in *The Weird and the Eerie*, the revelation that "I am It—or better, I am They." As Fisher points out, in Lovecraft, the shadow of the Other, Freud's uncanny double, terrifies but also fascinates; fascination "is integral to the concept of the weird itself."

3.

It was a train we were on,
    peripatetic tavern we
    were in, mind unremittingly
        elsewhere, words meaning
                                more
            than the world they
    pointed at,   asymptotic
        tangent...

—Song of the Adnoumboulou: 20

As many readers have recognized, movement through time and space is fundamental to Mackey's poetics. When we listen intently to music, we become aware of movement through time, which is one reason for the ubiquitous "box" with its endless stream of music from around the world which accompanies Mackey's "we" as they journey from place to place, sometimes exploring, sometimes escaping, sometimes seeking. For Mackey's "band of nervous travelers," these pilgrims, exiles, refugees, "[l]ocality and locality's discontent continue" endlessly, as they move past Lone Coast, Low Forest, through the desolation of Nub and Quag, toward a "blutopic" horizon called Mu or Atlantis, Zar or New Not Yet, always receding as they approach. Where, at this point in the serial poems, haven't these travelers been? Los Angeles, New Orleans, Georgia, Jamaica, São Paulo, Algeciras, Algiers, Bamako, Jaipur . . . Mackey uses the term "peripatetic" to describe the experience of his wanderers, but it applies equally to the experience of his readers, led on by the peripatetic nature of his words, his multivalent discourse that is not only always "elsewhere" but "asymptotic," approaching ever nearer but never completely defining the vision it seeks to name. This is a linguistic condition of perpetual loss and recovery. Mackey's language is as recursive and dilatory as the enigmatic events it records; like Freud's dreamwork, it is a language of displacement and condensation, in which the names of places and personages, acts of transport, acts of love, moments of pain and of ecstasy, performances of song and dance, learned disquisitions, flirtatious bar talk, and transcendent visions, are all in a constant process of metonymic and metaphoric exchange. As Patricia A. Parker puts it in *Inescapable Romance*, in a formulation which speaks directly to the condition of Mackey's poetry, "The melancholy of exile from the present or presence is the fact that they can only be 're-presented' in language, an activity which takes place in time." In other words, Mackey's poetry is one of our most recent occurrences, our most recent recurrence, of an ancient poetic mode: quest romance.

In *The Anatomy of Criticism*, Northrop Frye argues that "The essential element of plot in romance is adventure, which means that romance is naturally a sequential and processional form." But although the movement of Mackey's "wandering 'we'" certainly constitutes a "sequential and processional" adventure (as well as a migration, a flight, a pilgrimage, and so on), the idea that his serial poems partake of romance is not necessarily obvious. Traditional quest romance usually has a single protagonist or "hero," and while there is a certain heroic dimension to the adventures of Mackey's band, the very fact that it is a band, a group endeavor in which various characters appear and disappear, often under enigmatic circumstances, leads us to think of the poem as an exploration of community, rather than an unfolding vision of an individual's struggle and triumph. Furthermore, conflict is often considered a fundamental dimension of quest romance; an identifiable enemy confronts and engages the hero, and as Frye puts it, "the nearer the romance is to myth, the more attributes of divinity will cling to the hero and the more the enemy will take on demonic mythical qualities."

Again, Mackey's serial poems position themselves somewhat ambiguously in these terms. Does divinity cling to the figures in the poems? We have seen in our consideration of Huff that he both is and is not an avatar of Hermes. Another figure in the band, Sophia, may well be the divine Gnostic emanation of wisdom, but she is also, in *Whatsaid Serif*, "the Bedouin / hick you've heard about," and her erotic charms, the "Press of her / hips beneath a loose cotton / dress, / bright sun behind her. Graspable / waist, sinewy limbs," charges the spiritual quest for gnosis with a palpably human sexuality. Even more to the point, we may ask if there are really identifiable antagonists or "enemies" in the poems. To be sure, there is antagonism, but it tends to manifest itself in terms of place and historical circumstance rather than characters. I am thinking particularly of "Song" 60 and the vision of "Nub," involving an "Abducted future . . . Dearth Lake's dry / largesse / Dread Lake's aliases, alibis, / Death / Lake also there . . ." The "abducted future" is, in effect, that of the United States itself (cf. the stolen election of 2000), which Mackey calls in the preface to *Splay Anthem* an "imperial, flailing republic" in the wake of 9/11 and our subsequent wars. Rather than as a direct conflict, the corruption and violence of that period is represented in the poem as a condition that must be ritualistically suffered and endured by the band, and as commentary, Mackey notes "cycles of recriminatory assault further confirming a regime of echo the poem's recourse to echo would cure homeopathically if it could." Another instance of this representation of conflict is found somewhat later, in "Song" 62: "Planes flew . . . Bombs fell . . . / Operation Boast. Operation Lie. / Thug regime scrimmaging thug / regime, we were in the middle." This is "Kali's time," referring to the Hindu goddess of death and violence, "Operation / Gloat. Operation Slaughter. Name / after name after name . . . Not in ours / we / said, slapped heads ringing, not to be Andoumboulou again."

At this moment of confrontation, it makes a great deal of sense that Mackey not only renounces any possibility of identification with the warmongers ("not in our name"), but also invokes his central myth of the Andoumboulou, immediately insisting on its enduring truth: "*Not to / be Andoumboulou again but were, we / within we athwart we ad infinitum.*" Let us recall that Mackey interprets and reinterprets the Andoumboulou myth often in his work; as he tells Brent Cunningham in their interview, he sees the Andoumboulou "as a form of failed, flawed human being," which he then refines as "a rough draft of human being, the work-in-progress we continue to be." Human evil, even on an immense scale, is due, ontologically speaking, to the Gnostic truth that we live in a failed draft of creation and that at best, we are a work in progress, continually struggling to improve ourselves and usually failing, often spectacularly so.

Thinking, then, about Mackey's poetry as quest romance, we can see that if the category applies, it does so in dramatically revisionary terms. In a crucial early essay, "The Internalization of Quest Romance," Harold Bloom, still our greatest authority on revisionism in poetry, declares that "The hero of internalized quest is the poet himself, the antagonists of quest are everything in the self that blocks imaginative work, and the fulfillment is never the poem itself but the poem beyond that is made possible by the apocalypse of imagination." Could this in any way apply to Mackey's quest? We have already seen that per Jean-Luc Nancy, the poet, the myth-teller, becomes his own hero, but as in Mackey's case, is also part of a collectivity which finds its meaning through the myth's recitation. Bloom, like Frye before him, tends to think of quest romance in terms of a solitary quester, a Spenserian knight or a Childe Roland, and it could well be that one of the most significant revisions to the mode of romance which Mackey makes is the idea, embedded not only in content but in form itself, that collective life, collective experience, has a heroic dimension. This collective also experiences its "apocalypse of imagination," which is indeed "the poem beyond," the continual movement toward the utopian horizon that is never fully *revealed* ("apocalypse" literarily means "uncovering") in the "sequential and processional form" of *Song of the Andoumboulou* and "*Mu*." Commenting on Frye's formulation, Parker again observes, in a way that perfectly describes Mackey's work, that "One of the implications of the sequential, however, is that it remains, like time itself, within a frame in which presence, or fulfillment, is always in some sense placed at a distance." Likewise, "When the 'end' is defined typologically, as a Promised Land or Apocalypse, 'romance' is that mode or tendency which remains on the threshold before the promised end, still in the wilderness of wandering, 'error', or 'trial.'" Or as Mackey puts it in "Song" 110,

> *"Going forward" lay on every-*
>   *one's lips, wishful, a wand*
>   *we waved, would-be wand,*
>   *in-*
>   *sistent, spell we'd have cast*
>   *if we*
> *could*

Mackey presents this passage in the conditional; his magician's wand is a "would-be wand," and the spell is cast only "if we / could." In Mackey's poems, we are always in the state of "if," on the threshold of magic, moving toward that moment, that place, where magic becomes real. And it is on this threshold where the true magic of the poetry is to be found.

(2021)

III

Introduction to *Double Trio: A Restless Messengers Symposium*

This gathering of essays, all by longtime readers of Nathaniel Mackey, celebrates the publication of *Double Trio*, the three-volume "box set" that continues "*Mu*" and *The Song of the Andoumboulou*, the intertwined serial poems that Mackey has been writing for nearly forty years. Each volume of this enormous continuation of Mackey's "long song"—a total of over a thousand pages of verse—is, as he tells us, "composed of twice as many installments of '*Mu*' and *The Song of the Andoumboulou* as comprise each of the work's three most immediate predecessor volumes, *Splay Anthem* [2006], *Nod House* [2011], and *Blue Fasa* [2015]." *Double Trio* will undoubtedly win him many new readers, so for the record, let me note that of his six full-length collections, only the first, *Eroding Witness* (chosen by

Michael Harper for the National Poetry Series and originally published in 1985), contains poems outside of the two series, both of which begin in that book. *School of Udhra* (1993) consists of *Andoumboulou 8–15* and "*Mu*" 4–14; *Whatsaid Serif* (1998) consists entirely of *Andoumboulou 16–35*. "*mu*" reappears, completely intertwined with *Andoumboulou*, in the National Book Award–winning *Splay Anthem*, a volume that also contains the crucial preface in which Mackey explains his rationale for writing in serial form, naming some of his most important precursors in literature (H.D., Olson, Duncan, Creeley, Wilson Harris) and jazz (Ellington, Coltrane, Sun Ra, Pharoah Sanders, Don Cherry), and identifying some of the myths and beliefs from the worldwide cultures that inform his vision.

As Mackey tells us regarding the original Dogon funeral songs of the Andoumboulou, the music we hear emerging from this cross-cultural mix of traditions suggests "not only debts to history or the dead or the past, a neglect of history or the dead or past, but other non-observances only an alteration of mind might set right." And not only an alteration of mind, but a transformative work of the imagination: a great world-poem, a radical rethinking of both epic and lyric, endlessly expansive in its cultural frames of reference, endlessly moving in and out of history and geography, endlessly questing toward an unreachable utopian (or "blutopian") horizon. Since *Splay Anthem*, Mackey's band of pilgrims, his philosophic posse, his constantly morphing ensemble of lovers, singers, and Gnostic strangers, has continued to move through a global space-time continuum to the accompaniment of tracks from numerous musical traditions which this cast of characters hears "on the box." But always, as Mackey observes of his creation in the preface to *Blue Fasa*, "Locality and locality's discontent continue, as do identity and identity's discontent."

Never has this been truer than in *Double Trio*, which Mackey wrote in the six years between the summer of 2012 and summer of 2018, between the ages of sixty-five and seventy-one. As he tells us in the author's note to *Tej Bet*, the first volume, "It was a period during which earlier health crises continued to occur, with further complications and greater severity. In the summer of 2012 the U.S. was just around the corner from re-electing President Barack Obama, but by the summer of 2018 it was into the second year of having reasserted its white nationalist roots and begun a descent into neo-fascism. It was a period of distress and precarity inside and outside both." But as is sometimes the case with poets in such states of distress and precarity (think Keats, think Mandelstam), Mackey's muse, his Sophia, seems to have been with him constantly. "During this time," he writes, "a certain disposition or dispensation came upon me that I would characterize or sum up with the words *all day music.*"

The epic scope of this *all day music*, the breadth and depth of the long song, will amaze any reader who takes the plunge. What I have always found so moving in Mackey's poetry are his permutations on the themes of communal aspiration and utopian desire, themes which complement what, for this reader at least, has always been an *initiatic* tendency in his poetry. (I make this argument in my chapter on Mackey in *On Mount Vision.*) But listen to how these themes rise up clear and strong in "Lay of the Lifted Again"—*"mu" one hundred twenty-fifth part*—:

> ... *Lit by shipwreck we'd read*
>
>   *and*
> *so it seemed, rhapsodic resolve as it all*
> *fell apart ... Abstract music abstraction itself*
>   *made more concrete. Boxheaded exegete,*
>
>   *box-*
> *head ennui, box-had-there-been-one's be-*
> *quest. We gave a loud shout, beginning to*
> *be there again, the inconsequence it was not-*
> *withstanding ... There was a we we were on*
>
>   *our*
> *way toward regardless, no utopic elsewise*
> *too utopic, a we we would eventually be. "Let*
>   *the parts congregate and grow," we got up*
>
>   *insist-*
> *ing, a shout so loud it lifted us, our feet left the*
>   *floor, no matter it might've been mental at*
>   *most ...*

The reference to George Oppen's *Of Being Numerous* ("the bright light of shipwreck"), a precursor poem likewise informed by historical disaster and utopian communal hope, leads the more musically inclined Mackey, a "Boxheaded exegete" to be sure, to insist upon "a we we would eventually be," a we that cries out "Let the parts congregate and grow." Music and poetry lift us up and sustain us: this is Mackey's lay—a ballad, a story, a song.

But this is only one aspect of Mackey's project, for the nomadic "we" we are forever becoming meets with painful resistance, and the "utopic elsewhere" toward which we forever wander is often obscured by troubling shadows. I have in mind the poem which opens *So's Notice*, the second volume of *Double Trio*, called "The Overghost Ourkestra's Next"— "*mu*" one hundred fortieth part—. Inspired in part by the police killing of Eric Garner, this poem offers anger and hope, lament and persistence, all in equal measure:

> *"Nub held my neck in the crook of its arm," the*
>   *unworded song we sang said. "Nub took me*
>   *down*
>   *but I got up swinging." Could we only band*
>   *or bond we thought but it wasn't so, together*
>   *as we were we suffered, original sufferheads*
>   *for all eternity it seemed, wise ones and wounded*
>   *ones*
>   *it seemed . . .*

"Nub"—Mackey's shorthand for all that is hatefully, violently wrong with the world, and specifically with America—may take us down in an illegal chokehold, but we get up swinging—swinging our fists to defend ourselves, but also swinging as in jazz. "Hands up, wind- / pipes crushed, we blew . . . Notwithstanding we / couldn't breathe we blew." Here, the slogans in the streets renew themselves and take on lasting power in the Overghost Ourkestra's prophetic "posthumous release."

Gathered together, Mackey's prophetic books—yes, I do believe he is our William Blake, Gnosticism and all—constitute the scripture we read, to borrow the title of the third volume of *Double Trio*, in our *Nerve Church*. Written upon the nerves in a nerve-wracked time, Mackey's address to the congregation turns us into exegetes, mournful, joyful, always hungry for the Word. In "Song of the Andoumboulou: 245," dedicated to Robert Duncan (one of Mackey's most important precursors) and Peter O'Leary (one of his best commentators), "We slept inside myth but were stirred by ythm" (*Nerve Church* 237). "No redemptive narrative paved our way," yet "Out of the gold bell of many a horn . . . we rang / free- / dom." "*Ythm*" has long been Mackey's term for the strange, combinatory power of both ancient story and immediate song that wakes us from our slumber and sets us again upon our utopian quest. Ythm pulses through *Double Trio*, keeping in mind that the last part of the work was written out of the depths of some of the worst years our nation has experienced since the Civil War. Nevertheless, "in the nerve church, metaphoric boat / of soul metamorphic," Mackey calls to us to transform ourselves and join the band.

(2021)

Paul Bray

If there is such a thing as a born Gnostic, then Paul Bray (1951–2011) was surely it. Still almost totally unknown and unread today, Bray led a life comparable in intensity and self-destructive truth-seeking to that of three of his greatest literary heroes, Rimbaud, Poe, and Lovecraft. Yet as I note in the two pieces which make up this chapter, a few brilliant writers did indeed recognize his genius during his lifetime. I corresponded with Paul and spoke on the phone with him during the last years of his life. I'm honored to say that he admired my work as much as I did his, and I cherish the essays that he wrote about me. What follows are my review of his collected poems, Terrible Woods, *and a paper I gave on his work at a panel on "the New Gnostics" at the Louisville Conference for Literature and Culture in 2013. The first was written while Paul was still alive; the second two years after his death (he was found slumped over his computer). If any of the poets I have written about deserve a greater readership, it is Paul Bray.*

I

The Marvelous Adventures of Paul Bray

Paul Bray's poetry comes to us full blown, and that is one of a number of challenges in reviewing it. *Terrible Woods: Poems 1965–2008* is a collected poems, but unlike nearly all such volumes, most of the work here has not been previously published. Except for a chapbook or two, this is Bray's first book. Bray was born in Washington, DC, in 1951, and grew up in Maryland, Spain, and Central America. His father was a CIA operative, and worked undercover for much of his career. As an undergraduate at Bard, he won the Wilton Moore Lockwood Prize for Most Distinguished Creative Writing, and he holds a PhD from the City University of New York, where he studied with such distinguished scholars as Angus Fletcher and Allen Mandelbaum. He has taught at various universities, and published a number of academic pieces and reviews, including a study of Emily Dickinson as visionary which appeared in *Raritan*, but we are also told in an author's note that he was "an ominous presence on the New York art scene of the '70s and '80s," he collaborated on the film *Unmade Beds*, and he "was the lead vocalist and lyricist for the band Brains in Heaven" (which I could not find in the vast archives of rock bands now available on the internet). Bray currently lives in Santa Fe. In other words, his has not been the typical poetic career: no MFA in creative writing, no contest-winning first book, no long list of poems published in print or online journals, no appearances in prominent reading series, no history of critical recognition, no tenure. Yet he has had distinguished readers: in addition to Angus Fletcher, *Terrible Woods* has extraordinary blurbs from Victoria Nelson, Paul Auster, and Harold Bloom.

For good reason: at his frequent best, Paul Bray is a remarkable poet. His work is formal, erudite, bristling with arcane references, and shot through with words and terms that will send readers scurrying to the dictionary. Then again, it is witty and playful, with a fresh, lively appreciation for the vernacular and an instinct for turning even the most obscure historical events or metaphysical speculations into poised, seductive artifacts. In his preface (deadpan and utterly wacky), Bray calls himself the "channeller" of *Terrible Woods*. Yet I suspect there has been tremendous labor expended on these poems, precisely the sort of labor that Yeats, another channeller, describes in "Adam's Curse": "A line will take us hours maybe; / Yet if it does not seem a moment's thought / Our stitching and unstitching has been naught." This attitude toward writing—spontaneous, otherworldly dictation coupled with highly deliberate structural precision—is not something one sees much these days, and that is another reason why a review of *Terrible Woods* is a challenge. Bray's poems, in their elaborate dance of form, trope, and reference, deserve a great deal of careful scrutiny, and will yield all the more pleasure the more deeply they are read. They tend to be long and dense, and though Bray frequently uses a relatively easygoing iambic tetrameter line, his elaborate rhymes produce a high level of verbal concentration. Even poems of a page or two in length call for careful unpacking. And since Bray's work cannot be simply categorized (saying a poet writes "formal" verse tells us as little about the work as saying it is "free" verse), or readily placed in any contemporary

school or movement, readers will not be able to depend on many prefor-
mulated expectations or responses.

"Poetry is the scholar's art," Stevens notes in his *Adagia*, but even so,
I'm not quite sure he had a poet like Bray in mind. Aside from the sheer
range of literary and cultural allusions in these poems, a great many of
them have intellectual premises which may be unfamiliar even to serious
readers of poetry. How many such readers, for instance, have made their
way through Vico's *Scienza Nuova*, which posits a cyclical vision of history
(later appropriated by Joyce in *Finnegan's Wake*)? Bray's long poem based
on Vico is called "Ingens Sylva," referring, as he notes, to "the giant forest
of the earth through which the first men wandered in beastly ignorance
and solitude." Here are two of the work's thirty-five stanzas:

> By fictions and the empty masks
> melodious laws are petrified.
> Let in the pleb of straw who asks
> asylum from the cheetah-eyed
> insensate beasts who prowl the dense
> harpoon-treed forests, trapped in sense.
>
> Cold mutton paws unsheathe the key.
> The mute librarian lets him in
> to trace the etymology
> of orbis, language that folds in
> upon itself where puppets screech
> the used-up poem of their speech.

The third age in Vico's three-stage historical cycle, following the ages of
gods and of heroes, is the human age, an age of democracy and reflective
irony, producing, as Bray summarizes, "a second barbarism, the barbarism of reflection," which "was to be far more horrible than the first." As
we see in these lines, Bray's poem—indeed, perhaps all of his poetry—is
both an expression and a critique of this "barbarism." The "fictions and
empty masks" of systematized reason leave us "trapped in sense," limited to a "language that folds in / upon itself where puppets screech / the
used-up poem of their speech." But in a doubly ironic turn, such self-

knowledge produces not a "used-up" poem, but a brilliantly original one. Gesturing perhaps to Plato's Parable of the Cave, Bray declares that "The shamanistic power elite / rules all who sleep on that cave floor." Yet seeking existential freedom, the poet resists this elite: "We turn punctilious, steal their books, / ride out in chariots of war." "Strike out into the yawning glens / of overgrowth," he cries; "We'd / best move from here, keep silent, read // mute marks carved on the dancing stars."

The poet-scholar as romantic rebel is a figure that Bray finds irresistible; it recurs again and again in *Terrible Woods*. The pattern we have just traced in "Ingens Sylva" also appears in the first stanzas of the aptly named "Gothic Heaven-Storming":

We reach the mossy mental edge.
We reach the end of pilgrimage.
There is no way to go but up.

Instead we dare a stepping-back
into a verbal artifact.
It doubles on itself, no rope

is dangled. Help! The symbols point
to clockwork that is out of joint,
to watches crying for repair.

Once again, we are in crisis at the veritable edge of being. But rather than leap "up," the poet steps back "into a verbal artifact"—the poem which ironically expresses but also curtails the act of "heaven-storming" that is the poet's great goal. As in "Ingens Sylva," where we "read // mute marks carved on the dancing stars," poetic reflection again provides a source of insight. In the symbols of its inscription, we learn the clockwork of the universe is "out of joint," that the watches (our beliefs? our selves?) are "crying for repair." Yet by the end of the poem, we find ourselves struggling to get "outside the orbit of the limit // spaces that the words inhibit / us from knowing." Language, therefore, may aid us in uncovering our true condition but may also inhibit us in our quest for truth.

As some readers may have already guessed, Bray's quest has its origins in Gnosticism, and the knowledge he seeks is a spiritual gnosis that in its purest state will lead him beyond the starry limits of his cosmic fate. "There are many implicit Gnostic poets," observes Harold Bloom; "Paul Bray is overt. By a fine paradox, he is a vital and vitalizing Gnostic." When Bray is at his most overt, the result is a poem like "The Alien":

Beneath the boughs of weeping elms I wander.
I stagger under huge Druidic stones.
In strange cyclopean vales I stoop and ponder
what tribe of light left me so far from home.
From gate to gate unlocking every archon,
I carry in my tomb of flesh a portion
of captured light for fuel when I embark on
my bold escape from this immense abortion.
Watchmen and toll-collectors veil their faces.
My body-stump goes limping through the pillars.
Homesick and whored in terror's empty spaces,
stripped to my ribs by moth and caterpillar,
cast like live dice into the teeth of panthers,
I crouch in Tibil waiting for an answer.

This is wonderfully lugubrious, but it's textbook Gnosticism, and sounds more like H. P. Lovecraft than William Blake. The material universe is not the Gnostic's true home; it was created by a false demiurge, and hence the seeker of knowledge regards himself as an alien, longing to return to the fathering Abyss (about which Bray also has a short poem). The body is a "tomb of flesh"; the archons who block the initiate's ascent are "watchmen and toll-collectors"; the realm in which the quester crouches is "Tibil," which for the Mandaean Gnostics meant the earth, the limited, limiting natural world. Fortunately, Bray's Gnosticism, however serious, can also be very funny. In the same poem, he rails against fallen humanity, with "Your strange obsession / with watching men in uniforms hurl balls / at one another. This unholy passion / for platitudes that has allowed mere clods / and politicians to replace your gods."

A less overt but far more transgressive sort of antinomianism is at work in "The Harem in the Attic," one of the relatively few poems in

which Bray uses the first-person singular and writes more straightfor-
wardly about his early life—if he is to be believed. The American passion
for sports again gets skewered by the poet, a young Humbert Humbert:

Of all the tortures I endured when small
surely the worst was baseball. Boys with mitts
shouting, "Hey wake up, wake up, dammit, Paul!
You dropped the ball again, you stupid shit!"
As if my poet's soul should take the blame
for the outcome of their bland, moronic game.

So boys I grew to hate, but little girls,
now that's an equine of another color;
their dresses, underpants and falling curls.
Boys, by comparison, are somewhat duller.
Many a neighbor girl I would befriend
and many a happy afternoon would spend

up in the attic of my parents' house
undressing them: first come the shoes and socks,
and then the skirt and then the little blouse
and then the panties of my Goldilocks:
a fuzzless kiwi honey by the scent
of mischief, mirth, shame, fate and accident.

"Mischief, mirth, shame, fate and accident": in Bray's measured formula,
in the boy's shameful mischief, we see a refusal of his fate, a refusal of
the accident of birth, and a revolt against the neatly gendered order of
things. The poem's final stanzas are a strange blend of the judicious and
the outrageous:

I still remember all the fools who'd talk
about poor Paul "whose only friends are lasses."
I scan my TV in a state of shock,
watching the jocks pat one another's asses.
They call me sissy, but today as then
I'd take girls over grubby boys or men.

Nation of knuckled nances, put me down
for not orgasming in your blood and sand.
My eyes were on another pitcher's mound.
And so to Patsy, Candy, Cindy and
last but not least, to Babs, I say Thank you
and to the boys of Larchmont School, Fuck you.

The disturbing figure of the preadolescent muse recurs in a number of the poems in *Terrible Woods* which best demonstrate Bray's strengths. Bray has a strong affinity to popular song lyrics (he has a long set called "The Croons"), to the Protestant hymn tradition (another set, "Seven Hymns," are meant to be sung to various choral melodies by Bach), and to the romantic ballad. Two poems, "Meyer's Farm" and "Treatises in the Ground," are ballads of poetic initiation mediated by girls who possess, or are possessed by, eroticized supernatural powers that will lead the young man to visionary experience. In the first, the young man works on the farm of a family friend, encountering the granddaughter whom he first knew as a "Moonfaced and freckled, meadow-moist" child. Now thirteen,

. . . Her solemn eyes
had turned to chrysoberyl. They
could any farmboy hypnotize.
Her hair was like the summer hay.
Her flesh was like the Milky Way.

Despite the somewhat tongue-in-cheek tone, the narrative follows an authentically romantic trajectory:

. . . one strange night
while smoking reefer in the loft,
I spotted in the pale moonlight
my Megan with her nightgown doffed
between the silo and the trough.

About to be seduced by a demonic scarecrow, Megan is miraculously rescued by the spirit of William Blake, who recognizes the scarecrow as the demiurgic Urizen from his Prophetic Books. After driving him off, Blake leads the enchanted maiden home before dealing with the young poet, who complains "Why not inspire or enter me?"

"Relax," he said, "you'll get the girl."
Then added, "In, say, six more years.
I'll be right back." Then in a whirl
of wings they vanished. All my fears
returned and I was choked with tears.

When all at once I felt Blake shoot
up my left leg then straight into
my prong, my Vegetative root.
It hurt. I screamed, "You bastard, you!
John Milton would have used my shoe!"

But the pain soon subsides, leaving the young poet inspired: "I laughed and sang like one set free / and strolled into Eternity."

"Treatises in the Ground" takes us further back into childhood, uncovering, as the title indicates, even deeper sources of poetic power. The nine-year-old poet-to-be leaves home to visit the young witch Sally O'Neill:

She was ten years old with coal-black hair,
where Seven Locks Road met Tuckerman Lane;
she was ten years old with coal-black hair
        and ivory-colored skin.
She looked a sight in her dress so formal.
Like Wednesday Addams but not as normal.
Tell mortals nothing and the worm tell
        that you are his kin.

This delightful enchantress uses a divining-stone to lead the boy where "the creek sleeps over the thick black mud":

not two yards from the barn's hex sign,
where Seven Locks Road meets Tuckerman Lane;
not two yards from the barn's hex sign,

> *you waspy little prig,*
> *there's a willow tree with blood that drips*
> *and under that tree above the crypts*
> *a coffer of sacred manuscripts.*
> *We find it if we dig.*

Sally may find her companion a "waspy little prig," but the "coffer of sacred manuscripts" that the two dig up turns out to be her gift, "as if somehow," as he puts it, "she knew by right / the scrolls belonged to me."

But are these ancient texts (reminiscent, despite their American origins, of the Gnostic texts discovered at Nag Hammadi) a gift or a curse? As the boy concludes,

> *I scan those texts by the light of the moon,*
> *where Seven Locks Road meets Tuckerman Lane;*
> *I scan those texts by the light of the moon,*
> *bent over every page.*
> *By the light of the moon by the light of the sun*
> *I search each word. I've just begun.*
> *My studying will not be done*
> *till I am gray with age.*

In Bray's vision, poetic utterance is inextricably connected to the study of ancient texts. The poet is fated to practice an esoteric art, and Bray frequently insists that his initiation is both a joy and a disaster. As he says in "You Must Not Go to the Woods at Nights," section III of a poem called "Glyphs from Beyond,"

> *He found shards of meaning everywhere he turned*
> *and oftentimes he cut himself picking them up*
> *or caught himself thinking of what he had learned*
> *and then trying to unlearn it, to sip from the cup*
> *dipped deep in Lethe in the cypress zone.*

Not a chance: like Keats, who in his odes both does and does not want to drink from Lethe, the melancholy Bray both embraces his poetic fate and longs to forget it. For him, as he says in the great last line of "The Text

Beneath the Text," "The words are gates which open only to those who are willing to fall." A true Gnostic, Bray knows he has fallen; he knows the gates of words have opened for him; and he knows that in the end, the words can take him only so far.

"It will be clear to the reader," writes Bray in his preface, "how much TW owes to Wordsworth's 'Immortality' Ode. The only major difference is that it muses over multiple archaic and futuristic childhoods rather than over childhood in the singular." Granted, like Wordsworth, Bray is obsessed with childhood, and like him sees a progressive loss of divinity in the natural growth of the individual from infancy to maturity. And perhaps like Wordsworth in the Immortality Ode, Bray too can "find / Strength in what remains behind; / In the primal sympathy / Which having been must ever be." But as we have seen, in Bray, the childhood disaster that is at least as bad as the Wordsworthian loss of divine innocence and immediacy of experience is the fall into language, into a verbal expressivity that is both a gift and a curse. Bray's problematic view of poetic utterance is more akin to Coleridge than Wordsworth, as one sees in a different ode, Coleridge's "Dejection." Far more susceptible than Wordsworth to the "afflictions" of depression that rob him of "what nature gave me at my birth, / My shaping spirit of Imagination," Coleridge proposes a solution that is similar to Bray's. As Coleridge puts it, "And haply by abstruse research to steal / From my own nature all the natural man—/ This was my sole resource, my only plan." Like Coleridge (and later, like Poe), Bray engages in an immense program of "abstruse research" (seeking, as he puts it, "the text beneath the text") which is intended precisely to steal from his own nature the natural man. Wordsworth never needs to do this; his relationship to nature and to the natural man within is far less troubled, and concomitantly his relationship to language—and to poetry—more direct. His poetic identity and sense of vocation is less vexed.

Two questions follow from all this. First, what does Bray mean when he tells us that his poetry "muses over multiple archaic and futuristic childhoods"? And second, if he is indeed a Gnostic (and I really don't think there's any doubt about this), why should he be in any way concerned with the (Wordsworthian) natural man? After all, it is precisely the natural man that the Gnostics regard as irredeemably fallen, and it is the natural man in a fallen, natural world from which they seek to escape.

If *Terrible Woods* offers any answers to these questions, I think they may be found in a sequence of five poems called "Poems of Marvelous Adventure," dedicated to John Ashbery. In *Self-Portrait in a Convex Mirror*, Ashbery has a wonderful poem called "Märchenbilder" (Fairytale Pictures), drawing on Schumann's pieces for viola and piano as well as the German *märchen* themselves. Ashbery's poem begins like a typical *märchen*, "*Es war einmal . . .*" (once upon a time), makes reference to various fairytales, but then insists "I want to go back, out of the bad stories, / But there's always the possibility that the next one . . ." Bray, who has written one of the best recent essays on Ashbery, certainly knows this poem. His sequence acknowledges why one would want to get out of the "bad stories" but also understands the world of possibilities they hold. These poems do indeed muse over multiple archaic (if not futuristic) childhoods, for each one is based on a childhood classic (though not fairy tales): *Twenty Thousand Leagues Under the Sea*, *The Surprising Adventures of Baron Munchhausen*, *The Wizard of Oz*, *Peter Pan*, and (switching from book to film), *King Kong*. Like his "Ingens Sylva," they are all written in a six-line iambic tetrameter stanza rhymed ababcc, which Bray deploys with particular effectiveness, since the verse form works in counterpoint to the narrative movement of the poems.

Although it appears that Bray simply retells the plots of the stories, on a deeper level he transforms these familiar narratives into sites where he can reflect upon the existential and spiritual tensions to which he is so sensitized, and which serve as his greatest inspiration. He is particularly sympathetic to such antiheroes or Gnostic questers as Captain Nemo or Captain Hook. For Nemo (whose name means "no-man" in Latin, indirectly referring to the wandering Odysseus, who tells the Cyclops his name is "No-man"), "The sea is everything. It is / the Living Infinite and not / unlike this library of his," a trope which certainly resonates for Bray. With his submarine caught in the Norwegian Mokstraumen or maelstrom, Nemo faces his doom:

I write this damping violent fires
of lava and obsidian,
convulsions of diluvian

immensity where islands rise
from terra firma under reefs.
If I can part the mermaid's thighs
tattooed with hearts and bas-reliefs
then surely all that's left for me
swims under this dark gallery.

Likewise, Hook (who, it should be recalled, is a disgraced gentleman who attended Eton) also goes to his destruction in a confrontation with primal forces, embodied in the figure of perpetual youth, his nemesis Peter Pan:

Hook rushes forward when the noise
as of a ticking clock is heard:
the crocodile forever lured

to Hook who cries, Pan, what art thou?
I'm youth, I'm joy, the innocent,
the heartless, the eternal now,
the bloodrush in the long ascent
to ecstasy, the loutish horn
that sprouts on foaming Capricorn.

I am tempted to say that Paul Bray, in the mythic depths of the Neverland that is *Terrible Woods*, plays the roles of both Pan and Hook. Attracted to the dark souls who give cosmic meaning to their rebellion in Gnostic arcana and hermetic research, Bray is also inspired by a more playful Eros, by exuberant spiritual forces if not entirely innocent, then still charged with natural joy. Like Blake, his poetry is possessed of both the Prolific and the Devourer. At his best, he is an irresistibly magical tempter:

Yes, many girls still hear the crow
of Pan outside their bedroom doors
and cry, if only I could go
down all your tragic corridors.
Pan, god of Panic, in the woods,
co-fosterer of angelhoods.

We readers are more fortunate than these girls, for we can respond to Bray's "crow" and follow him down his "tragic corridors," which may prove a less tragic fate than it first appears. If we read him deeply enough, perhaps he will foster our angelhood too.

(2009)

II

Glyphs from Beyond: Paul Bray's Gnostic Poetry

I think it is particularly appropriate, given the subject of my paper, that I should be the very last presenter in our two panels on the New Gnostics. If Gnosticism as we have come to define it today is an undercurrent in recent (and not so recent) American poetry—strong but not always palpable—then the poetry of Paul Bray makes a good endpoint. A true *poète maudit*, Bray made no secret of his Gnosticism, and would frequently sign his emails to me "Yours in the Pleroma." But personal jokes aside, he returned continually to those Gnostic themes, symbols, and gestures which lend themselves most effectively to literary expression. Like the half-mad seekers of Poe and Lovecraft, the visionary speakers of Bray's poems, sometimes in the company of enchanting, prepubescent witches ("She looked a sight in her dress so formal. / Like Wednesday Addams but not as normal"), pore over "Glyphs from Beyond" or "The Text Beneath the Text," in which "The words are gates which open only to those who are willing to fall." Yet for Bray, we have always already fallen; the poet's textual obsessions are intended to help him escape from the material world, "this dark prison planet" where "I move along the furious Equator / And suffer the remorse of the Creator." Against that Creator—the Gnostic Demiurge—Bray, like some comic book superhero, conducts a hilariously transgressive linguistic campaign.

In *The Ringers in the Tower*, Harold Bloom famously argues that Romanticism may be understood as the "internalization of quest-romance." "The movement of quest-romance," Bloom observes, "before its internalization by the High Romantics, was from nature to redeemed nature, the sanction of redemption being the gift of some external spiritual authority, sometimes magical. The Romantic movement is from nature to the imagination's freedom . . . redemptive in direction but destructive of the social self." This formulation, which already verges on Gnosticism, no doubt applies to Bray, but not in a direct fashion. Arguably, Bray's poetry represents a "re-*externalization*" of quest-romance. The redemption it seeks is certainly a matter of imaginative freedom, and indubitably, indeed flamboyantly, destructive of the social self. But archaically, it is also sanctioned by an external spiritual authority, magical in itself and capable of granting magical powers to the questing poet, even when he is unable to master them. Again and again, the poet finds himself thwarted by the archons, the psychic and spiritual blocking agents which only Bray's outlandishly triumphant rhetoric can overcome in his search for gnosis.

Bray's quest consists at least in part of undoing what he calls our "unholy passion / for platitudes" through the invocatory power of the poem, and consequently restoring our lost knowledge of the divine. These two goals are intimately connected. Consider, for example, "Alien Alphabets," the first of three sonnets in the set called "Glyphs from Beyond":

His technique of mystical exploration involved
projecting his consciousness into blank, embryonic
sectors of the matrix until waiting was resolved
by a sense of something moving along the tectonic
vectors of the grid where the paradigm shifts
into third and a whole world is lurking in the plasmic
halo that shimmers on the leaves and glyphs.
He adjusted the trodes and allowed the orgasmic
waves to wash over the sands behind his face
and the photisms changed into the green of the mantra
and he asked the bright beings who linger in that place
of the emblematic meaning of the giant sriyantra-
crop circle found in the Maryland field.
What was its genesis? What had it concealed?

Typically for Bray, we have a deadpan, ironic humor, a pastiche of science, science fiction, and New Age mysticism, combined with formidable technique. In his piece on *Terrible Woods*, in *Notre Dame Review*, Henry Weinfield notes that this poem works so well "because of the extraordinary use of enjambment, especially on feminine rhymes, and because the meter is accentual but not syllabic—the anapestic rhythm coincides with four strong beats per line, but extra syllables are allowed, and these contribute to the continual sense of flowing over that produces a river of sound." Weinfield concludes his analysis by noting that the sonnet's innovative form is in turn "a figure for the confrontation between the mundane and the esoteric that Bray is working with in terms of the poem's content." And this leads me back to Bray's textual gnosticism or gnostic textuality.

Despite the manifold ironies in poems such as "Alien Alphabets," I think that Bray is quite serious when he tells us that "the paradigm shifts / into third and a whole world is lurking in the plasmic / halo that shimmers on the leaves and glyphs." (Here, by the way, the enjambment is very sly, since we think that "shifts" is a plural noun but it is then revealed to be a verb.) Bray's "technique of mystical exploration" is a textual practice that declares itself to be in search of lost, hidden depths which actually come into existence through its own composition. There *is* a whole world lurking on the leaves and glyphs: Bray enters it through his poetry, and he calls upon his readers follow him. "I slid down a mossy bank," he declares in "The Text Beneath the Text," "until I found myself in a sea / of hieroglyphics and Vedic brushstrokes. The sea vomited me / up onto a distant beach and from there I came to a dark wood / where the secret life of poems brooded over me." The secret life of poems broods over him still; indeed, the life of his poems is now all that remains of Paul Bray, but that is more than enough. As for his readers, they are at "The Edge of the World," where he half-seriously informs us that

> *Rapports with the Beyond*
> *are established. There is an oneiric upsetting of the world,*
> *a universal collapse*
> *of their whole picture of space-time, a reliving of an experience*
> *they had eight or perhaps ten trillion years ago when they*
> *knew where they were going:*
> *to the lifeless, arctic, final desolation. They have become*
> *wavelike*
> *and seem to melt into the shrieking air . . .*

Beyond nothingness there is something even more horrible,
and beyond that there is Heaven.

There is something strangely comforting in this vision, for one comes to trust Bray to establish our rapport with the Beyond—and point our way to Heaven.

(2014)

Lawrence Joseph

Lawrence Joseph is one of our most astute political poets. A law professor with a deep understanding of the nature and role of testimony, his poems move rapidly from one register of speech to another, creating a dazzling collage of contemporary voices in a constant search for justice. Yet his hunger for the truth of our current social circumstances is also insistently prophetic, charged with religious zeal but tempered by modern skepticism. Raised in Detroit, the child of Lebanese and Syrian immigrants, and a longtime resident of lower Manhattan, Joseph writes an urgent, streetwise poetry, tough but profoundly compassionate. This chapter presents my readings of two of his most recent books.

I

Ground Zero Baudelaire: Into It and the Poetics of Shock

1.

The word "apocalypse" comes from the Greek for "to uncover," and one of the most apocalyptic passages in Lawrence Joseph's Into It is the first section of "Why Not Say What Happens?" It reads as follows:

Of icons. Of divination. Of Gods. Repetitions
without end. I have it in my notes,
a translation from the Latin, a commentary
on the Book of Revelation—"the greater
the concentration of power on earth,
the more truth is stripped of its power,
the holiest innocent, in eternity,
is 'as though slain . . .'"
It has nothing to do with the apocalyptic.

The seven-headed beast from the sea,
the two-horned beast from the earth, have always—
I know, I've studied it—been with us.
Me? I'm only an accessory to particular images.

Despite the poet's assertion that "It has nothing to do with the apocalyptic," something is definitely being uncovered here. If "it" refers, as I
believe it does, not only to the events of 9/11 (toward which the poem,
and much of the rest of the book, inescapably gravitates), but to the catastrophic "concentration of power on earth" and the resultant stripping
of the power of truth which constitutes recent history, then the utterly
profane nature of the world itself becomes a revelation. Icons, divination,
gods—the traditional religious concepts through which we figure earthly
disaster—may repeat themselves without end, but the fact of the matter
is that human corruption is, and always has been, the one subject truly
under discussion. And the poet? "Careful!" (as he says of capital later in
the poem): the poet claims to be "only an accessory to particular images,"
the images which, presumably, are presented to us—imposed upon us—
throughout these poems, in all their elliptical violence. Accessory? Was
John of Patmos only an accessory when the angel called upon him to eat
the little book? The poet, Joseph implies, is no prophet, nor does he have
to be, since the beasts which symbolize evil in the Book of Revelation are
all too human, and have always been with us. At best, the poet is a commentator, or a student of the commentaries. Be that as it may, like John,
he still testifies.

Following Joseph's lead in his essay "Theories of Poetry, Theories of
Law," critics of his work have given a great deal of consideration to his status as attorney and law professor, particularly in regard to his use of terms
like "accessory." John Lowney observes that "To be an 'accessory before
the fact' or 'an accessory after the fact' in legal terms implies complicity
but not presence in the commitment of an offense. For a poet to claim
that he is an 'accessory to particular images' suggests a somewhat different subject position, a position that is subordinate or supplementary to
the images, a position that decenters the poet but does not remove his
agency." Agency is always a concern in discussing contemporary poetry,
since so many poets seek to displace or undermine the agency that is
traditionally associated with the voice of the lyric subject. Joseph's posi-

tion in regard to this matter is particularly nuanced. As he explains in an interview with Charles Bernstein, "For me, a poem's telling is in the voice or voices of compressed, condensed thought, feeling, observations, perceptions—compression that is achieved by employing various sorts of refracted language, including prosody—what Stein and Williams called 'grammar.'" Joseph's "refracted" or dissociative procedures, which he refines in *Before Our Eyes* and employs with such startling power in *Into It*, indeed decenter the poet, but I would argue that, through an ironic turn, they actually strengthen his agency. Behind the abrupt voices, the interrupted reportage, the ominous, fragmented recitations of public and private disasters, the poet forcefully makes his presence known. Again, from the interview with Bernstein: "The self who is speaking in the poem is a self who exists with an identity or identities—or, more accurately, as a self who is identified in certain ways. The self or selves who speak in the poem are constructed through various vocal languages that reflect thoughts, perceptions, feelings, often in terms of identity." Outraged, indignant, but still given to bursts of compassion and startled love, the poet regards himself, as he declares at the end of "Woodward Avenue," as "So many selves— / the one who detects the sound of a voice, / that voice—the voice that compounds / his voice—that self obedient to that fate, / increased, enlarged, transparent, changing."

So the poet's fate is to be possessed of a voice that compounds his voice, enlarges him, changes him even as, to use the title of another poem in *Into It*, "The Game Changed." "Give me the voice / To tell the shifting story," runs the volume's epigraph from *The Metamorphoses*. Through the changes in the "game" and in himself, Joseph seeks to fulfill his "intent to make a large, serious / portrait of my time"—and this despite his frustrated observation in "Inclined to Speak" that "The immense enlargement / of our perspectives is confronted / by a reduction in our powers of action." Yet this corrosive self-consciousness does not in any way detract from the book's pervasive urgency. If anything, the self-consciousness of the compounded voice adds to the sense that we are reading a document that, despite *and* because of its uncanny artfulness, is propelling us into history. And by history, I do not mean the accounts or even analyses of given events as produced by normative historiography. Rather, I mean events pushed to the point of crisis interacting with the vagaries of human subjectivity. Or as Joseph himself puts it in "History for Another

Time," "Pressure is what / it's about, and pressure's incalculable— / which eludes the historian." Thus it becomes the poet's task (but then, it has always been the poet's task) to acknowledge that pressure, to find the means by which it may play itself out in the poem, and to accommodate that pressure in himself as well as in those around him, as he tries in turn to give us a large, serious portrait of the time.

In an attempt to situate Joseph's poetry in relation to the shifts in style and reader expectations in the past two to three decades, Lisa M. Steinman notes that *Before Our Eyes* "neither gives up on subjectivity (in the sense of representing interiority) nor abandons the suggestion that however difficult to represent or malleable they might be, there are both social and physical worlds with which subjects interact and by which they are formed even as they reform what is seen in language." Steinman observes that the arc of Joseph's career parallels the move from what Charles Altieri calls the "scenic style," with its quasi-autobiographical, centered voice, often given to the task of witness, to the more disruptive, linguistically and epistemologically oriented poetry that has by now made its way into the mainstream—though even in the eighties, when Joseph's first two books came out, these two modes were already in conflict. I agree that there is a shift in Joseph's style between his first two books and his second two, and that in the latter, a greater linguistic self-consciousness and a more jagged, dissociative technique predominates. But I would also note that, important as these changes may be, Joseph's poetic goals have in some respects remained the same: he wants to tell the story of the "pressure" placed upon us by history, of how we have placed that pressure upon ourselves. "For me," he observes in the interview with Bernstein, "an—if not the—formal issue in making a poem is how, compositionally, to express, to explain, both interiorized and exteriorized realities." These are indeed matters of what Steinman calls the "social and physical worlds," matters of linguistic representation, and of interiority—all of which, given modern and postmodern conditions, are under assault, all of which are registering shock. One could say that ever since he was, as he declares in his first book, "*pulled from a womb / into a city*," Joseph has sought increasingly more effective ways of "mixing / emotional perceptions and digressions, // choler, melancholy, a sanguine view." And even as the need "to see everything simultaneously" has grown more urgent, the righteous anger of the prophet who takes umbrage at his calling (and what prophet does not?) remains the engine of the poem. The suffering of the immigrant Joseph family, the wreckage of Detroit, the criminality in the streets and skyscrapers of New York City, and finally, the destruction of the World Trade Center and its global aftermath—Joseph's poetry is the existential seismograph of personal history and of history writ large. Or as he understates the matter in "When One Is Feeling One's Way," "Two things, the two things that are interesting / are history and grammar."

2.

In his magisterial essay "On Some Motifs in Baudelaire," Walter Benjamin argues that the menacing spectacle of the urban crowd, described by mid-nineteenth-century writers as diverse as Poe and Engels, "became decisive for Baudelaire. If he succumbed to the force by which he was drawn to them and, as a *flaneur*, was made one of them, he was nevertheless unable to rid himself of a sense of their essentially inhuman make-up. He becomes their accomplice even as he dissociates himself from them. He becomes deeply involved with them, only to relegate them to oblivion with a single glance of contempt." Benjamin goes on to analyze the shock effect of the crowd for Baudelaire, and how, for the individual, "nervous impulses flow through him in rapid succession, like the energy from a battery. Baudelaire speaks of a man who plunges into a crowd as into a reservoir of electric energy. Circumscribing the experience of the shock, he calls this man 'a *kaleidoscope* equipped with consciousness.'" Taken all together, I can think of no better description of Joseph's stance in *Into It*. Attraction and repulsion, sympathy and contempt, identification and alienation—these are the antitheses which determine the key in which Joseph's book is written. Joseph's response to the crowd, which is to say the people of Manhattan, changes moment to moment, line by line. Like Baudelaire's man registering the experience of urban shock, Joseph is a kaleidoscope equipped with consciousness, but a kaleidoscope equipped with language as well. This instrument is repeatedly brought to bear on individuals in the crowd; the poet attempts to keep his distance, struggles with his contempt, but, as Benjamin understands, inevitably becomes an accomplice. George Oppen, writing about New York City in *Of Being Numerous*, likewise faces these "ghosts that endanger // One's soul" and pointedly declares that "one may honorably keep // His distance / If he can." Living and writing through and after 9/11, Joseph's work has a verbal speed and intensity that contrasts dramatically with the meditative deliberation of Oppen's masterpiece. But both poets understand the problem of honorably keeping one's distance, and their poetry records their struggles.

Into It, then, may be understood as the intricate verbalization of a kaleidoscopic vision of historical catastrophe, even as the poet constantly questions his role. A poem such as "What Do You Mean, What?" (a quintessential New York expression, which reminds me of the title of Hugh Seidman's wonderful volume *People Live, They Have Lives*) caroms from one instance to the next of what Joseph calls "this individual and collectivized looting / of the most astonishing complexity, / each point of an imagined circuit / attached to each of the others..." Movement along this "imagined circuit" follows immediately thereafter:

In the King James Hotel in a bath towel,
solicitous with the interviewer
who crosses her long, tanned legs, smiling at him
when he says you need a billion
just to get into the game; on my way downtown
(no, he answers, he doesn't own his own taxi),
his name is Thomas Saint Thomas, a green card
is what he owns, a working man from Haiti—
he'll play for me (I, perhaps, have not yet heard)
a tape cassette of a speech
concerning the imminent coming of Jesus Christ
Word Incarnate, Second Person of the Triune God,
who'll whip the moneylenders out of the temple.

Note how the narration in this stanza (Joseph is fascinated with the possibilities of narration in lyric poetry) literally turns on the semicolon and resultant caesura in the fifth line. It both divides and links the two vignettes (in the hotel and in the taxi) and the four figures (the man in the towel, the interviewer, the cabbie and "I"). The news of Christ's imminent return as announced on the cassette sends us back to the billionaire giving the interview, who undoubtedly deserves whipping. The poet, the first-person speaker in the taxi, is situated simultaneously inside and outside of the action. Benjamin's term is "accomplice"; Joseph's term, as we noted earlier, is "accessory." In the "shifting story" that is the poem, the poet insists on his distance from the corruption he perceives around him, but his sympathy draws him continually into the crowd and the physical spaces—particularly those of lower Manhattan—that they occupy. There is something honorable about Thomas Saint Thomas, this "working man from Haiti," whether we can accept his religious fervor or not. There is something unbearably poignant about the poet's observation of a "lavender (green for youth, blue for love) sky— / a shadow, distinct, beautiful pink detail, / of all places on the pier with wooden benches / near Canal Street . . ." And there is something terribly scary and sad about the poor soul with whom we are presented as the poem ends:

The rain was like ice. The umbrella placed
over the phone booth. "I'm all right."
"What do you mean, what?" "Why don't you leave it
at that?" "Are you sure?" "Don't think that way."
"Yes, forever." And so on, the script proceeded.

In "Notions of Poetry and Narration," Joseph quotes William Carlos Williams from *A Novelette*: "Conversation as design . . . actual to the extent that it would be pure design. . . . Purely what? Conversation of which there is none in novels and the news." The scraps of the phone conversation that make up the last stanza of the poem are indeed a design, presented briefly and imagistically, unlike such presentation in a novel or the news. The vignette is more, perhaps, like a very brief scene in a movie, and as Benjamin demonstrates, film is the preeminent modern art because it embodies the experience of shock: "The spectator's process of association in view of these images is indeed interrupted by their constant, sudden change. This constitutes the shock effect of the film, which like all shocks, should be cushioned by heightened presence of mind." There is, then, something shocking about the way Joseph suddenly thrusts this man in the midst of an obviously stressful conversation into our field of perception. Nor does he offer any sense of closure or resolution. "And so on, the script proceeded"—because the catastrophe is continuous. Once again, Benjamin, from *The Arcades Project*: "The concept of progress must be grounded in the idea of catastrophe. That things are 'status quo' *is* the catastrophe."

3.

Joseph's poetry is suffused with this awareness, resulting in a deep historical pessimism, and an equally deep sense of poetic responsibility. Although there can be no doubt that (as we have observed apropos of Joseph's title), "The Game Changed" after 9/11, in another respect, 9/11 was only a continuation, or an intensification, of "the game." The poetic result, paradoxically, is "A continuity in which everything is transition."

The fundamental instability of history, of the flow of events and their violent impediments, matched by the perceived instability of the poetic speaker positioned both inside and outside of that flow, produces a unique tone in *Into It*. It is a tone that conveys—again, paradoxically—a sense of both inevitability and contingency, or what Joseph identifies near the end of "Metamorphoses (After Ovid)" as "A poetry of autonomies, / bound by a transcendent necessity." Writing such a poetry presents tremendous epistemological and formal challenges. Dissociation, condensation, heteroglossia, rapid shifts across diverse discursive registers: these modernist and postmodernist procedures are a given, but in *Into It*, they are subordinated to something more, something toward which the poet can only gesture. "Metamorphoses" concludes with these lines:

> . . . *Plato's idea*
>
> *of anamnesis, what is in us is remembered,*
> *that which we are destined, in thoughts and in images,*
>
> *to give expression to. Concentration*
> *aural and visual. A table covered with pages of notes*
>
> *I compose as I feel. Through my beginning*
> *through to my end, my moira, my allotted part.*
>
> *When this time comes to an end, what I don't write*
> *will not exist. I did my work, lived*

as if the day, my own day, had come. I was, I am,
who I will be. I will not be eternally condemned.

Here, the poet insists on his integrity, guaranteed, as it were, by that "tran-scendent necessity," which is in turn related to the Platonic anamnesis, the remembering of something otherwise lost, and its expression aurally and visually "in thoughts and in images." The poet in his time, of his time, rightly insists that "When this time comes to an end, what I don't write / will not exist." In the face of an endless forgetting—a forgetting, I would venture to say, exacerbated by the contemporary media, through which all is recorded, archived, and lost—he willingly accepts the role of recorder as his "moira," his fate. The sense of historical, perhaps even divine judgment grows palpable, in the face of which poet declares that "I did my work."

The concept of judgment, of course, leads us back to Joseph's complex self-awareness as a lawyer-poet, his sense of himself as an instrument and a critic of the law, which also returns us to his status as both insider and outsider. Nowhere is this more apparent than in the opening lines of "The Game Changed":

The phantasmic imperium is set in a chronic
state of hypnotic fixity. I have absolutely
no idea what the fuck you're talking about
was his reply, and he wasn't laughing,
either, one of the most repellent human beings
I've ever known, his presence a gross and slippery
lie, a piece of chemically pure evil. A lawyer—
although the type's not exclusive to lawyers.
A lot of different minds touch, and have touched,
the blood money in the dummy account
in an offshore bank, washed clean, free to be
transferred into a hedge fund or a foreign
brokerage account, at least half a trillion
ending up in the United States, with more to come.
I believe I told you I'm a lawyer. Which has had
little or no effect on a certain respect
I have for occurrences that suggest laws

of necessity. I too am thinking of it
as a journey—the journey with conversations
otherwise known as the Divina Commedia
is how Osip Mandelstam characterized Dante's poem.

This passage merits an essay unto itself, and here I can only point to a few of its most important features. Again we see Joseph's reliance on Williams's "conversation as design." If we assume that on a literal level, the conversation in question is about the "blood money," then we are dealing almost immediately with a breakdown in communication, a failure of conversation which ironically becomes the design. The poet, the first-person speaker, offers an abstract critique of the situation and its causes: "The phantasmic imperium is set in a chronic / state of hypnotic fixity," to which his interlocuter responds with "I have absolutely / no idea what the fuck you're talking about." This response makes perfect sense: although both are lawyers, the two individuals are speaking different languages, representing very different worldviews, which include two different ways of understanding the law. For the man whom the poet calls "a piece of chemically pure evil," being a lawyer is a matter of power and expediency, and the law is to be manipulated to further for one's self-interest. For the poet, being a lawyer grants him highly refined insights into such manipulations. But he also acknowledges something higher: the "laws / of necessity" (that is, the "transcendent necessity" we observed previously), about which poets have traditionally had the deepest understanding.

This accounts in part for the poet's role not merely of lawyer but of judge, and he judges the other lawyer to be "one of the most repellent human beings / I've ever known." Indeed, the design of conversation is a design of judgment, a necessary judgment. Hence the invocation of the *Commedia*, and Mandelstam's observation that the poem is a "journey with conversations." The description applies to Joseph's writing as well, both in his poetry and, of course, in his prose work *Lawyerland*. Dante the Pilgrim is on a journey which consists largely of conversations in hell, purgatory, and heaven. But in the *Inferno* particularly (and Joseph, for the most part, remains a poet of our secular Inferno), Dante is also a judge, and he (or Virgil) both articulate and sometimes question the laws of necessity that have led to the vision of divine judgment that lies before him. Joseph too is a severe poet of judgment, and if *Into It* is not quite our *Inferno*, as it is not quite our *Fleurs du Mal*, Joseph may rightfully claim to be part of that classical lineage.

4.

My use of the term "classical lineage" is quite deliberate, and it is in the light of Joseph's classicism that I will conclude. In his very brief essay "A Note on 'That's All'" ("That's All" is a poem which appears in *Curriculum Vitae*), Joseph discusses his desire "to achieve a sense of control, balance and lucidity, a classical *claritas*," as he juxtaposes New York City, Detroit, and the Shouf mountains of Lebanon from which his grandfathers originally emigrated. The "I" of the poem is intended to be a figure "who both reacted to and was a part of these worlds." The poem, written in loose ten-syllable couplets designed to achieve the control and balance Joseph seeks, leads the poet to conclude that "Its formal lineage is classical." It is a brave claim, but I would argue that it applies not only to "That's All" but to much of Joseph's poetry, including the poems of *Into It*. Nor is it only a matter of form as this term is usually understood.

In "What Is a Classic?," T. S. Eliot associates the classic with the notion of "*maturity*," and argues that a "classic can only occur when a civilization is mature; when a language and literature are mature; and it must be the work of a mature mind. It is the importance of that civilization and of that language, as well as the comprehensiveness of the mind of the individual poet, which gives the universality." As for "maturity of mind," Eliot observes that "this needs history, and the consciousness of history. Consciousness of history cannot be fully awake, except where there is other history than the history of the poet's own people: we need this in order to see our own place in history." American civilization, American literature, and the American language may all be reaching a point of maturity; and there is no doubt that the events of 9/11 and their aftermath have made Americans more conscious of their history, and of the history of other nations. When the planes hit the towers on 9/11, Joseph was at work at St. John's University School of Law in Queens, where he teaches, while his wife, the painter Nancy Van Goethem, was in their apartment just blocks from the World Trade Center. But even before 9/11, Joseph was refining a style that comprehended some of the most balanced, intelligent, and effective qualities of American and of international modernism. The events of 9/11 gave Joseph a subject that could match that style and brought it to a level of maturity and verbal intensity that to my mind constitutes the classic.

"Once Again," the last, magnificently Stevensian poem in *Into It*, unfolds its couplets in lower Manhattan, on the "The esplanade. High summer," just a few blocks from ground zero. It reflects upon "Fate's precisive wheel revolving," generating, through the "dream technique" of the poem, the myth of "new types of half-monsters," balanced against "a woman, a man, / love's characters, the myth // their own." Monsters and lovers: what Joseph names "the primary soul-substance" of the human story is revised continuously by history, which for all its reworkings, manages to remind us, through the voice of the poet, that in another respect nothing has changed at all.

Eliot, whose classical touchstones include Virgil, Dante, and Baudelaire, notes that Baudelaire was "a classicist, born out of his due time. In . . . his sensibility, he is near to Dante." Whether Joseph is also "a classicist, born out of his due time" is an open question—what does that mean, after all, for any artist who successfully tells the fate of his time? Be that as it may, it does seem to me that however acutely Joseph registers the violent shocks to America in this first decade of the century, his poetry has also maintained its equilibrium brilliantly, achieving a classic balance. And in this respect, on "Fate's precisive wheel revolving," he helps us regain our balance too.

(2012)

II

Lawrence Joseph's Credo

In his last book of poems, *Into It* (2005), Lawrence Joseph describes his work as "A poetry of autonomies, / bound by a transcendent necessity," which paradoxically produces "A continuity in which everything is transition." In his new collection, *So Where Are We?*, Joseph remains faithful to these notions, pushing them to a further extreme. The code switching that marks the poems' discursive "autonomies," which one would expect to be more disorienting in their state of continuous "transition," actually binds the work to a greater extent, resulting in a style that is more unified, fully achieved, and even monumental in its scope. The "transcendent necessity" becomes all the more urgent: the poet holds nothing back, and yet in doing so, the language becomes even more sculptural, more poised, and more ruthlessly efficient in its presentation and analysis of historical catastrophe. Joseph, deep reader of Louis Zukofsky, understands the older poet's idea that "Each writer writes / one long work whose beat he cannot / entirely be aware of." "How long will it be, // the one long poem?," Joseph now asks in "An Ancient Clarity Overlaid." And what should we readers now expect of this "expansion of tendentious language, / an ancient clarity overlaid"? In *So Where Are We?*, the expansions and continuities in Joseph's work become increasingly clear, as he struggles heroically with

> *. . . Too much consciousness*
> *of too much at once, a tangle of tenses*
>
> *and parallel thoughts, a series of feelings*
> *overlapping a sudden sensation*
>
> *felt and known, those chains of small facts*
> *repeated endlessly, in the depths*
>
> *of silent time. So where are we?*
> *My ear turns, like an animal's. I listen.*

In these lines from the title poem of the collection, the poet's instinctive sensitivity to "those chains of small facts," his ability to parse the "tangle of tenses" and to sort those "parallel thoughts," are increasingly challenged by historical exigencies that push language to the breaking point. As he tells us in "Of What We Know Now" (the titles of many of these poems are like phrases from the news or from bureaucratic or legal documents), we face

> *the violence along social fracture lines, anarcho-capital*
> *circulating at infinite speed, returning to itself even*

before taking leave of itself, on its own plan of intelligence,
warping, dissolving nature—the poem in its voracities
of contemplation—the poem's judgment proven, exact—
thought to thought, configurations, in fifty years these words
will be written fifty years ago, that is, now.

In order to deal with such phenomena, the poem responds with "voracities / of contemplation," an oxymoron indicating how the poet's thought and language can cope with, can respond to, unprecedented levels of organized global violence. "Here in a State of Tectonic Tension," a poem that honors and mourns Detroit—the city where Joseph was born, raised, and lived until his early thirties, when he moved to New York City—forces us to confront "Narco-capital techno-compressed, / gone viral, spread into a state of tectonic tension and freaky / abstractions—it'll scare the fuck out of you, is what it'll do . . ." Indeed it will, though the very twists and turns of the language, the discursive metamorphoses of the poem that are precisely commensurate with the metamorphoses of these dangerously "freaky / abstractions," actually provide us with the understanding of, if not the control over, these prevailing global forces. For Joseph, in "A Fable," we are ensconced in the world of

Technocapital, permanently, digitally,

semioticized, virtually unlimited
in freedom and power, taking

billions of bodies on the planet
with it. . . .

If technocapital is "semioticized," presenting itself as a constant play of empty signs, behind which ruthless political and economic power endlessly accumulates, then the poem, risking reification, must become "semioticized" as well. This is one of the great gambles—and uncanny pleasures—of Joseph's current work. Many contemporary poets employ a lexicon of this sort, and follow somewhat similar signifying procedures, but few do so with the probing self-awareness, to say nothing of the formal skill, of Lawrence Joseph. The most powerful poems in this collection move at a relentless pace, especially when they recount the abstract powers of digitized "technocapital," only to abruptly shift and describe the terrifying results of the worldwide struggles that the expansion of such powers entails. "Behind / the global imperia is the interrogation cell," declares Joseph in "Syria"—"It's not / a good story." And so we are told that

... Neither the Red Crescent
nor journalists are permitted entry; the women tell
how men and boys are separated, taken in buses
and never seen again, tanks in the streets
with machine guns with no shells in the barrels
because the army fears that those who will use them
might defect.

This horrific moment in the present resonates powerfully with catastrophic events in the past. Joseph's early life and work, it should be recalled, was shaped by the immigrant experiences of his Syrian and Lebanese grandparents, who settled in Detroit, and of his parents, born in Detroit, who experienced, as did Joseph himself, the upheavals of that city, including the 1967 riots. Furthermore, he has lived in lower Manhattan now for many years, and *Into It*, as well as a number of poems in this new book, obsessively return to the events of 9/11—and let us not forget Lawrence Joseph's personal experience of those events. "So Where Are We?" opens with the following lines:

So where were we? The fiery
avalanche headed right at us—falling,

flailing bodies in midair—
the neighborhood under thick gray powder—

on every screen. I don't know
where you are, I don't know what

I'm going to do, I heard a man say;
the man who had spoken was myself.

In the aftermath of the attack, Joseph and his wife were eventually reunited and live to this day in the same apartment, a few blocks from the World Trade Center. Yet the threat of lasting trauma pervades nearly every line that Joseph writes, whether drawn from personal experience or the extensive research into history, politics, and economics that forms a crucial element of most of the poems. But amid these seemingly endless horrors, which extend from Detroit and lower Manhattan to locations, as Joseph puts it, "On the Peripheries of the Imperium," what *does not* occur in these poems is the helpless congealing of chronology into the perpetual present, what Walter Benjamin describes in his *Theses on the Philosophy of History* as the homogeneous, empty time of capitalist domination and ideological blindness.

Why is this the case? "On Utopia Parkway" provides some clues. Like many of the poems, this one moves kaleidoscopically from one scene, one thought, to the next, its free verse couplets and sinewy enjambments controlling its abrupt shifts in affect and imagery. Jumping from the names of the roses in the front yards of houses that the poet sees on his way to work (St. John's is on Utopia Parkway in Queens), to the homicide of Eric Garner by New York Police Department officers, to the CIA's "legally justified means / of enhanced interrogation" (i.e., torture), to the strange art of Joseph Cornell (who spent his whole life on Utopia Parkway), to the Federal Reserve's control of monetary policy, Joseph asks near the end of the poem, "in what places, violations // of which forms of which eternal laws? / Is it error, the idea that no place, too, is a place?" "Utopia," of course, comes from the Greek for "no place"; it is our word for the perfect society that can only be imagined, usually with a high degree of irony. Joseph is not really a utopian thinker (usually he is quite the contrary), but the invocation of Utopia here, even as he plays on the location of his workplace, a law school, is especially powerful. As a lawyer and a professor of law, he is also acutely sensitive to violations of laws, whether eternal or not. The poem ends

On the corner of Utopia Parkway and Union Turnpike,
in red-blue twilight abstracted into an energy

blowing it apart, in spaces of language transformed
and coded, to be decoded and recoded in the future.

The corner of Utopia Parkway and Union Turnpike is a real location (I grew up not far from there), but it is also an imagined space which twilight abstracts into energy, transforms, and codes into language—the poem—"to be decoded and recoded in the future." The poem holds out a promise to futurity, maintaining a faith in its communicative power as a well as a faith in a readership yet to come. This future readership, willing to decode and recode the text, to interpret it and reconsider its meaning, underwrites Joseph's role as a chronicler, a role upon which he has insisted for the entirety of his career. "The Recording Angel // completes the exactest chronicle," declares Joseph in "A Fable," the opening poem in *So Where Are We?* In the traditions of all three Abrahamic faiths, the recording angel writes down the thoughts, prayers, and deeds of every individual, as testimony to their ultimate fate. That angel is Joseph's divine role model, calling him continually to his appointed task.

The recording angel is one of a number of religious references that appear in Joseph's new book, for as in his earlier work, Joseph is never far from his Maronite Catholic roots. Thinking, as is so often the case, about the events following 9/11, Joseph observes in "So Where Are We?" that

Ten blocks away the Church of the Transfiguration,
in the back a Byzantine Madonna—

there is a God, a God who fits the drama
in a very particular sense. . . .

What that "very particular sense" is, exactly, is never fully articulated in these poems. Perhaps it never can be: in Joseph's work, we encounter the poet as historian, the poet as political analyst, the poet as legal scholar, but however much he seeks to rationalize the incessant flow of data that constitutes current events, he is still a keeper of the mysteries, insisting on the presence of the divine in human affairs. As he declares in "Syria," "Who knows what has happened, / what is happening, what will happen? God knows / God knows everything." "I, too, see God adumbrations. I, too, write / a book on love" he insists in "On Nature," though how we may think of this book, with all its terrors, as a book on love remains to be seen. But to be sure, it may be read, as in the poem "In Parentheses," as

A theological-political fragment,
a mythographical, scriptural, text,
and sorrow, to understand the meaning
of sorrow, Saint Sorrow;
the addressee of my avowal,
Saint Sorrow's stern vigil necessary to keep.

Here, Joseph alludes to Walter Benjamin's *Theologico-Political Frag-ment*, a text in which Benjamin, like Joseph, seeks to comprehend "a mystical conception of history," which involves the relationship between "the order of the profane" and the order of the Messianic, a relationship that can only be represented figuratively. Benjamin uses the image of two arrows:

> If one arrow points to the goal toward which the profane dynamic acts, and another marks the direction of Messianic intensity, then certainly the quest of free humanity for happiness runs counter to the Messianic direction; but just as a force can, through acting, increase another that is acting in the opposite direction, so the order of the profane assists, through being profane, the coming of the Messianic Kingdom. The profane, therefore, although not itself a category of this Kingdom, is a decisive character of its quietest approach.

This passage strikes me as an important key to much of what is going on in Joseph's poetry, especially in the poems of *Into It* and *So Where Are We?* Although it is hard to reconcile the horrors that Joseph chronicles with "the quest of free humanity for happiness," they are still part of "the pro-fane dynamic," the dialectical chronicle of human happiness and sorrow that current political circumstances have pushed to an extreme. Mean-while, the poet, like Benjamin's figure of the revolutionary historian in his *Theses*, seeks for traces of messianic time. One site for the possible appearance of such traces is in human creativity itself, in literature and the arts, as in Joseph Cornell's weird and mournful assemblage *Medici Slot Machine*, which in "On Utopia Parkway" the poet calls "the expres-sion / of an ascent from the temporal to the spiritual." That ascent, how-ever hopeless is may appear, is a powerful motivating force in Joseph's work, which in itself, perhaps, may be part of the profane counterforce that brings on the Messianic Kingdom in its "quietest approach."

But whether or not that Kingdom may make its approach, Joseph's poetry is still suffused with a this-worldly sense of abiding affection and beauty that remains an inspiration, however momentary it might be. Thus, the poet is true to his claim that "I, too, write / a book on love." We see this love expressed in his passionate affair with New York, as in "A Fable":

But is there a more beautiful city—parts
of it, anyway? Another path to the harbor,

the border between sea and land
fluctuating a line, a curve, Peck Slip

to Water Street to Front Street
to Pine, to Coenties Slip to Pearl

to Stone Street to Exchange Place,
the light in majestic degrees.

Place names produce a sort of magic spell in Joseph's poems, which is to say that they create a sense of romance, but also function pragmatically, grounding the poet and securing the self in a space that is physical but psychic as well. "Water Street" opens with Joseph observing

Nothing between us and Brooklyn Bridge
seen from our windows—on the other side of Pearl,

Dover is Frankfort, along the Bridge toward
City Hall—Governors, Staten, Liberty islands,

the harbor, violet and gray, a passing barge
piled with sand, ebony, the East River, the Heights

gold, rain pouring down, massed angles washed
by spacious light, air cleared, an amber luster . . .

The place names release a gracious lyricism, "afterimages, in aftertime, remembered // time, in love's optic, love's characters" (32). And in "Here in a State of Tectonic Tension," the lost world of battered Detroit is remembered through a litany of streets as well:

> . . . Drive Woodward to Seven Mile,
> west on Seven Mile to Hamilton, Hamilton south to the Lodge
> Freeway, then the Lodge downtown, and measure the chaos,
> drive Mack Avenue east to Seminole, south on Seminole
> to Charlevoix, then west on Charlevoix to Van Dyke, south
> on Van Dyke to East Jefferson, and remember what isn't.

What remains present to the poet, or what is gone and can only be remembered: in either case, as Joseph tells us in the last poem of the volume, "What More Is There to Say?," "in the envisioned heart / inmost issues take the form // of a credo." Envisioning his heart and its inmost issues—this is the way in which Lawrence Joseph remains true to himself, and to his poetic calling.

(2018)

Total Midrash

This essay was written for a forum on contemporary midrash which Alicia Ostriker edited for the journal Religion & Literature. *"Midrash" is a term that was once the exclusive province of Jewish religious writers—traditionally, rabbis and scholars. But more recently, it has been adopted by literary theorists to denote certain modes of interpretation, and by poets, mostly but not exclusively Jewish, who write poems that address and revise biblical material. The occasion of the forum led me to reflect on my midrashic practices, and what it means to be a poet who often considers his poetry a form of commentary. It also raised a bigger question: What is the cultural significance when a religious concept and practice like midrash expands beyond its original boundaries? Does its earlier religious significance get lost? This remains, for me and others, a question that has yet to be settled.*

Although I have written a good deal of what could be construed as "midrashic" poetry, and, in my criticism, have applied the term "midrash" to various works of modern Jewish literature, I have always been a little nervous and distrustful about the concept when it is applied to modern, secular writing. A certain sense of unease comes over me, despite my enduring enthusiasm for all that midrash has traditionally implied in regard to Jewish textuality, Jewish modes of interpretation, and the Jewish literary imagination. My knowledge of Hebrew is rudimentary, and I have relied on scholarship in the field to provide me with the knowledge I need to apply the midrashic model to literary analysis. In my criticism, I have always asked myself if I am using the idea and all that it entails in a responsible and credible fashion. In my poetry, where I feel free to take far more liberties, I have recognized and given rein to what I believed to be a midrashic impulse, wondering all the while if what I was experiencing was nothing more or less than the play of the verbal imagination in relation to a particular biblical story or figure, or even more broadly, a particular Jewish theme. In writing such poetry, I felt that I was engaged in the midrashic process of creative commentary, while still asking myself if that was even possible in a language other than the one in which midrash came to be.

Granted, I think I came to be interested in midrash in a legitimate fashion. Starting in the 1980s, I became increasingly aware of the rich but always vexed discussions of midrash in the fields of literary theory and Jewish studies, even as I was "returning" to my Jewish sensibility through extended but still rather haphazard readings of poetry, fiction, scholarship, and traditional religious texts. The results of that "return" is the poetry in *Restless Messengers* and *Passing Over*, and the critical study *The Ritual of New Creation: Jewish Tradition and Contemporary Literature*, a title which itself midrashically plays on the title of Gershom Scholem's essay "Tradition and New Creation in the Ritual of Kabbalists." During that time, I was particularly concerned with the relation of text to commentary in Jewish writing, and so was naturally fascinated by the descriptions I read of midrashic exegesis. But what held me more than anything else was not biblical commentary per se, but the way in which, according to at least some scholars, midrash seems to allow for remarkably innovative textual moves and extraordinary assertions of imaginative invention, while at the same time appearing to operate within the bounds of tradition and normative belief—however such notions come to be defined.

In retrospect, much of my writing at that time arose in part from my desire to understand my Jewish identity in relation to my poetic identity. Jewish authors, texts, and themes presented themselves to me in ways that I believed could be imaginatively transformed and claimed for my own. I struck a precarious balance between devotion and independence, between sincerity and chutzpah. I was torn between homage and transgression, nostalgia and revolt. I recall reading the chapter on midrash by Barry Holtz in the volume he edited called *Back to the Sources*. "Primarily," writes Holtz, "we can see the central issue behind the emergence of Midrash as the need to deal with the presence of cultural or religious tension and discontinuity. Where there are questions that demand answers, and where there are new cultural and intellectual pressures that must be addressed, Midrash comes into play as a way of resolving crisis and reaffirming continuity with the traditions of the past." Although I was not sure that I wanted to reaffirm continuity with tradition, I was viscerally aware of cultural and religious tension and discontinuity, which, if not producing a sense of personal crisis, was at least leading to the composition of what Harold Bloom might call a "crisis-poem." Here, for instance, is the last stanza of my poem "Aliyah":

The soul falls back into the world of the mirror,
as across an infinite distance the Word withdraws,
        leaving only a trace of itself,
                illegible and exiled . . .
        They shake hands all around;
        shake hands and kiss each other
                as they kiss the Book.
It is the birth of irony, born once again
from the dissatisfactions, meager compensation,
        strong fragments, broken speech.

For me, then, writing midrashically meant writing ironically, but with an irony that tended to turn itself inside out, opening to and resisting the traditions, texts, and rituals to which it obsessively returned.

Holtz cites the Passover Haggadah as an instance of extended midrash with which most Jews are familiar, even when they do not recognize the text to be midrashic in nature. His presentation of the rabbis discussing the departure from Egypt resonated deeply for me, for as a child, it was one of most intriguing moments in the seder. It was not too long after reading Holtz (as well as the essays in the collection *Midrash and Literature*, edited by Geoffrey Hartman and Sanford Budick) that I wrote what proved to be my most ambitious "midrashic" poem, the long sequence based on the Haggadah and related Pesach rituals called *Passing Over*. It is, in effect, a midrash upon a midrash. Here is part of a journal entry I wrote (27 May 1992) while contemplating the poem and doing preliminary research:

> But no amount of reading and research can provide me with a way in; at best, they can provide clues as to where the key might lie. Obviously one cannot "rewrite" the whole of the Haggadah; one must approach it more obliquely, and yet, however dispersed and various the results, still capture the essential. But what is the essential? One wants to use the text and

occasion midrashically, to fill in, to address, to argue. The Seder contains past, present and future as history and myth. It is entirely appropriate to my current views and procedures. It is sensual and textual, common and refined. Within its ritual and its tale of bondage and freedom, it has room for all.

Reading this passage many years later, I am struck by my insouciant tone. I was certainly aware of the debates about the applicability of the midrashic model to secular literary interpretation. What led me to believe that my poetry—secular poetry in American English, however Jewish its concerns—could be written in accord with midrash, with the midrashic spirit or sensibility, if not with traditional midrashic procedures? True, I understood that the ostensible verbal and generic indeterminacy of midrash, the free play of the signifier which midrash presents as a challenge to the unity of the text, could be construed as an encouragement to new midrashic writing, taking place under very different historical and religious circumstances. Midrash was upheld by literary theorists to be a form of commentary that was something more than commentary. As Geoffrey Hartman puts it in the essay "Midrash as Law and Literature," "It may be strange to call Midrash literature since it remains a mode of commentary explicitly linked to the very words of Scripture. Yet we recognize the creative and parafictive result of its interpretive elaborations. Moreover, at a certain level Midrash is *not* satisfied with the text as it stands, and while it refuses to produce a new or transformed writing it looks for more of the original in the original, for more story, more words within the words." So perhaps *Passing Over*, along with a great deal else of my poetry, could be understood in terms of that midrashic desire for more of the original in the original, more words within the words. From the "Dinnertime Interlude" in *Passing Over*:

Seamlessly falling
into a rhetoric of completion
you imagine the scene:

the numinous objects
that must remain unnamed
like faces in shadow

and faces in shadow
on the border of recognition
—they too must fade away.

So you refuse the bribe
that the past has to offer,
hold out for more

as the fathers grow anxious
and the mothers sigh,
longing for the oblivion

to which they would return,
the night of tradition
signified by their absence.

What is it they want
that they offer you so much
and still not enough?

They smile indulgently
at the weary child
up past bedtime,

wandering in the desert
laden with matzah
and an ancient promise.

Like the child holding out for a few more coins in exchange for the afi-koman, the poet longs for more words, words that are both his and those of the tradition, that both confirm the tradition and call it into question.

But there were problems then, and there are problems now, and we writers of modern midrash need to acknowledge them. Hence the anxiety—what I take to be, paradoxically, a *healthy* anxiety—to which I alluded at the start of this essay. My study of the scholarship that was written during that particularly rich period of some twenty to thirty years ago impressed upon me the importance of understanding midrash from within, of trying to appreciate, as best I could, what constitutes the inner forces (historical, psychic) that lead the rabbinic commentator to open the biblical text in that unique spirit of innovative reverence. Procedurally, artistically, *poetically*, I was and remain dazzled by the midrashic perspective on the total interpretability of the text. For me, it was never a matter of rethinking scripture, "updating" it or making it more "relevant" to the modern reader. I have no great desire to retell bible stories—most of the time, I am perfectly content with the original telling, which is why, for instance, Robert Crumb's illustrated Genesis impresses me much more than most modern poetry derived from the intrigues of the patriarchs and matriarchs. I understand, as Erich Auerbach famously demonstrates in the first chapter of *Mimesis*, that the biblical narrative is "fraught with background" and calls out for commentary. But it is the *process* of midrashic commentary that I hope imbues my poetry, no matter how far the work may seem to wander. Indeed, as I insisted in *The Ritual of New Creation*, the writing is always a matter of wandering meaning.

But how does the writing wander, and in what ways may it be legitimately understood as midrash? I recall an extraordinary controversy which unfolded in 1985 in the pages of the journal *Prooftexts*, an argument between the distinguished scholars Susan Handelman and David Stern. From my perspective as a relative outsider, the erudition on both sides continues to amaze. Stern, in some respects a more conservative thinker in regard to midrash, takes Handelman severely to task in his review of her book *The Slayers of Moses*, accusing her of an ahistorical perspective on rabbinic interpretation in the complex parallels she draws between rabbinics and contemporary theorists such as Jacques Derrida, Paul de Man, and Harold Bloom. Handelman, in a detailed rejoinder, argues in turn that from a traditional perspective,

> Because God's language is self-reflexive, it can be turned over and over on itself, and these turns create pockets, enclosures, openings where man and God speak together, where human and divine language meet. But contemporary literary theory does not assume a divine guarantor of language, a stable connection between word and thing, or sign and meaning; on the contrary, it focuses on the gaps and voids. Where a de Man would perceive only emptiness, the rabbi would perceive an opening to the divine. But perhaps one needs to empty out in order to open up.

Handelman refers here to a concept that underwrites the traditional rabbinic perspective, the concept that for the rabbis, the divinity of the Torah guarantees and indeed encompasses, unifies, all possible interpretations—a concept which does not apply in the case of most contemporary theorists, or for that matter, poets. The "gaps and voids" of language, the instability of the sign, is understood differently by most contemporaries; as Betty Roitman puts it in her essay "Sacred Language and Open Text," for recent theorists, the midrashic "opening of a text . . . presupposes an a priori renunciation of any 'truth' of meaning." But as Roitman goes on to explain, "To describe midrash accurately it is important to acknowledge the force of the paradox represented by the classic midrashic position, which enacts at the level of interpretation a dialectic formulated on the ontological plane by Rabbi Akiva: 'All is foreseen, but freedom of choice is given.' All is determined, and yet all is open." Furthermore, as David Stern points out in his essay "Midrash and Indeterminacy" (published not long after his debate with Handelman), the polysemic writing we encounter in rabbinic discourse "attempts to capture or to imitate in writing the oral exchanges that took place between sages in both formal debates in the academy and less formal occasions elsewhere." In his historical analysis, Stern notes that in rabbinic midrashim, "editorial policy was elevated to the order of exegetical ideology. . . . Polysemy in midrash, then, is to be understood as a claim to textual stability rather than its opposite, an indeterminate state of endlessly deferred meanings and unresolved conflicts."

Where does this leave contemporary midrashists—not only those who seek to reinscribe biblical texts, but those who, like myself, think of midrashic processes as applicable to any intertextual composition, however seemingly secular its concerns? I, for one, do not subscribe to the traditional belief in the radical unity of Scripture. In this regard, I return continually to Gershom Scholem's great essay "Revelation and Tradition as Religious Categories in Judaism." As Scholem notes, the rabbinic tradition holds that "revelation comprises everything that will ever be legitimately offered to interpret its meaning." Yet he also insists that this notion is "a historical construction whose fictitious character cannot be doubted but which serves the believing mind as a crutch of external authentication." As a nonbeliever who remains deeply immersed in tradition, for me it is this construction, however fictitious, that remains most compelling. Through midrashic commentary, the gaps and voids may not open on the divine, but they also do not necessarily lead to the textual nihilism of which deconstruction has often (and often irresponsibly) been accused. Again, Geoffrey Hartman: "It is as if the original text had become unreadable except through an extreme fragmentation that paradoxically confirms its unity." And as for belief? "Even when, as in [Edmond] Jabès, the absolute authority of Scripture is lost, words of the other are recalled, or simulacra that continue to haunt us." If my poetry is not devotional in any normative sense, it still recalls the words of the other, and remains haunted by the simulacra of ritual. Indeed, I think of my recent poems, overtly Jewish or not, as uncanny enactments on the shifting border of the sacred and the profane.

In a provocative essay called "Midrash and the 'Midrashic Condition': Preliminary Considerations," Ithamar Gruenwald seeks to understand midrash epistemologically, as "a form of thinking and expression" that has proven "to be an important factor in the development of the religious tradition of the Jews and not merely a literary form and exegetical technique use in the interpretation of Scripture. Even beyond that, Midrash is a form of cognition that supplies terms of reference and channels of perception for people who organize their lives in accordance with a scriptural world of ideas." Although this model does not really apply to me, I still like to think of my art, if not my life, as organized in accordance to a scriptural world of ideas—if the scripture to which we refer consists not only of Jewish religious texts, but of the wide world of secular literary texts as well. Gruenwald asserts that when new meaning is midrashically incorporated into a preexisting text, "new possibilities are opened for the text and its new setting of meaning. It becomes at once the source of further speculations and the basis for new traditions." Hence, "*Midrash is a mode of cognition and the major component in the creation of religious tradition.*" Gruenwald also observes that "Midrash-like modes of relating to a scriptural or canonical text can be extended to any type of mental relationship that entails the concern for establishing relevance or relatedness to any given fact or piece of information." Epistemologically, and therefore compositionally, imaginative writing seeks the kind of mental relationship Gruenwald describes. If, as Walter Pater says, "All art constantly aspires towards the condition of music," perhaps all writing aspires to the condition of midrash. We are approaching a condition we might therefore call *total midrash*.

In closing, I will wander back to the center of the traditional midrashic enterprise, that is, biblical commentary, by simply presenting a recent poem that points to the troublesome, restless midrashic imagination. The poem is called "Adam," and it is by Harvey Shapiro, a great master of the midrashic mode in Jewish American poetry:

It is possible Adam
was bored in paradise,
the leafy green settling
in his mind like fog.
I have a taste for something
else, he thought, but what?

All the rest is midrash.

Secular Jewish Culture and Its Radical Poetic Discontents

This deep dive into Jewish thought and writing, and how they have shaped my poetry, was written for the collection Radical Poetics and Secular Jewish Culture. *The title, playing on Freud, indicates my sense that such terms are wanting or inadequate, and need to be refined and reexamined. The result is my most comprehensive statement on Jewish poetry.*

1. Moses, Zusya, and Me

> The very first task of each man is the actualizing of his unique possibilities, without precedent and never renewed, and not the repetition of something that someone else, were he the greatest person of all, would already have accomplished. It is this idea that Rabbi Zusya expressed shortly before his death: in the other world I will not be asked, Why were you not Moses? I will be asked, Why were you not Zusya?
>
> —MARTIN BUBER

The question has been posed; the books surround me. I have been asked to reflect upon the relationship between secular Jewish culture and radical poetic practice, or more broadly, how Judaism and experimental poetry relate to each other. As is my wont, I prepare for the task by turning to my bookshelves, seeking the new texts with which I am currently engaged as well as the old, reassuring works that have guided me in the past. As I dutifully read and research, I come upon Buber's anecdote about Zusya in Marc-Alain Ouaknin's *The Burnt Book: Reading the Talmud*. Ouaknin then takes us to a commentary on Buber by Emmanuel Lévinas: "This suggests that the totality of truth is made up of the contributions of multiple persons: the uniqueness of each reaction bearing the secret of the text: the voice of Revelation precisely inasmuch as it is inflected by the ear of each person, would be necessary for the Whole of Truth!" After which Ouaknin himself comments: "The same idea is expressed in the texts of Hasidism in the following manner: each man is a letter or a part of a letter. The Book has been completely written when there is no longer any letter missing. Each man must write his letter, must write himself, that is to say, create himself by renewing a meaning: his meaning."

I am both encouraged and dismayed: encouraged because my immersion in the world of the text leads me to understand that it is my own meaning, my unique contribution, that ultimately counts; dismayed because, paradoxically, it is only through that very dutiful, habitual, obsessive immersion, that I am led to this discovery. Because I am so much a creature of the Book, I am able to learn that I am myself. Yet I am myself only insofar as I am a part of the Book, completing something infinitely greater than myself. Where, I wonder, am I to be found? Where does my practice—my reading, my writing—begin, and where do those of others end? How will the textual play in which I constantly engage answer the question that awaits me (whether I really believe it will be posed to me or not): Why were you not Norman?

But wait. According to Ouaknin, "Rabbi Nachman does not like answers. In that respect he is faithful to the whole Talmudic and Cabalistic tradition that defines man-Adam as a 'what?' (*Mah?*). Man is a 'What is it?' As [Edmond] Jabès remarks very well: 'The Jew not only asks questions: he has himself become a question.' He is a question without an answer." Needless to say, I read this with some feeling of relief. Furthermore, have I forgotten the Talmudic adage which I have encountered and repeated now in so many contexts, but which still remains my goad and my comfort?: "You are not required to complete the work, but neither are you free to desist from it" (*Aboth* II: 21). Each of these passages stresses the radical incompletion of the human being in the work of understanding the Word. None can encompass the whole, yet it is in the spirit of the whole that the work goes on. Furthermore, the Talmud insists upon the equal importance of each individual in his devotion to the Book and to his scholarly responsibility, which in turn represents a communal responsibility. Hence another famous passage: "If I am not for myself, then who is for me? And if I am only for myself, then what am I? And if not now, when?" (*Aboth* II: 14).

Called to ask the existential question, who am I?, but also charged to participate in an endless textual community and a process of culture through which I take responsibility both for myself and others, I am led to wonder at my conduct and my stance as Jew, as poet, as Jewish poet. To pose the question of Jewish culture is to enter into the process of Jewish culture. To pose the question of poetry is to enter into the experiment of poetry. If I do not pose those questions, however unanswerable, then what will I answer if asked, why were you not yourself?

(And yet I already anticipate what my answers might be. This premonition comes in the form of an allergic reaction to the terms *experimental* poetics and *secular* Jewish culture. I reach for an antihistamine. Wallace Stevens, from his *Adagia*: "All poetry is experimental poetry." Jacques Derrida, from *Of Grammatology*: "the intelligible face of the sign remains turned toward the word and face of God." Ah, I feel better already. It would follow then that Jewish poetry is always experimental poetry; and that Jewish poetry—if not Jewish culture in general—can never be fully secular. Perhaps. Let us see . . .)

2. Cadaverization and Undeadness

In the Talmudic tradition, the work of self-actualization, of discovering the integrity of the individual, the person, takes place in the vertiginous world of endless textual play, a world of total hermeneutical and exegetical freedom bound only by the fact of divinity: "And the tables were the work of God, and the writing was the writing of God, graven upon the tables. Read not *charuth* (graven) but *cheruth* (freedom), for no man is free but he who labours in the Torah" (*Aboth* VI: 2). Recent accounts of traditional Jewish textuality present compelling analogies to poststructuralist theories of reading and writing, which we may relate in turn to modernist and postmodernist poetic practices. Thus, to stay with Ouaknin for a while longer, "*Mahloket* [controversial or polemical discussion between Talmudic masters about the same subject] produces an interruption into which is introduced a waiting, a suspension, which measures the irreducible distance between the two masters. *Mahloket* research is not unifying; on the contrary, it seeks separation, a breach, the interval, which are the other's possibility of being." What interests me about these disruptive and deconstructive practices is the Talmudic notion that they do not undermine a sense of identity or personhood, as in the case of some versions of postmodernism, but rather help to reveal and affirm the place of the person, both in the text and in the world at large. What might be the modern Jewish poet's inheritance from this religious tradition? For me, it is just this notion: that the linguistic indeterminacy and extreme hermeneutical procedures of traditional Jewish textuality may lead us to a deeper and more genuine or authentic sense of self. We live in a world that is increasingly characterized by totalizing modes of thought and discourse, facile and manipulative cultural production, insidious forms of political coercion, and institutionalized violence. Perhaps what we think of as experimental poetry, radical or avant-garde writing, at least as practiced in a Jewish context or in a self-conscious relation to Jewish scriptural tradition, can provide access for us today to personal and social truths opposed to such administered forms of modern life. How can this be the case?

(I pause, led to reflect upon my last two sentences. First: who do I mean by "us today"? Obviously not observant Jews who still follow the Law fully and lead a more prescribed way of life than most. Broadly speaking, I suppose I mean readers of poetry, or readers of Jewish poetry, or readers of poems by Jews [*all poets are Jews* whispers a ghostly voice], or those who seek to become, as Jerome Rothenberg would say in *Poland/1931*, a "connoisseur of jews." But I also mean, more specifically, nonobservant Jews, *secular* Jews—though for the moment, I set aside the question of whether such Jews really take part in what is an identifiably *secular* Jewish culture. Second: do I honestly believe that poetry of any sort, in relation to any tradition or set of beliefs, can lead us to self-understanding and to truths that oppose or even dispel the violence and illusion of modern life? To which I can only respond, in the words of George Oppen's "The Building of the Skyscraper," "It is the business of the poet / 'To suffer the things of the world / And to speak them and himself out.'")

We think of innovative writing as providing a liberating perspective on reality—otherwise, why "Make It New?" In his discussion of Rabbi Nachman's contribution to Jewish hermeneutics, Ouaknin focuses on Nachman's interpretation of the concept of divine *tsimtsum* (contraction or withdrawal) that is fundamental to Isaac Luria's kabbalistic theory of creation. According to Ouaknin, Nachman's concern is with the process of textual innovation, how it is possible and how it may be encouraged, since in Talmudic interpretation, "the plural speech of *Mahloket*, room is left for each person to create his own world." Nachman associates innovation with *tsimtsum*: "When someone wishes to innovate new words (new meanings), he should limit his knowledge (literally: accomplish the *Tsimtsum* in his mind), that is to say, evacuate, not hurry into the known preliminary considerations that confuse his mind and are not necessary for innovating. He should act like someone who does not know and only then can he progressively, and in order, innovate new meanings." The rationale for this procedure implies a critique of institutional thinking and of the status quo. As Ouaknin puts it, "Man has to withdraw from 'himself' in order to attain himself. The first 'self' is not the real one; it is constructed, prefabricated by institutions." *Tsimtsum* is thus a process of *designification*; the innovative reader (or writer) "attacks the semantic actuality of a speech, or, in other words, rediscovers for himself the power of words through their 'designifying.'" Withdrawal from conventional signification transforms one into a "simple man," one who says "I know nothing"—a notion that I cannot help but see as analogous to Keats's negative capability, which went on to inspire ideas of open-form composition in poetry over a century later. Ouaknin asserts that "The 'I know not' of designifying removes language and the text from a sort of cadaverization where the words would no longer have the power to signify an affective or emotional actuality." Against this condition, innovative writing organizes a repertory of designifying or defamiliarizing techniques—poetic techniques—in the production of new meaning.

Ouaknin's emphasis on the writing self's withdrawal and his use of the term "cadaverization" to denote the stultifying force of institutionalized language have extraordinary resonance for me, for they relate directly to some of the most important insights in Eric L. Santner's *On the Psychotheology of Everyday Life: Reflections on Freud and Rosenzweig*. On one level, this magisterial book is an analysis of the ways in which two of the greatest modern Jewish thinkers have reconceived (but by no means "secularized") Judaism so as to redeem us from the "undeadness" imposed by the surplus power of social institutions, those "sites that endow us with social recognition and intelligibility, that produce and regulate symbolic identities." The *"too much of an address"* by these sovereign powers leads in turn to a defense mechanism producing a condition that Santer names "Egyptomania," a "'too much of demand,' [that] most powerfully captures life, undeadens it, makes it rigid with energy." Freud and Rosenzweig variously offer the therapeutic means necessary for us to enact an "Exodus" from this condition, renewing our capacity to love and allowing us to open to the Other whom we previously feared. This, for Santner, constitutes "Revelation": "an opening of a space in human possibilities organized around the claims made upon me by the Other insofar as he or she is singularly out-of-joint with respect to the social intelligibility produced by this inscription in law." Indeed (at this point Santner opposes Rosenzweig to Freud), "Judaism, this first religion of revelation, can rather be understood as a kind of therapy directed precisely against the fantasmatic pressures of the superego and its tendency to keep the subject at a distance from his or her answerability within the world."

For Santner, one of the most potentially effective human creations through which we may overcome our undeadness is *poetry*. "What poets establish," he argues, "is not some sort of vision or consciousness of the All; rather they introduce into the relational totality of social existence— into the social body divided into parts—the perspective of 'non-all.'" Like Ouaknin's view of innovative writing as a designifying practice, Santner understands artistic production (i.e., "the beautiful") "conceived not as a harmonization of parts within an ordered whole but rather as the representation of an interrupted whole—or better, a *self-interrupting whole*—one animated, as it were, by a 'too much' of pressure from within its midst. . . . beautiful objects are *disarming* not in the sense of releasing us, and once for all, from the 'too much' of excitation that is, at some level, constitutive of human life, but rather in the sense of loosening our defenses, opening beyond our stuckness in the especially rigid and defensive organization of this pressure." As in the case of Ouaknin and Nachman, here we see some form of negativity, some sense of the "non-all" intervening in a totalizing structure of signification. Of particular importance for me is the notion of the poem as *self-interrupting whole*, for Santer's formulation startlingly resembles my own reflections while working on *Track*, my long serial poem. I quote the first of my "Statements for *Track*":

> *Track* is a series of controlled discontinuities, the self-conscious dilapidation of the structuralist's dream as it ascends toward the transcendental signifier. The poem as "field of action" or "park of eternal events" applies to my work only insofar as the action or events can be both

determined *and* left open to happenstance. Linguistic and experiential
pressures brought to bear on the writing (and again, this is a matter of
deliberation *and* accident) set off "articulations of sound forms in time," or
lyric moments arising in spite of themselves. *Track* is the lyric of disaster,
the disaster of lyric. It inoculates itself through measured sequences of
verbal shocks, which then reveal themselves as parts of a larger pattern.
It becomes a totality in spite of itself, and it is under this condition that
it continues to be conceived and composed. Always at odds with itself, it
requires a grandiosity that must be continually punctured, sufficiently
punctured in an act that is still a shaping, still formal. Its place in the
course of my work in general is thus inevitable and extreme.

Although I was not thinking in specifically "Jewish" terms in this passage (my reference points are drawn from the "radical" poetics of modernism and postmodernism), I would argue that the sense of form I was
attempting to articulate is related in principle to what I was later to learn
about Jewish writing from the authors I have been discussing here. In
Track itself, I frequently have recourse to Jewish content or references,
sometimes engaging in what amounts to full-blown poetic midrash,
even on biblical passages. But regardless of the particular matter or content under hand, *Track*, as a "*self-interrupting whole*," operates through
what I now conceive to be not only "experimental" but also "Jewish"
textual procedures. And as a serial poem in the tradition of such poets
as Oppen, Creeley, Duncan, Spicer, and perhaps further back, Whitman
and Dickinson, it is contoured to the shape of a life lived, taking on the
search for definition of that life's path or track. Here again, I find congruence between Jewish textuality and "radical" poetic composition. The
designifying procedures we associate with both traditions constitute the
open work of self-discovery, the renewal of meaning and answerability,
the overcoming of undeadness. Again, from my "Statements for *Track*":
"The incursion of a certain kind of pleasure/terror, akin to the strong
incursions of eros into one's life, is registered through a shift in the verbal
patterning, until it potentially becomes a part of the patterning." Or as I
put it in one of many such passages in the poem itself:

#

Sometimes there are numbers
and sometimes there are ruptures

Sometimes the rules
break the continuities

And sometimes the continuities
break the rules

Sometimes a seventh is added much later.

As I think of the movement from one point to the next in *Track*, the incursions, ruptures, discontinuities and abrupt revelations, I recall Franz Rosenzweig's words at the end of *Understanding the Sick and the Healthy*: "The world's assurances should prevent one's eyes from closing. Nor do they close. They peer ahead to find what the hands must grip next and where the feet must step."

3. Language, World, and Thought

What Rosenzweig lovingly calls "the world's assurances" come to us through language, "the companion of everything, including every event which takes place in the world, and yet is external to them all: the Word." Language is "a bridge between the world and these other things. . . . To utter a word is to affix a seal as a witness of man's presence. The word is not part of the world; it is the seal of man." Through our engagement with language, we span the gap between self and world. Rosenzweig's model of being is tripartite: world, man, and God. Thus, he goes on to tell us that "language stamps the sign of God and man upon all the things of this world. . . . The thing is and as such immediately acquires a name. Its name bears it into the flow of things . . ." The power of the word to bear the thing into the world, to secure it in the cognizance of the subject, whether human and divine, calls to mind one of the most significant qualities of modern poetry, as one finds, for instance, in Rilke, or in a different register, in Stevens, Oppen, or Bronk. I am thinking of a poetry of worldly presence in which language in its naming of things grants them (or unveils in them) a sense of the numinous, even when the work generally tends toward the agnostic. Bronk: "This tree! This tree! Look, there are parts of the world / not ever wounded, within whose light, the world / is always changed with light. This tree, tree." Oppen: "The small nouns / Crying faith / In this in which the wild deer / Startle, and stare out."

For Rosenzweig, poetry, more than any other art, holds out what is in effect a redemptive promise through the aesthetic experience that it has to offer. As he explains in *The Star of Redemption*, "Poetry is not a kind of art of thought, but thinking is its element as space is that of the plastic arts and time is that of music; and from thinking, it ends also by putting at its service the world of inner and outer intuition, space and time, the extensive 'epic' breadth and the intensive 'lyrical' depth. It follows that it is the living art in the proper sense." "Because it is the most alive," Rosenzweig declares, "poetry is the most indispensable art . . . every man who is fully man must have a sense for poetry."

But although poetry is indispensable, its power and ultimately its redemptive significance lie in its relation to thought, not what Rosenzweig calls its "tonality" (i.e., musical qualities) or the "language" (i.e., style) of the individual poet. "It is only the 'idea' that gives life to the poem," he insists; ". . . it is that which is perceptible from an aesthetic point of view for the senses, that which is actually real and effective in the work. . . . The idea is that which 'speaks' in the poem to the spectator, like the melody in the musical work and the plastic figure in the visual work. The idea is not somewhere behind the poem, it is in it." This certainly poses a problem for any sort of formalist or language-centered poetic, including those which posit their "radical" nature in the play of the sign. We have already noted that the designifying practices of traditional Jewish textuality function as a means of self-determination: language may be regarded as indeterminate, but that indeterminacy renews, rather than disperses, the unique meaning of each individual. Now we observe that for one of our most important Jewish philosophers, language in its formal capacity, however much it makes manifest the poem—indeed, constitutes the poem—is ultimately subordinate to the idea of the poem, which, as Rosenzweig concludes, is that element "where life itself stirs most of the time."

It is very much in this spirit that Michael Heller, one of our best commentators (in prose and in verse) on Jewish thought and modernist poetics, criticizes the formalism of language-centered writing. In "Avant-Garde Propellants and the Machine Made of Words," Heller argues that the problem of this work lies in its "fetishizing not reality but language, as though language were now suddenly capable of becoming an object where all else had failed." By contrast, he proposes that "The power of poetry . . . is that it puts a word back into the voice of an Other, that it is a power for him or her and so confronts my particular empowerment of it. The word again becomes an object of thought." And in "Diasporic Poetics," an essay on his relation to the Objectivists that also draws from Rosenzweig and Lévinas, Heller writes of the Jewish poet "as transmuter of a worked-upon physiology into language, the re-namer. Implicit in this line of thought is that the poet is not perceived as an experimenter with language *per se*, for there is nothing more confident than the experimenter in the laboratory who can objectively manipulate materials (language in this case) in a fanciful manner. On the contrary, Lévinas's poet is anguished and exposed . . . does not perform but is performed upon by experience, by adversity, by love and history."

Both Heller's critique of experimentalism and his own position (which he likes to speak of as offering a "counter-history," or "counter-memory," producing "countercontinuities") stem from a strong belief in the primacy of thought, the product of a thinking subject which both mediates and is mediated by language. In Heller's nuanced and dialectical view, language, self, and world are constantly assayed, valued, and recalibrated at the site of the poem. And when he asks himself "how a particular Jewishness informs a poetry," his answer takes much the same dialectical form, in which the poet both performs and is performed upon in a continuous process of becoming, and poetry is both revelation and commentary: "becoming begins in exposures and antecedents: those poets that I read, the life their words lead me to. This is very much in keeping with the Jewish notion of revelation which begins in overhearing the revelatory nature of the text before one's eyes, its imports and prophetic hopes." In terms of both content and form, thought and language, I am reminded of another instance in *Track*, when passages from Oppen and Bronk, two poets who mean a great deal to me, suddenly take on a force akin to revelation, and the poem acknowledges its status as commentary, and the responsibility that lies therein:

#

Gathering, arranging
the endless repetitions

At risk of ending
at any moment

Any moment suffused
with ending or beginning

"Now that tremendous
plunge"

#

Any moment suffused
with endless quotation
Quotation as translation
beyond all strategies

Lifting the text
in and out of time

"these certainties against
the all-uncertain"

(Once again I pause and reflect. "Quotation as translation / beyond all strategies"? The procedures or strategies we associate with modern and postmodern poetry, insofar as they relate to Jewishness, must take up the risk, the challenge, of revelation: revelation of the self, of the world—and of God? Inevitably we are led back to the question of divinity, in terms of poetic practice and Jewish culture. But I am not quite ready to deal with the question head on, which would not, in any case, be a particularly Jewish move. Let's engage in commentary just a little longer ...)

4. Rothenberg *contra* Grossman; Or, the Secular and the Holy

More than any other recent Jewish poet, Jerome Rothenberg has self-consciously appropriated traditional religious writing procedures and formal strategies for the production of secular poetry. As he explains in the "Post/Face" to *Gematria*, one of his most radical experiments along these lines, "Unlike the traditionalists of gematria, I have seen these coincidences/synchronicities not as hermeneutic substantiations for religious and ethical doctrines, but as an entry into the kinds of correspondences/constellations that have been central to modernist & 'post' modernist experiments over the last century & a half." Note the ease with which Rothenberg moves from "religious and ethical doctrines" to "modernist and 'post' modernist experiments." As he sees it, the complexity, variety, and dizzyingly contradictory nature of Jewish culture and history is best understood as an evolving continuum of creation, of *poesis*, which means that "religious and ethical doctrines" are not, ultimately, the driving forces behind traditional Jewish writing. This view is elaborated in the "Pre-Face" to *A Big Jewish Book* (reworked as *Exiled in the Word*), his monumental anthology of "Poems & Other Visions of the Jews from Tribal Times to Present." For me, this Pre-Face remains one of the most important documents in the annals of Jewish literature. At the center of the text, Rothenberg tells us that

> Work for this book has accordingly been drawn from both "sacred" & "secular" sources, with the link between them *my* stress on a poetic/ visionary continuum & on the mystical & magical side of the Jewish tradition. And since poetry, in the consensus of my contemporaries, is more concerned with the "free play of the imagination" than with doctrinal certainties *per se*, I've made no attempt to establish an "orthodox" line or to isolate any one strain as purer or more purely Jewish than any others. Instead my assumption has been that poetry, here as elsewhere, is an inherently impure activity of individuals creating reality from all conditions & influences at hand.

Not only does this account for the remarkable heterogeneity of the material in the anthology, it also definitively establishes Jewish *poesis* as a sort of visionary secularism, since Rothenberg disregards the fundamen-

204 I TO GO INTO THE WORDS

tal distinction in normative Judaism between the sacred (or more accurately, the holy—*kadosh*—difference or separation) and the profane. The
resulting "promiscuity" (a term Rothenberg himself uses) in regard to
Jewish writing allows for previously repressed linkages and filiations in
apparently contradictory traditions and ideologies to reveal themselves,
so that kabbalistic spells and Dadaist performance pieces, passages from
Torah and from heretical messianic texts, shed light on each other in
an immense modernist collage. From this perspective, the shaman, the
prophet, the Talmudist, and the poet are all engaged in the same activity,
whether the cultural artifact is presented as a spell, a sermon, a scriptural
commentary, or a "word event." Under the aegis of modern ethnography and religious historiography (Rothenberg is the inventor of the term
"ethnopoetics"), we discover "the poetic *mainstream* . . . magic, myth, &
dream; earth, nature, orgy, love; the female presence the Jewish poets
named Shekinah." The marginal and the avant-garde, in Rothenberg's
anti-authoritarian and decentered view, reveal themselves to be the hidden or repressed center of the culture: all Jewish writing participates in an
endlessly evolving process of experimentation which is, to reiterate, "an
inherently impure activity."

As Rothenberg well knows, this inherently impure activity poses a
serious challenge to any sense of normative, not to mention orthodox,
Judaism. Thus, Jewish poetry, indeed, Jewish cultural activity of any sort,
regardless of how it understands itself in regard to traditional Jewish
belief, is ultimately secular, profane, *treyf* [unclean], *asur* [forbidden]. If it
is to be understood as having any relation to the "sacred" (as in the invocation of "magic, myth & dream; earth, nature, orgy, love"), it is an understanding of that term that could actually be *opposed* to the fundamental
Jewish concept of holiness. As Emmanuel Lévinas explains in his severe
Talmudic essay "Desacralization and Disenchantment," "The sacred is
in fact the half light in which the sorcery the Jewish tradition abhors
flourishes. . . . Sorcery, first cousin, perhaps even sister, of the sacred, is
the mistress of appearance. She is a relative slightly fallen in status, but
within the family, who profits from the connections of her brother, who
is received in the best circles" (141). Lévinas defines sorcery as "looking
beyond what it is possible to see. It is to go beyond the limits within which
one must stay when truth approaches, not to stop in time. . . . Sorcery is
the curiosity which manifests itself when the eyes should be cast down:

indiscretion regarding the Divine; insensitivity to Mystery; clarity projected unto something the approach to which requires some modesty.... Sorcery does not come about because of bad influences; it is the excess of knowledge itself, that which is beyond what can be borne in truth." This is why, as Lévinas puts it, "I have always asked myself if holiness, that is separation or purity, the essence without admixture that can be called Spirit and which animates the Jewish tradition—or to which the Jewish tradition aspires—can dwell in a world that has not been desacralized." And in Lévinas's view, the sacred tends not toward desacralization, but toward degeneration, and in its degeneration, becomes sorcery: "That is why the sacred is not sacred, why the sacred is not holiness."

Much as I admire Lévinas's brilliant integration of Jewish tradition and modern philosophy, I would simply note in passing the tension between his view and that of Rothenberg, were it not for another crucial poet who adopts much the same view as Lévinas in his understanding of Jewish poetry. I refer to Allen Grossman, whose poetry and poetics I regard as equally significant as Rothenberg's, but who stands, it seems to me, diametrically opposed to the ethnopoetic position which Rothenberg represents. Rather than take an anthropological perspective on Jewish culture, in which the Jewish writers, however they define themselves, are ultimately *bricoleurs* ("individuals creating reality from all conditions & influences at hand"), Grossman assumes that Jewish culture is, by definition, a *culture of holiness*:

> . . . the supreme human work (man's service and creativity) is the voluntary performance of the transactions of holiness, which reciprocate and complete God's creation of the world by restoring it day by day, fact by scattered fact, to his nature. The specifications of such work, as in the 613 *mitzvot*, or commandments, defines a *culture of holiness*, a system of transactions by which through the mediation of holiness man and God come to be included within the precinct of the same term.

This passage comes from "Holiness," originally published as a chapter in a volume called *Contemporary Jewish Religious Thought*. Grossman focuses on a number of basic Jewish prayers, but it's clear that he has poetry in mind when he notes that "From the point of view of human experience, therefore (the point of view of language), *holy* is not in the ordinary sense a predicate, a word that asserts something about a term, but a sign of the withdrawal of all reference into its source, a determinator of the radical disablement of metaphor and the absolute preemption of the truth of discourse at the supremely privileged moment of reference to reality." Thus holiness, as the signifier of ultimate difference between creator and creation, is that which simultaneously inspires but also shuts down linguistic production. In Jewish culture, "transactions of holiness," especially linguistic transactions, enable humanity to interact with the Absolute, for God both constitutes and creates reality. This is why, as Grossman tells us in his great essay "Jewish Poetry Considered as a Theophoric Project," "The Jew's word, strictly speaking, is One (holy, sacred, *Kadosh*), and is unlike all other words in that it does not signify by difference [as does gentile poetry] but rather serves the Master who is difference—which is to say, existence itself."

According to Grossman's paradigm, although poetry has always been associated with the sacred (that is, the holy), "for the Jew *there is always a sense* (a profound understanding beneath all other understandings) *that the category of the sacred and the category of the poetic repel one another.*" Yet Jewish poetry still strives to be a "theophoric" or God-bearing enterprise. And with remarkable irony, the mediating power that Grossman names as the inspiration for Jewish poetry, the power through which the transaction of holiness, of *purity*, between God and the Jewish poem takes place, is the Shekinah, the very figure that Rothenberg identifies with the *impurity* of poetic activity: "The Jewish poet who invokes the Shechinah has an obligation to construct the place where 'Light and Law are manifest,' to which the nations may come because it is where they are. The obligation is the same as the obligation to the intelligibility of experience, the covenant." In other words, that figure which for Grossman distinguishes Jewish poetry from the poetry of other peoples is the same figure that for Rothenberg aligns Jewish poetry with the poetry of other peoples. For Grossman, the Shekinah assists the Jewish poet in approaching a covenantal state of holiness. For Rothenberg, she leads the Jewish poem into what he calls in regard to his own *Poland/1931*, "some supreme yiddish surrealist vaudeville" of the utmost heterogeneity.

Although Rothenberg is usually associated with "avant-garde" modernism and postmodernism, in terms of both technique and affiliation, while Grossman is seen as a more "academic" poet with roots going back to Romanticism via such precursors as Yeats and Crane, what I would argue is that both practice versions of a radical Jewish poetics. I say this because although their styles and theoretical positions are diametrically opposed, both are radical in their *idea* of the Jewish poem. Both formulate their approach through a deep and sustained engagement with Jewish beliefs, Jewish history, Jewish traditions of writing and discourse. This in turn manifests itself in each poet's style, technique, and attitude toward language, though as we observed with Rosezweig in section 3, beneath style, technique, and attitude lies the idea, the concept, derived from a Jewish worldview. Modern Jewish poets, like Jewish writers and thinkers in the past, enter into dialogue with that worldview. Even when they struggle against it, perhaps even seeking to negate it, it remains foundational to the Jewish poem.

5. "My secularism is not secular": Tentative Conclusions

In an interview originally published in 1975 in *On Jews and Judaism in Crisis*, Gershom Scholem was asked to account for the varying responses of religious and secular students to his classes on kabbalah at the Hebrew University. The secular students seemed to be seeking for "some living spark," while the religious students saw kabbalah "as no more than a chapter in the history of religion that had no significance for their own faith." Scholem's response led him to reflect on his own stance:

> I don't consider myself a secularist. My secularism fails right at the core, owing to the fact that I am a religious person, because I am sure of my belief in God. My secularism is not secular. But the fact that I addressed myself to *kabbalah* not merely as a chapter of history but from a dialectical distance—from identification and distance together—certainly stems from the fact that I had a feeling that *kabbalah* had a living center. . . . Something unknown of this sort must have motivated me beyond all the philological games and masquerades at which I excel. I can understand that something of this sort inspired my secularist listeners the way it inspired me.

Scholem raises a number of points that I find very helpful and personally appealing. The first is the "dialectical distance" in his immersion into a deeply Jewish subject which at the time he began his research was either dismissed or repressed. This may be close to the attitude that appears in all my work, not only in regard to kabbalah, or to Jewish religious matters in general, but to all matters involving issues of religion, faith, and spirituality. Yet my very ambivalence, or sense of identification and distance, has led me to some of the most challenging and rewarding moments in my poetry and criticism. This leads me to the second point, which is the idea of Scholem and then his *secular* students being attracted to a living center or some living spark in the Jewish mystical tradition, as is certainly true for me as well. Unlike Scholem, I am not at all sure in my belief in God: if one were to ask me, nine times out of ten I would probably say that I'm an atheist. But if what I profess can be called atheism, it is an atheism that circles around some living center, perhaps an *absent* center which still has compelling power. Elsewhere, Scholem comments on the kabbalistic *tzimtzum*, comparing it to the "emptying of the world to a meaningless void not illuminated by any ray of meaning or direction [that] is the experience of him whom I would call the pious atheist. The void is the abyss, the chasm or the crack which opens up in all that exists. This is the experience of modern man, surpassingly well depicted in all its desolation by Kafka, for whom nothing has remained of God but the void—in Kafka's sense, to be sure, the void of God." In this respect, at least, I think of myself as more of a modern rather than postmodern writer.

The third point with which I identify is Scholem's sense of something unknown motivating him "beyond all the philological games and masquerades"—and let us recall that Scholem was a serious if not prolific poet as well as a great scholar. Jews, of course, have excelled in language games and masquerades for a very long time. But as we have seen (pace Rothenberg), they are usually put in the service of some religious or ethical idea, if not doctrine. Whether we cast it in religious or secular terms, we continue to yearn for some form of transcendence, some experience of the numinous, with which poetry has been traditionally associated. Scholem remains a paradigmatic figure for me partly because the volatile categories he explores (messianism, gnosis, counter-history, redemption through sin, nihilism, etc.) continue to manifest themselves today, not only in the frightening versions of religious fundamentalism that so dangerously shape global politics, but even in the most apparently secularized of cultural formations. In *Religion After Religion*, Steven M. Wasserstrom notes that for Scholem, "Secularization revealed novel religious forces. . . . The crisis of tradition is still tradition, both remaining within its spirit and yet leaving its current form behind." About Scholem and his colleague Henry Corbin, Wasserstrom tells us that "What they championed as the most 'traditional' theosophy appears as an expression of a curiously emphatic modernism: antinomian, individualistic, and secular. One may call their paradoxical approach *religion after religion*."

The figure of Scholem as a paradigmatic modern Jew of culture, engaged in *religion after religion*, is in some respects even more attractive to me than the more well-known "non-Jewish Jew" first identified by Isaac Deutscher nearly fifty years ago. Akher, the Talmudic heretic still revered by his former rabbinic colleagues, and Spinoza, whose philosophy led to his excommunication by the Jewish religious leaders of Amsterdam, are Deutscher's models for a tradition which includes Heine, Marx, and Freud: "They all went beyond the boundaries of Jewry. They all found Jewry too narrow, too archaic, and too constricting." The marginal status of non-Jewish Jews, their being "in society and yet not in it, of it and yet not of it," their dialectical determinism, their understanding of "reality as being dynamic, not static," their rejection of moral absolutes, their revolutionary optimism despite their acceptance of the tragedy of Jewish history—all these qualities remain relevant to any discussion of secular Jewish identity and culture. And yet when we study individual figures or specific intellectual or artistic tendencies in what is broadly called secular Jewish culture, we often discover it is precisely the volatile, dialectical engagements of "non-Jewish Jews" with "narrow," "archaic," or "constricting" aspects of Jewry that lead to their most bold, radical, and innovative contributions. The transformations of this sort—one sees them throughout modern Jewish literature, including the most innovative Jewish American poetry—may, on one hand, be considered instances of "secularization," insofar as they constitute, to use Rothenberg's term again, "an inherently impure activity." On the other hand, we may think about Jewish culture in the way Scholem describes the Jewish religious tradition: "Tradition undergoes changes with the times, new facets of its meaning shining forth and lighting its way. Tradition, according to its mystical sense, is Oral Torah, precisely because each stabilization in the text would hinder and destroy the infinitely moving, the constantly progressing and unfolding element within it, which would otherwise become petrified."

This passage, from Scholem's "Revelation and Tradition as Religious Categories in Judaism," has provided a guiding principle for my understanding of Jewish culture—and for my understanding of myself as a Jewish writer—ever since my "return" to Judaism over twenty years ago. The indeterminacy, the designification, the dialectical play of this concept has repeatedly helped me negotiate matters of belief and practice. My secularism is not secular—and my religion is not religious.

Nowhere is this more true than in the combinations and permutations of *Track*:

#

But to profane
this sacred history

But to sacrifice
this deserted writing

To call and call
knowing he will answer

To answer
not knowing if he calls.

In *The Burnt Book*, Ouaknin quotes Henri Atlan: "The primary preoccupation with biblical teaching is not the existence of God, theism as contrasted with atheism, but the fight against idolatry. In all theism there is the danger of idolatry. All theism is idolatry, since expression signifies it, thereby freezing it; except if, somehow, its discourse refuses itself and so becomes atheistic. In other words, the paradoxes of language and its meanings are such that the only discourse possible about God that is not idolatrous is an atheistic discourse."

"The Text," declares Ouaknin, "which is the primary relation to God, must not turn into an idol." Hence Rabbi Nachman, whose belief in God was as tortured as his textual innovations were inspired, seeks to write a book "that is written in the margins, the one which, through its writing, becomes margins. The book is burnt; it becomes margins, empty space—*Hallal hapanui*—which creates the absolute separation between man and God." That separation, that space, is the space in which Jewish writing occurs. It is the space that defines a radical Jewish poetics.

The Master of Turning

This final reflection surveys the most important changes and passages in my poetry in terms of Jewish thought, and stays with the problem of the secular, as discussed in the previous chapter. It takes me up to the present, and, perhaps, serves as a launching pad for whatever is to come.

In Judaism, the Hebrew term *ba'al teshuvah*, or "master of the return," traditionally refers to a repentant sinner (*teshuvah* also means "repentance"), and more recently applies to a Jew who turns, or returns, to a greater degree of orthodoxy. Such Jews are more observant, they follow *halakhah*, the Law, a word in Hebrew which literally means "the way." I am not an Orthodox Jew—on the contrary, in most respects I regard myself as a secular Jew. I do not keep kosher; I do not pray; I avoid synagogue services; I do not fast on Yom Kippur; and for what it's worth, I'm an atheist. At our house, we have a Passover seder, partly because of the traditional foods, partly because I love the text of the Haggadah, and partly for the sense of extended family that the ceremonial meal implies. Much the same is true of our celebration of Hanukah, when we light the menorah, fry up a batch of latkes, and give the grandchildren an enormous load of gifts. Yet I am deeply committed to the continuance of Jewish culture. I am fascinated by Jewish history, and the ways in which Jews have shaped and interacted with the forces of modernity. I have studied and written extensively about Jewish literature, especially Jewish American poetry. In today's climate, when the vexed concept of "identity" comes into play, not only in politics but in the arts, I "identify" as a Jewish American poet, which is to say that a great deal of my poetry is identifiably Jewish.

The concept of identity takes me back to the figure of the *ba'al teshuvah*, which in a very idiosyncratic way I feel myself to be. In college, as a fledgling poet and literary critic, my Jewish upbringing and rather spotty Jewish education were not especially meaningful to me. Poetry became my religion; my experience of spirituality (an annoyingly vague word), or better, of inwardness, became connected, or cathected, to the power of verbal expression, especially in verse. Gradually I learned that the roots of poetry and religion were deeply entangled (I had intuited this from an early age), but I also saw that poetry and religion were often at odds, not only in the individual, but in culture as well. Thus conventional or normative Jewish belief and practice was a challenge to my poetic development, especially because the poetry that I was writing was in in some sense visionary or prophetic, but not identifiably Jewish. It posited a transcendental horizon which it posed against institutional structures of all kinds. That was certainly the case in regard to religious institutions. Subconsciously, I was conflicted about this, not because I wanted to write a specifically Jewish poetry (that would come later), but because I felt I was embodying a contradiction. This, however, is not a bad thing, especially when the zone of conflict and contradiction is poetic language.

What to do? My daily life was, and still is, conducted almost entirely on a secular plane, although I found myself attracted to Jewish customs and beliefs as to a rather remote but still intimate and beautiful poem. Eventually, I came upon a passage in the work of Harold Bloom (from *Ruin the Sacred Truths*) which helped me understand, though certainly not resolve, my situation. As Bloom argues,

> The scandal is the stubborn resistance of imaginative literature to the categories of sacred and secular. If you wish, you can insist that all high literature is secular, or, should you desire it so, then all strong poetry is sacred. What I find incoherent is the judgment that some authentic literary art is more sacred or more secular than some other. Poetry and belief wander about, together and apart, in a cosmological emptiness marked by the limits of truth and of meaning.

Encoded in Bloom's remarkable statement are two concepts which are worth elaborating. First, the idea that poetry and belief *wander*. This in itself is a very Jewish notion. My first book on Jewish literature, *The Ritual of New Creation*, was premised in part on what Bloom, following Olivier Renault-d'Allones, calls "wandering meaning," a fundamental instability of language, a constant movement through registers of discourse (including poetic and religious discourse) that is analogous to exilic and diasporic Jewish life. Second, such wandering takes place in a *cosmological emptiness*. Here the reference is to what the Gnostics call the *kenoma*, the lower, fallen world of phenomena—our world. We seek meaning or substance in this emptiness. If I were an Orthodox Jew, I would, of course, reject this existential situation, especially because I would be following *halakah*, the Way. I would know my way forward, understanding that there was a path for me in a creation that may be fallen, but is still full of divine goodness. But as I said, I find this way of life to be in contradiction to my most basic creative impulse, the restless source of my poetic imagination.

Thus my "return" to Judaism was and remains only a partial return. My obsessive textuality and mystical yearning are both quite Jewish. My disinclination to follow the Way, however, is transgressive. And these contradictory impulses expressed themselves and began to work themselves out in my poetry as soon as I sought to incorporate Jewish material in my work. Orthodox Jews, as I mentioned above, are *observant*, which is to say they observe the laws and rituals. But poets must also be observant: they must observe the world around them and the world within them, and transform those observations into poems.

The contradictions and overlapping impulses I am adumbrating here manifest themselves in my poems continually. "The Master of Turning," from *Restless Messengers* (1992), my first full-length collection, is suffused with Hasidic and kabbalistic imagery and a vaguely Eastern European setting, but also it has a political dimension, an anarchistic tone derived in part from messianic thought, codified by reading Gershom Scholem's studies of Jewish messianism. Here are the last two stanzas:

> And I came that day to the fountain
> about which I have been forbidden to speak,
> so that there are blanks in the writing
> as if a divine censor had struck out the words,
> leaving me with nothing but the etceteras of history,
> while the apparatchiks chortled into their beer,
> taking it all for a sign.
> If I were to upbraid them, my most extravagant claims
> would be fulfilled:

> *upon such conditions, soup cooks,*
> *bread rises,*
> *and stories remain to be told.*

Is this an observant poem? Does it follow the Way? It makes its own way, suffused with a secret wisdom (*gnosis*) which it has gained by looking within and without. But in its contradictory state, its struggle with a "divine censor," it can only say so much.

Later, I would confront and seek to name that divine oppositional power more directly, though as I discovered, this is only possible through a language both of saying and of unsaying. Such language is to be found, strictly ordered through numerical and combinatory procedures, throughout *Track*, my long serial poem:

"He is the place of the world
but the world is not his place"

Walking into a picture
"fraught with background"

Three days walking
out of myth into history

Endlessly walking
into the history of our response.

Track (1999–2005), as I wrote in a notebook entry published as an appendix to the single-volume edition (2012), "is a series of controlled discontinuities, the self-conscious dilapidation of the structuralist's dream as it ascends toward the transcendental signifier." These discontinuities may appear to cease (which is to say I decided to bring the poem to an end), but the ascent, the endless walking that is the history of our (the Jews'?) response never really does. And as for the transcendental signifier? See how it is addressed in "Desert," from *Scribe* (2009):

Called back, returned, and so went forth
again. From the edge of the abyss, "the

deep places of the imagination," retrieved,
rescued, redeemed. Fronted, confronted,
conspired, conspired against, usurped
stolen, sacrificed. Bidden, forbidden.
Dreamed, prophesied, spoke to, with,
against. Visited, was visited, was visited
upon. Throned. Dethroned. Written
upon the sky and upon the ground.

Grammatically speaking, there are no subjects or objects in these lines; they consist mainly of verbal and adverbial phrases. Who is bidden or forbidden? Who is throned or dethroned? My poetry has always confronted me as a mystery, almost in a religious sense—or as Jack Spicer writes, "What I mean is words / Turn mysteriously against those who use them." Spicer is one of a number of poets from whom I have learned that poetry is always a veiling and an unveiling, a ritual in which poets participate with the utmost seriousness, however they may find themselves the butt of uncanny jokes. The "ghosts" that Spicer entertains tend to be Christian (he also had his ugly antisemitic moments), but perhaps more than any other poet, he gave me "permission" (as his erstwhile friend Robert Duncan would put it) to write poems which embody both spiritual gravity and cosmic zaniness.

What this implies is a "turning" of a different sort, though one that is strangely connected to Jewishness. We speak of the turn (volta) in a poem, most often a sonnet, as the point at which the rhetoric shifts, the thought changes gear, the argument moves in a different direction. More recently, some poetry, following the concept in linguistics, is found to engage in various types of code switching, rapid turns from one register of discourse to another. This kind of linguistic turning is especially common in minority communities, as in the African American community, where it has been frequently studied. Growing up, I heard a good deal of code switching in my own family. My mother would frequently move between English and Yiddish while conversing with my grandparent. Standard English (my mother was an elementary school teacher) mingled with *mamaloshen*. There was also a kind of vernacular English that was peppered with Yiddish phrases, a vernacular I associate especially with the tough-guy discourse of business, spoken by male relatives in diners on Seventh Avenue and in front of football games on TV. Together with allusion, puns, occasional rhyme, and repetition, various sorts of code switching have become increasingly important to my writing style. The first of my books that fully represents this style is *Inside the Ghost Factory* (2010). Consider the poem "Urgent":

You must undertake this mission, this
rescue. He is waiting to be taken under, to
be taken home. He is in the precincts of

the living, he is wandering from house
to house, he is restless, he is dis-
eased, he does not know what to do. Do

you love him that much, do you love
life that much? He was a great
poet, he was your uncle, he was under

a curse. Take this and this. There
will be impediments, incidents, you may
or may not go in a straight line. There

will be two, maybe three. I do not
know, I cannot see, but it does not
matter. Take this. The books are a ladder

you may climb, from which you may
leap, but do not look for him in any
library. Try the shops, the diners,

the stock exchange. Try the garment
district. There is money to be made
but not if you do this right. This rite

calls for you to understand the order
and after you place your order, after you
eat the meal, they will bring the bill.

Inside the cookie will be a piece of paper,
it will tell you where to go, tell you your
lucky number. Tell the number to the man

who is greeted by all. It's payday. Why
do you linger here? He is slipping away,
there will be shame, stress, a sudden

downturn. His name is that of a priest
or prophet. Take him to a bar and get
him a drink—half Jack Daniels, half tears.

Is this a Jewish poem? Probably not in any obvious way, but I think of it as quite Jewish, or quite Jewish American, or at least closely bound up with my Jewish American childhood. I think of the fortune cookies in the local Chinese restaurant, where we would go when my mother, after teaching all day and then helping my grandparents, was too tired to cook. I have a vivid memory of my Uncle Aaron's dry-cleaning store in the Garment District, where the numbers runner would come through on payday. Jack Daniels and Seven-Up was the drink of choice among the men in my family, and I still have a taste for it. From the perspective of the poem, it is as if the family were under a spell. The ghosts, the dybbuks, are wandering from house to house, psyche to psyche, as in Nathaniel Mackey's *Song of the Andoumboulou*. But here, the child seeks to rescue the older generation from the stresses and anxieties of that frantic post-immigrant life. I think the word that hovers over the poem, though it is never spoken, is *tsuris* (trouble). A Yiddisher shaman, the poet seeks to free his family ghosts from their *tsuris*. As Hans Loewald, the great psychoanalytic theorist, writes, "the ghosts of the unconscious are laid and led to rest as ancestors whose power is taken over and transformed into the newer intensity of present life."

What Loewald calls the desire for "the newer intensity of present life," the desire to free oneself from a condition that the psychoanalytic critic and philosopher Eric Santner calls "Egyptomania," has become a fundamental theme in my recent work. Given what I learned about the uncanny and the psychic power of the outside in writing *Ghost Factory*—especially in regard to their effect on voice, tone, and shifts in discourse—it seems inevitable to me now that I would seek a more expansive imaginative domain, a "park of eternal events" (as Olson calls Dogtown in *Maximus*) with more acreage. On August 10, 2009, my wife Alice and I were in Virginia Beach, visiting her family, and we had slipped out for a drive. Quite accidentally (though perhaps nothing of this sort is really accidental), we came upon the headquarters of the Association for Research and Enlightenment, founded by the psychic Edgar Cayce (1877–1945) in 1931, and still going strong. Cayce, the so-called "sleeping prophet," had an immense following during his career. That afternoon, we took a tour of the Association, spent a lot of time in the huge library of psychic and occult books, and even had our telepathic powers tested. Shortly thereafter, I wrote the poem "Tour." The Immanent Foundation was born:

Welcome to the Immanent Foundation.
Our headquarters are located in a large house
on a hill above the beach. Our headquarters
are located on a large estate in a forest of oak
and beech. This estate is called Arcady,
or the Memory Palace. After the house
burnt down, it reappeared in a grove
adjacent to the garden. This is the Reading Room.
Here we conduct the tests that measure
sensitivity to light, to time, to daemonization.
This is the Room of Lost Manuscripts
and this is the Room of Manuscripts Recovered.
After the notebooks were gathered and burnt,
they were found beneath the cherry trees by the gardener,
who then climbed into the sky and disappeared.
This is the Master Bedroom, where the Master
sleeps and speaks. This is the Ballroom,
which is adjacent to the Chapel, where we
celebrate the marriage of the sun and the moon.
The light from these globes has been captured
on nights when the moon is full, when she comes
to her husband. They converse and make love
all night long. At daybreak there is a procession,
there is a celebration, there is a moment

of utter stillness in which all evaporates.
Let us retrace our steps. That door leads
to the labyrinth, which is currently under repair.
The walls are painted with images from
the Psychomachia, but they have faded
and need to be restored. We are presently
seeking support, earnestly seeking, the scryer
peering into the stone even on moonless nights.
There are angels in the stone. All their names
begin with the letter A.

Once in a rare while, there are poems that come to us with hardly any labor, poems which, as Jack Spicer tells us, are acts of dictation, which Spicer understands as a kind of grace. I too think of them as gifts. For me, "Tour" is one such poem. It opened the door, to use the images from the poem, to the Rooms of Lost Manuscripts and of Manuscripts Recovered, to poems that borrow and combine a range of discourses, from the sciences, from bureaucracies, from myth and religion, from everyday slang and conversational speech. The result is an off-kilter, mysterious poetic sequence, increasingly narrative in its trajectory, producing uncanny effects, familiar and defamiliarizing, ritualistic, enigmatic, linguistically unstable, but still oddly connected to ordinary language acts. I began to use certain names, which is to say, certain characters began to introduce themselves to me. They are not fully developed characters, as in a novel, but more fleeting figures, fugitive, engaged in mysterious pursuits related to the Foundation, working for it, working against it, subversive but also subordinate to its secret motives. The tone of many of the poems is highly controlled, but at the same time borders on the hysterical. (Not accidentally, I was also a research candidate at the Cincinnati Psychoanalytic Institute during that period, and yes, the Institute may also be related to the Foundation.) Connected to all this is my fascination with the conventions of popular genre fiction—fantasy, fairy tale, science fiction, steampunk, detective and police procedurals, and the so-called "new weird." Judaism too gradually makes its way into these poems, sometimes obliquely, sometimes overtly. By the end of the sequence, we've encountered a golem, an aged rabbi, and a wedding beneath a chupah made by nanobots at the base of the kabbalistic Etz Hayyim.

From the Files of the Immanent Foundation was completed in May, 2016, and published in January, 2018. But all was not well. Even as I finished the sequence, I felt unsettled, uneasy. In my mind's eye, I saw the estate in ruin after some gnostic disaster, some great fall. As I prepared the book for publication, I wrote a few more poems that seemed related to it, but also seemed oddly disconnected. Then, in February, 2018, my wife Alice bought a pair of flowered Doc Martens, a model called "Pascal Wanderlust." I found the name quite amusing in an oxymoronic way, given Blaise Pascal's famous saying that "All of humanity's problems stem from man's inability to sit quietly in a room alone." Suddenly Pascal Wanderlust stood before me—a mysterious character who had a life to lead and places to go. A story! I had been thinking of quest-romance and rereading parts of *The Faerie Queene*. A densely allusive, highly elliptical philosophical adventure began to unfold, a graphic novel translated back into words, referencing H. P. Lovecraft and Neil Gaiman, Robert Browning and the *Pirke Aboth* and the *Zohar* (which, not accidentally, Arthur Green calls a "sacred fantasy").

A magical adventurer, Pascal Wanderlust travels through strange realms, perhaps through the Kenoma, the void or fallen world, all the while wishing to be back in that quiet room. Pascal would not be tied down, not even to gendered pronouns. Only the rigorous syntax I had developed in *Immanent Foundation* could keep Wanderlust on course. Over the next few months, I slowly but steadily hammered out twelve twelve-line stanzas: Book I. Not long after, I knew that *The Adventures of Pascal Wanderlust* would consist of six books, each book in the same twelve-by-twelve form. (Such stanzaic numerology has always been my habit since writing *Track*.) Both the character and narrative of Pascal Wanderlust have numerous links to the Immanent Foundation. It gradually emerges, for example, that the androgenous Pascal is an alchemical creation of the Foundation, but also a sort of avatar of a mythic being, just as the Foundation embodies archaic powers as well. Wanderlust's fate is bound up with that of the Foundation. The adventures continue.

The Adventures became the central part of *In a Broken Star*, published early in 2021, that most plague-ridden year. The imposed isolation of the pandemic was made even stranger for me because I retired from teaching in May of 2020, at the pandemic's early and perhaps most intense stage, both medically and culturally. Like so many of us, Alice and I kept in touch with friends and relations as best we could. I was already corresponding with the poet Tirzah Goldenberg, whose first book, *Aleph*, had been published by Verge, the press coedited by my friend Peter O'Leary. Tirzah and I discussed Judaism and Jewish life continually (she came from an Orthodox background, but had left Orthodox life years before). In one of her emails, she sent me the draft of a new poem. I picked up the last line and used it as the first line of a poem I wrote, sending it back with two words: "Your turn?" Months later, we had written a set of thirty-six poems, eighteen—חי—*chai*—life—each. I had never before collaborated on a book of poems, but *Thirty-Six / Two Lives*, published late in 2021, proved to be one of my deepest explorations of Jewish life and letters:

Belonging to an invisible acrostic,
the scattered letters call to each other,
caught up in the exhausted sentences
and longing to spell out a new name.

"Look at / what passes for the new."
Take warning from one who knows!
The risk grows with every quotation
and the spaces widen on the page.

But there is a politics embedded
in every citation, and even the dead
are not safe. Zakhor! The Torah strips
the future of its magic, but the allure

remains. The Angel of History hovers
over disaster, the pen of the Recording
Angel is suspended over his Book.
What is the weather report from Paradise?

Clear and calm, soft rains, gentle
breezes. Adam and Eve (who were never
expelled) take a stroll. We are welcome,
if only we could get there.

I had turned once again.